THEODORE DREISER

THEODORE DREISER

A New Dimension

Marguerite Tjader

Silvermine Publishers Incorporated

Norwalk, Connecticut

Table of Contents

Introduction—My Creator

by Theodore Dreiser

Part I

Part II

INTRODUCTION

Theodore Dreiser was a challenging, controversial figure. His novels are now a part of literary history. Other writings are not yet fully evaluated. For critics and biographers, Dreiser has never been easy to understand. His thoughts and actions were often contradictory and madly emotional, and there were heights and depths in his nature which are beyond the experience of the average mind.

Whatever one may think of Dreiser as a writer, his impact as a man was tremendous. Here too, was contradiction, paradox. People were drawn to him or repulsed by his peculiar way of being himself, without compromise.

No photograph could capture the rough-hewn fascination of Dreiser. He was a big man with a round, dynamic head that was like an object coming at you through space. He had strong sculptured features, mobile, sensual mouth, haunting eyes. Add to these the vibrant tones of his voice, the magnetism of his touch, the emanation of a presence, scowling or laughing from some depth of being not often sensed—and you have the phenomenon Dreiser, alive still in the hearts of many who knew him.

But for a younger generation, Dreiser must be recreated through many pictures and through words, words preferably his own.

Most people who know his name, think of Dreiser as a novelist, a pioneer in the field of modern American writing. His daring realism—a part of his search for truth in human relationships—gave us *Sister Carrie* at the turn of the century;

then came *Jennie Gerhardt, The Genius,* and the two sweeping portraits of *A Triology of Desire: The Financier* and *The Titan.* The average reader considers that Dreiser's career culminated in the success of *An American Tragedy.* Young people have usually learned of Dreiser, at least in their literature classes, in connection with this almost contemporary classic. Some may have seen it in its latest film version—*A Place in the Sun*—which at least revealed Dreiser's sympathy with youth if not other subtleties of his novel.

In it was the social theme of Dreiser's strong feelings for the *underdog,* an insistence on human *equities* which colored all his thinking. This concern made Dreiser's life not only that of a literary man, but also that of a crusader for justice, a seeker of truth in social relationships; a *publicist,* as he is sometimes called, scornfully by the right, affectionately by the left.

Twenty years after *An American Tragedy,* Dreiser's long-delayed story of the revolt of youth and tragedy in a Quaker family, *The Bulwark,* was finally published. I do not believe that this novel has yet come into its own. It is like Bach music, which waited long for full recognition. But it has been accepted as a unique, minor work and has been re-issued in paperback. Many of Dreiser's concluding ideas are found here in disarmingly simple form.

For few realize that Dreiser spent a good part of his last twenty years collecting facts, plodding in and out of libraries and laboratories, consulting with scientists and thinkers in many fields, seeking to formulate his own philosophy of life. Novel writing and even social causes had become secondary to him, compared to his passion to reach the truth. *Why* he did not complete his work and what it was like in the making, is part of the story of this book.

Little account has been taken of Dreiser's philosophic probings in his prose-poems, *Moods.* Instead, he has in general been labelled a cynic and a devastating pessimist. After his many, earlier iconoclastic statements, the fact that he finally arrived at a belief in a Creator seems almost incredible and it is certainly not very well known. Indeed, a remarkable twelve-page essay which Dreiser wrote as a sort of *Apologia*

for former attitudes and which he first had typed in 1943—
two years before his death—has not yet been published. Although the concluding page has been quoted in other books
on Dreiser, it is not as convincing as Dreiser wished it to
be, placed in the rich context of his scientific—philosophic
studies.

With the kind permission of the Dreiser Committee of the
University of Pennsylvania, guardians of Dreiser's collected
manuscripts and unpublished materials, I will give a somewhat longer quotation below.

Here one can recognize the old Dreiser, more mystery-
loving, more original than ever in his complicated but exact
wordings, his widening cosmic perceptions, his *Moods* of the
latter years. Yet his thought was changing—how natural for
one who said that "change was the essence of life." He was
becoming more patient, more full of love and awe, more
transparent to the whole, illumined glory of the universe he
sought to show.

As an introduction to this book there can be no more
beautiful theme than that which Dreiser announces himself
in his *Apologia*—belief in a Creator.

My Creator

*Many, many times in my semi-industrious life I have
been asked by one person or another what I thought of
life (?) or whether, if ever, I sought to interpret the Creative Force by reason of which all of us find ourselves present—numbered among the living? At that time my brash
and certainly most unpremeditated reply was that I took
no meaning from all that I saw unless it was some planned
form of self-entertainment on the part of the Creative
Force which cared little if anything for either the joys
or sorrows of its creatures, and that, as for myself, "I
would pass as I had come to be, confused and dismayed,"—
a very definite statement which, for some reason or other,
seemed to register sharply on the minds of many, and
which since, and up to this very day, has been thrown
at me whenever I have chosen to claim any clear under-*

*standing of any of the amazing processes that I see in full
function about me in the world. And yet here they are—a
minute number of them.*

Dreiser then continues for ten pages, describing the contrasts
of living and the wonders revealed each day by science and
observation pointing clearly to a master-designer, and concludes:

*The fact is, however, that more than anything else in con-
nection with the Creative Force which brings us and all
other phases of life into being—at times for so little time
as (in the instance of some flowers or insects) an hour or
a day; in the case of some trees or vines, for hundreds of
years, is, as I have said, this matter of design. For design,
however one may feel concerning some of it, is the great
treasure that nature or the Creative Force has to offer to
man and through which it seems to emphasize its own
genius and to offer the knowledge of the same to man.
Design! Design! Design! And with each astounding variation, either of beauty or practical wisdom or both.*

. . . .

*And so studying this matter of genius in design and beauty,
as well as the wisdom of contrast and interest in this so
carefully engineered and regulated universe—this amazing
process called living—I am moved not only to awe but to
reverence for the Creator of the same concerning whom—
his or its presence in all things from worm to star to
thought—I meditate constantly even though it be, as I see
it, that my import to this, my Creator, can be but as
nothing, or less, if that were possible.*

*Yet awe I have. And, at long last, profound reverence
for so amazing and esthetic and wondrous a process, that
may truly have been, and for all that I know, may yet
continue to be forever and forever. An esthetic and wondrous process of which I might pray—and do—to remain
the infinitesimal part of that same that I now am.*

Theodore Dreiser, Hollywood, Nov. 1943

Part I

I. MY CITY

—encounter with Dreiser in New York, 1928-29

Dreiser in a black dinner suit, soft white shirt and black bow
tie was still not a figure reduced to any social scale. He was
force dormant in a man, and flashing out, as his glance flashed
under heavy, iron-gray brows, seeking some contact sacred
or profane.

That was my first impression of Dreiser as I found myself
sitting next to him at a dinner party of eight around a square
table at the home of Laetitia and Wallace Irwin, his good
friends. I must have been introduced to him before we went
into the table, but I do not remember it. Perhaps he had given
me one of those downcast glances or mumbled greetings behind which he sometimes hid, deliberately muting his own
personality. But I will never forget the physical reaction I
had when I found myself beside him and he turned to look
down at me as if I were a glass and he wanted to see what
sort of liquid was in it. I felt as though I were transparent, or
at least totally unable to dissemble anything about myself,
under that x-ray gaze.

Here was a human being, super-sensitive; a doctor of souls,
knowing them and seeing their secrets. So I felt him to be,
instantaneously, before the influence of his later words. I
have often wondered about it since—why was I so struck by
him, so sure of his understanding? At the time, I am ashamed

1

to confess, I had never read any of his works. Enthralled by French and Russian novelists, I had a stupid lack of interest in American letters.

But here was Dreiser, the shock of his personality, his presence radiating some kind of glow. His works? If he had never written a line, he was himself, literature; some concentration of human understanding both giving out and intensifying life.

Conversation around the small table was intimate, gay. Our host, Wallace Irwin, a successful writer, and Laetitia, his handsome wife were old defenders of Dreiser and there was ease and humor in their remarks. Dreiser did not get into argument, as he frequently did, I discovered later, in less congenial company. But his mind seemed like an open plain across which he could gallop or cavort in any direction. Several times he said things which made us laugh and he could clothe his words in a rich, sarcastic tone that would sound tragic or comic, as he wished.

After dinner, we sat on a stiff studio couch and talked casually for a time. But then Dreiser asked me what I was doing. It did not seem enough to him that I was married and took part in the rushing social life of New York.

"Nothing but a parasite," he teased, "I can put you to work."

He said he had just written a prose-poem called *My City* which was to be published in a special art edition. He needed illustrations which might fit into the mood of his text. Would I help him find some?

I promised to do so, since I frequently made the rounds of the New York galleries. He told me that there was also literary work with which I might help. His hand was on my knee in a way which was both paternal and confident. He said we would be friends and that he liked my Swedish face.

That is about all we said, but that first encounter with Dreiser was like a crossing of lines on a chart; there was a fatal and beautiful precision about it. For many years, we were to cross and re-cross at certain far-distant points in our lives like the courses of a great and a small ship, lost to each other for long periods and then meeting again, to exchange cargoes or render each other passing assistance.

The next day, Dreiser called at my apartment to bring the poem for which he sought illustrations. He strode about the living-room, looking at the fireplace of masonry and brick, flanked by French peasant wood carvings, and finally settled in a big, blue couch, scrutinizing me with his hypnotically deep, scowling eyes.

I perched on the arm of the couch beside him, reading his poem. Again, his presence was so intense that it aroused a strange defiance in me, like the threat of an impending storm. Finally, I jumped up, giving him back the poem. "I love it," I said, "but there's a poet I like better—whom I would rather know than anyone in the world."

"Who?" demanded Dreiser.

I went over to the book-case. He followed me, as I took out a small volume, entitled *Samphire,* by John Cowper Powys. "You probably never heard of him," I said. He took the book out of my hand:

"*Jack*"—and the way he said that word lingers in my memory like the sound of an oath or a vow. Dreiser had a manner of using his voice almost as a musical instrument, to envelop some syllable and give it emotion. No actor could give more impact or richness of meaning to a name than Dreiser gave this one with his warm, purring, scoffing, down-falling tone of love; it was like a word whispered by initiates, a pass-word for the recognition of secret ties of fraternity or blood.

For now Dreiser began telling me that Powys—the idol of my adolescence, of all the writers whose works I had devoured with a first hunger for life, the one who seemed to come nearest to some ultimate truth—this was his great friend and at that time, quite frequently, his companion of an evening.

So—that explained Dreiser's magic. There was the quality of dark genius in him too, the strange radiance which Powys seemed to give out in his work, and especially as a lecturer. I used to listen to him spell-bound when he came to our school

standing before us in his black college gown and stretching
his arms out for emphasis, like wide, dark wings. He had been
like a prophet, or a dread angel of ultimates, describing the
inner moods of Dostoievsky, or denouncing modern man for
not being able to believe in supernatural forces beyond his
limited understanding.

Response to the beauty and power and mystery of life
so strong, that the lover-of-life gets literally carried by his
emotion into identification with the *Thing* loved; this Powys
had. And now, obviously, as he talked, Dreiser had. Here
was some essence-of-life in a person, articulate, tangible.

When Dreiser left that day, I felt that a new world was
opening up to me. What a privilege it would be to work for
such a person—for he told me that he would train me and trust
me, in spite of my inexperience, and forgive me for not
knowing his books because I loved *Jack's*.

So, from the beginning, our friendship was based on a
love of things outside ourselves—Powys, Russian literature,
a probing into the mysteries beyond life; an impersonal element, sometimes chilling—like the thought of interplanetary
space. Yet also something that did not fade nor die.

Dreiser was like a whirling dynamo that winter of 1929.
After his success with *An American Tragedy,* many demands
came upon him. He was involved in new literary projects, he
handled a huge correspondence, with the help of his able secretary, Evelyn Light, and he was always being asked for articles and for his opinions on everything from the divorce laws
of New York State, to the doings of the Soviet Union, which
he had visited the winter before.

Besides this, he saw a great number of friends, old and
new, critics and admirers, and many who were drawn to his
magnetic person and sought to crash the gate of his big studio
on 57th Street.

Here was Helen, the beautiful hostess who shared his days.
She had left a promising career as an actress in the silent
films, because of her love for this strange companion, who
wanted both love and freedom.

Dreiser had been married for a number of years to a

woman from the Middle West. She had been a pretty school-teacher when he first met her, travelling on a train to visit the Columbian Exposition in Chicago to which he was being sent as a newspaper reporter. I have often felt that the sense of drama which Dreiser could convey about a train-ride—such as those in *Sister Carrie*—may have stemmed, in some degree, from this experience. He fell in love with this young girl, who, he thought, represented the education and culture for which he longed. But it was almost eight years, before he had enough money to marry her, and the romance had faded before its consummation. The climax of his disillusion came when he found that his wife was *shocked* by his first novel, *Sister Carrie,* failing to understand any of his serious intentions as a writer.

Finally, Dreiser broke away from his wife, but she would not give him a divorce, so for the greater part of his life, he was officially married to her. I do not think this made much difference to Dreiser, since he often said that he did not wish to marry again. The *varietistic impulse* which he attributed to so many of his characters, was very strong in him.

So it was that when, earlier, his lovely cousin, Helen Richardson, had come to call on him, and their romance developed into a serious relationship, Dreiser felt no compulsion to offer her marriage. She herself had been divorced and was eager to continue her acting and singing. Indeed, both Dreiser and Helen were artists of that period after the First World War when, for the first time in New York, there developed a free, Bohemian life, mostly centered around old Greenwich Village. Eugene O'Neill, Ernest Hemingway, Edna St. Vincent Millay, and many others had begun to express this new freedom in their writing, and in the circles where Dreiser then moved, defiance of convention was almost a rule of life. Thus it was that Dreiser and Helen had lived together, and sometimes, apart. Now, after the success of *An American Tragedy,* they felt prosperous and relatively secure. Helen had persuaded Dreiser to take a spacious apartment because of their many new friends and sudden high spirits.

Dreiser loved people and Helen did, too. She was a delight-

ful hostess, warm and generous in her appreciation of talent
and personality. It was exciting for both of them, at this
period, to see how easily they could gather really fascinating
groups of writers, publishers, painters, musicians, profes-
sionals of all sorts, who came to the regular Thursday evenings—at—home, to which Dreiser now consented.

The first evening we had met Dreiser at the Irwins, Helen
invited me and my husband, who was a handsome Southerner,
to come to the next big party at the studio. Entering, we first
saw an impressive cathedral-like window, running up two
stories to the baronial ceiling of the duplex apartment.
Smaller rooms opened off a balcony which crossed the inner
wall. At the bottom of this huge, dim, smoke-filled space, was
a piano, a big square desk, and some immense chairs. Large,
crudely painted reddish nudes ranged along another wall.

Guests came in evening clothes or sport jackets, long skirts
or more Bohemian get-ups, batik blouses, gay colors. Helen
took on a special glamor in a long, white hostess gown which
she often wore on these occasions. It molded her graceful
figure, and she moved around the room like a princess in a
fairy castle, greeting her friends and introducing them to
each other, with evident joy. There may have been fifty or
sixty people standing in groups, or milling around Dreiser;
there was animated exchange of thoughts, arguments, a welter of ideas and suddenly, music—a man's strong baritone
rang out, and people fell back, glasses, cigarettes in hand or
took chairs, thoughtful, attentive.

Dreiser liked to retire to a preposterously high-backed
ducal chair, an antique some admirer had given him. He
looked out through the fog of smoke and many personalities,
his eyes glowing under the domed brow, the unruly iron-gray
hair and thick eye-brows. How many women in the room that
night, felt their particular lure and penetration? Yet he could
keep them all at a distance because of a certain impersonality
of mood which he could wrap around himself, like a protective
cloak.

Among many interesting people there, were Sherwood Anderson, heavy-set and thoughtful; the handsome, Spanish-

looking Horace Liveright; blond, small-faced Martha Ostenso, Norwegian writer, with her Irish husband of the baritone voice; the enigmatic Russian Doctor, Boris Sokoloff; the dark, thin, high-strung Dorothy Dudley Harvey whose brilliant book *Dreiser and the Land of the Free,* had just been republished.

Late in the evening, Helen sang, as she often did at the end of a party. There was a Gypsy charm about her long, oval face and soft black hair. She sang in a low, husky voice, crooning her favorite spirituals, *Water Boy,* or *Sometimes I feel like a Motherless Child.* When she stopped, there were always people to urge her on and she would give a warm chuckle, a gracious, ingenuous laugh and gesture. And Dreiser was proud of her and the night would end warmly, because life was held there, somehow, in this room full of many artists and many temperaments, eddying around the rock that was Dreiser.

Day by day contacts with Dreiser were a different matter. Occasionally, I was summoned to the big studio, to pick up an assignment and there I would find Dreiser sitting solemnly behind his large, square rosewood desk, often gruff in manner and not in a mood for wasting time. Gradually he gave me so much to read and type that I took a room nearby where I could keep a typewriter and papers relating only to him. It was a gray room in an old house, with a photograph of Powys stuck in the mirror.

Dreiser came there only rarely. He was secretive about his ways, seldom planning ahead, according to any formal schedule, but preferring to remain free to respond to the urgency of the moment. When he called on the telephone, I was not always free to meet him. Sometimes I worked all day in the little room, not knowing whether he would come or not. It did not matter. When he did come, there was always some exciting new project to discuss, and more work, so that there was little time for sentiment.

Yet sometimes, Dreiser would be in such a happy, mellow mood, that he would throw himself down and begin to talk irrepressibly, about things having nothing to do with the work at hand. With women he was often more expansive than with men, and loved to share his reactions, good or bad.

"Imagine," he might begin, "So-and-so said *this* to me." Or, "Did you *see* what it said in the paper this morning?" Then he might go off on some tirade against snobbery or injustice. In other moods, he would indulge in an outlandish sort of humor, such as that in an exchange of letters with the English writer Gilbert K. Chesterton, who had attacked him in an article in *The Forum* of Feb. 1929, chiefly because of Dreiser's scorn for organized religion. Chesterton was himself a Catholic and this was a church for which Dreiser had particular antagonism (probably because he himself had been brought up as a Catholic, and revolted against churchly restraints, yet deep down, had remnants of a guilty conscience about it!)

Dreiser's reply, published in the issue of *The Forum*, for February 26th, was as biting, original and far-fetched as Dreiser could be himself, in clownish moments. He had utter scorn for conventional patterns of speech or thought, combined with readiness to laugh mercilessly at himself, as well as others, which led to the most ludicrous, not the most subtle, wit. Thus, in his letter, Dreiser picked up a suggestion of Chesterton's that "We might, indeed, meet on the street and fall on each other" .... and makes the most of it, for some four columns of type:

> *For neither his (Chesterton's) faith in revealed truth, nor that excellent business organization, the Catholic Church, nor his generally superior educational and other standards, appear to restrain him from this unhappy desire for violence. . . . Yet, I would not fall on Mr. Chesterton—not ever—not as evil as I am. For, as I hear, he is a man of weight in England, some two hundred odd pounds, on the English scale . . . Besides, I am small and of a retiring, apologetic disposition and would not risk myself in any such unarranged contact.*

> *But I have a suggestion, a most profitable one as I see it, for both of us. For only consider the standing of Mr.*

Chesterton, and the Barnumesque or Tex Rickardish
possibilities of such an arrangement as I am now about
to propose. By a single agreement and contract which
might involve little more than a fairly carefully simu-
lated violence—what publicity, what shekels—the names
of each of us spread across the front pages of all our
English and American papers—our fortunes made! Via
the courtesy and consent of Mr. Chesterton, of course, I
propose the receipt by myself, of a black eye—and since
my situation is as it is—that is, not too prosperous,—
in a public way and for money. For who am I? Am I
rich? Am I looked after? Am I liked, in America or Eng-
land? I am not. Yet, as I view it, with one swipe, if not
one stone, Mr. Chesterton might render me, and at the
same time achieve for himself, an almost incalculable
boon. Oh Lord! I scarcely know how to present it, but
actually it appears to involve fame, fortune, the outright
sale of my neglected works, the rejoicing of the entire
American body politic in some form of punishment for
me. . . .

So Dreiser goes on, *ad absurdum* in his picturing of this
literary prizefight with Chesterton. I remember the day when
he brought me this *lunatic* letter—he liked that word, and
used to call life a *lunatic* game. I was to make copies of it,
and he scribbled in some more nonsense in the margins—and
laughed and laughed, until his eyes filled with tears. He could
really see the whole thing happening, as in some old-fashioned
comedy—the incident was typical of the clumsy humor he
could use in talking, as well as making comic effects with his
actor's voice; it is evocative of the contradictory, controversial
figure he represented, that winter of 1929.

There was another matter concerning the Catholic Church
with which he worked with me at the time. It was a manuscript someone had procured for him, which was written
by a Catholic priest for other priests, on the subject of collecting monies from various types of people, including those
about to die. It gave some pretty callous advice which, of

course, Dreiser pounced upon as typical of cold-blooded materialism on the part of the Church.

"Ah, this will really show them up," he chuckled, laughing at my fears that such material might harm simple, faithful souls. But no—Dreiser, for all his love of humanity, was never one for protecting the morals and beliefs of the religious and the young—much as he himself treasured dreams and illusions. It was perhaps fortunate that he did not procure a publisher for his exposé of this manuscript, but he put it away in his files for future use, never doubting its value as some kind of argument against religion. In those days, he did not seem to understand the concept *religion* as one might define it from a philosophic point of view. Yet he was full of conflicting ideas, dark beliefs, and a driving force which he believed came from outside of his physical makeup.

Always a rebel in thought and feeling, a great volcano of emotions, erupting and quieting down, only to rumble and break forth again at the most unpredictable moments, he had never been a clear thinker. Now that his fame had raised him to a higher vantage point—heaved, as it were, this whole human volcano another hundred feet above sea-level—meaning the level of the average—he could amaze and bewilder and delight more minds—and also reach further to antagonize others not able to tolerate or cope with a mentality so original, so undisciplined, so little in line with any system of established thought.

That was his fascination, as it was Powys's. But where Powys had gone far, intellectually, toward explaining his own mysticism and intensity of life-experience, Dreiser simply *was* his own emotions, his own instincts, or intuitions, attempting to communicate them directly, often in terms contradictory to each other.

One thing that caught me off guard was his utter simplicity. In spite of all the words that he could weave around himself, there was inside the core of a man, direct, ruthless, and yet completely vulnerable, rawly sensitive, as ready to weep as to rage. Intense in his personal feelings, he could also withdraw into a mood aloof, and launch into speculations about the universe, at the slightest provocation. Perhaps it was his instinctive belief in the supernatural that protected him from being bogged down in the mire of sensuality. There was always something that leavened his realistic nature, raising it to a higher understanding than was always visible through his words or actions.

So it was that at the same time that he ranted against religion, he was going to see a famous Medium on the West Side and preparing a story for *A Gallery of Women* on *Giff,* —the strange little fortune-teller, whose predictions came true because of "something which is far more solidly real, if less material or electrical, than that which appears here: i.e. knowledge, direction, control." This is from Dreiser's introduction to *Giff,* in *A Gallery of Women.*

Sometimes we indulged in a kind of religious badinage meaning little to us at the time, yet in our near-blasphemous conversation there was a dark eagerness to defy ordinary forms of thoughts and get at some mystical understanding of life. Perhaps it was only expressed in a sardonic remark or a phrase in a letter. Dreiser might start a business memo, pinned to the top of a sheet: "Did Black Angel have copies of these?" Or once he scribbled: "This note is for Lodge A of the Sons and Daughters of Israfel." He often signed himself: "St. Theodore the Nubian" (without apologies to Anatole France!) It puzzled me that he used religious concepts without connecting them in any way with an ethical system.

Another thing that bewildered me at the time was that Dreiser believed man's will is not free—but that he is driven by a force, or ruthless destiny, call it what you will. But when I asked him if this was the *Fate, Ananke* in which the Greeks believed, he said, *no, not exactly*—simply that there is no such thing as *free-will* to believe *with.*

Such was Dreiser, paradoxical, vehement, not afraid to shock young minds or old, and yet how tolerant, how sympathetic to every human need or weakness. The first person I had ever known who seemed a completely free liver of life, prowling through all the colorful, flower-hung swamps and jungles of sensual experience, savage and subtle as a great cat; gentle and curious, purring with affection for all beauties, yet ready to turn and snarl at any moment, *your will is not free* or *religion is the bunk,* as if that other element in him— the psychic or cosmic (these words he would admit) were totally unrelated to faith, religion or God.

But people, men, women, were ever fascinating to him, whatever they believed or said they believed. He loved to study them, caught in the web of their multiple behavior patterns; whatever activated them, or inspired, he accepted them at their face value, as phenomena.

Women's characters and experiences interested Dreiser endlessly. He loved to question them about themselves, their impressions, their reactions to this and that. He was never tired of studying the likes and dislikes that made up, what was to him, the mystery of feminine behavior. It was fun to answer him, because he was so understanding—a strange confessor who did not blame but encouraged any sincere emotion. Women were tremendously stimulated by him, because he always wanted to build them up to whatever superior qualities they might have, wanted them to be their best, most daring, selves.

At the same time, he had come to be afraid of making commitments to any woman who might want to depend on him too much. He had had some devastating experiences with women who wanted to possess or dominate him. He did not want to attach himself to anyone, especially now that his work was his life, as never before.

This odd confessor was always unwilling to give advice on matters of personal behavior, no matter how inquisitive or serious he was about his soul-searching. He did not like making decisions for himself, much less for others. I told him that I might have a child, and asked him what he thought about this, as an expert on human experience. He hesitated a long time before he would give any kind of an answer. Finally, he said: "Well, I can't give you any advice on a subject like that. The only thing I can say is that I can't remember that a woman ever told me she *regretted* having one."

Similarly, when another friend of his asked for advice

about a man she was considering as a husband, he would not counsel her, but indirectly goaded her into marriage because of his apparent indifference. Yet, after she was married, he wanted her to explain *why* she was not happy!

It was at this time that Dreiser was collecting his sketches for his forthcoming *Gallery of Women*. I did certain confidential work for him in this connection and saw how carefully, and also how carelessly, he put together some of these stories. Between the lines, however, can be read his understanding and compassion for many entirely different types of wives and other women, many of whom he had known personally.

Odd little characteristics of Dreiser's came out on various occasions. Once, for all his scorn of society, he wanted to spend an evening with me, in complete luxury. I was to wear an elegant evening gown, and he, his tuxedo, and we would dine in a fashionable restaurant. Another time, I took him to lunch at the exclusive *Turf and Field Club*, at the Belmont Park Races. Dreiser enjoyed sitting at one of the gay tables on the lawn, eating delicacies and listening to the old-time orchestra, as he watched the smartly dressed women come and go. Afterwards, he lumbered happily about, rubbing elbows with Bernard Baruch, the Coreys, the Alexandres, Raoul Fleischman of the *New Yorker,* and others of the racing set.

Rich people had a certain glamor for him which, inspite of his scorn for a parasitic class, or for *ruthless* capitalists, never completely faded. He had struggled against poverty so long that he had never entirely satisfied his boyhood cravings for the "gay life" which he had seen pictured in the *Police Gazette* and the social notes of the newspapers he used to read, hanging around a bookstore in Warsaw, Indiana. Those were his own first desires that he put into the mind of the young Stewart, in *The Bulwark,* when he longs to be, in the language of the day, a *young blood,* attractive to girls, a figure in the social notes, a *man-about-town.* This little lust was in Dreiser, still.

When he came back from Russia, he passed through London, and ordered several expensive new suits, including about fifteen beautiful, soft, white tailored shirts for evening wear. Later, when he did not have enough occasions to use them, and they became crinkled and yellowed, he finished them off by wearing them as night-shirts!

One of the society matrons who often invited Dreiser was Alma Clayburgh, a warm, dark, exuberant dealer in personalities, who often managed to get into the social columns. Dreiser went to her parties for years, though he was usually bored by formal invitations. But Alma was delightfully clever and casual. She had a good voice, and once entertained her friends with Russian songs, imitating the words so well, that few realized she did not know the language.

The Russian Ballet

One of Dreiser's dominating interests that winter was his project of bringing the Russian Ballet to New York. The winter before, in 1927-28, he had made his much-talked-of trip to the Soviet Union and said, in a statement he was now releasing:

> *The keenest artistic impression that remained with me was that of the new Russian Ballet in Moscow. Here was an organization of the greatest dancers and pantomimists assembled by the leading musicians in a country which, for years, has taken precedence over all others in this form of creative art. . . .*
>
> *For six months I have carried on a cable correspondence with the highest authorities and after overcoming numerous difficulties, I am glad to say that the new Russian Ballet—one hundred of the leading dancers, musicians and scenic designers, etc. are ready to come to America for a four months' tour, beginning next fall. . . . My own interest in the Ballet is strictly an artistic one.*

But he went on to say that in order to raise money for this, he was organizing the *All Russian Ballet, Inc.* to issue $150,000 worth of preferred stock which he hoped to sell at $1,000. a share to America's leading cultural patrons.

Dreiser had already enlisted the support of the famous financier and art-lover, Otto Kahn, in this venture, and he had purchased $25,000. worth of stock. With this encouragement, it did not seem impossible to raise the rest of the money. It was truly an adventure for art's sake, and Kahn and Dreiser became fast friends in their common enthusiasm.

One fine afternoon, I was despatched to Kahn's office, to be considered as a sort of salesgirl for their project. I was frightened and suddenly shy although I had bought a new dress for the occasion, and did not want to disappoint Dreiser. But I arrived late, and spoke badly and though Kahn received me with the greatest cordiality, I am sure he was not impressed with my potential ability as a saleswoman. But I was amazed at his warm feeling for Dreiser. He sent me back with two suggestions for contacts—and Dreiser's conviction that we could soon sell the rest of the stock was little short of *Cowperwoodian.*

For the first time, he was connected with a cultural enterprise which also partook of the nature of big business and dealings with world famous financiers, such as Kahn, and it really went to his head.

All that winter, he was glowing with the thought of bringing this big Ballet Company to *his* city. He strode along with a dream about it in his heart as he passed the entrance to Carnegie Hall, only a block from his studio. He loved to talk about things Russian, eat in Russian restaurants—of which there were a great many in New York at the time—and tell his friends about those fantastic productions, *The Hunch-Back Horse, Notre Dame,* or that new one, *The Red Poppy,* which they were going to see before their own eyes, very soon. Then they would see, too, the greatness of the new Russia that had risen from the Revolution. . . . There were things which he criticized about the Soviet Union at that time, and his book, *Dreiser Looks at Russia,* was full of divergent views, but the excellence of Soviet artistic production, he felt, was something above politics.

The manager of the Ballet project was a young man, Hy
Kraft, who had produced several plays and had asked Dreiser's permission to dramatize *Sister Carrie*. This production
did not materialize, but it brought to Dreiser's attention
Kraft's live, young talent, so different from his own that it
fascinated him. Brought up on the East Side of New York,
Kraft had the toughness, ingenuity and sophistication of a
city boy, as well as the subtlety and potential creativeness
of the Jewish temperament. He had a highly nimble, individual mind which could dance circles around Dreiser's,
delight him with endless stories, tease him, discuss art, sex,
politics—and the Ballet.

Both Dreiser and Kraft, at this time, fancied themselves
as professional balletomanes, although they had hardly seen
more than a couple of ballets before the Russian scheme
struck them. One night, they went up to see an older man
who really knew something about the art of the ballet, but
was not as enthusiastic about their project as they were.

They argued about Russia and the ballet, until far past
mid-night, Dreiser and Kraft, with their raw enthusiasms
certainly aggravating the old connoisseur. The next morning,
this older man was found dead in his garage, whether from
excess emotion, heart failure, carbon monoxide poisoning, or
some other cause, they never knew. But each accused the
other that they had argued too hotly, a sense of guilt over-
hanging them both.

Indeed, Dreiser's arguments were no little matter. They
could fill a room like a thunder-storm, frightening every one
around. Right, or wrong as he sometimes was, the basic emotion driving him was in itself worthy; love for his fellow-man,
anger at injustice, desperate knocking at the doors of truth
without patience, but with an eagerness to break through,
even at the risk of injuring himself, in his reckless quest
for the absolute.

Yet in his quieter conversations, what warmth there was,
and understanding of human beings in their illusions, limitations, loves . . . and always the willingness to help another,
toward self-expression or what he considered freedom.

Kraft, for one, could never forget how Dreiser encouraged him, talked to him about writing, and about his own early life, his struggles and lack of recognition. Once they estimated that if all the money that had now come in to Dreiser as a result of *An American Tragedy,* his first financial success, was spread out over the fifty-odd years that he had been trying to write, his earnings would be from 10 to 15 dollars a week. So that, perhaps, could be called the earning capacity of the greatest American writer since Poe and Whitman.

Music
Dreiser's attitude toward music was as original, stubborn, warm and contradictory as everything else about him. To say that he loved music was not strong enough; he was inordinately susceptible to emotion coming through music, to a point where music could irritate him quite as much as it could please him, if he did not understand it—could not translate it, at once, into emotional terms.

The *great* symphonies enthralled him, particularly those of Beethoven and Tchaikovsky, although he would not attempt to understand their structure. Grieg delighted him and immediately brought to mind the tragi-romantic figure of the man "hunchbacked and prophetic, struggling to say so much with his music." . . . Thus Dreiser described him in an interview with R. H. Wollstein for *Musical America.* He continued: "At once, I see Fjords and ice-capped horns, bleak winter light and buxom peasant girls in bright dresses. As a matter of fact, it takes very little material for Grieg to create a mood, compared to the hundreds and hundreds of words Ibsen has to use to say the same thing . . ."

This reaction to Grieg, shows Dreiser's entirely subjective and emotional approach to music. Indeed, he was an ideal "sucker" for program music, and what program notes he might have written himself, judging by the above on Grieg!

It was in the province of the tragedian—tragic music— that he came nearest to understanding this art, not his own. I remember sitting next to him in a box which had been given to us for a Boston Symphony concert at Carnegie Hall.

Through the grave movement of Beethoven's *Eroica,* he sat immobile, his brow bent, his mouth hanging open—absorbed completely in tragic trance. As the music ceased, he was too stirred to clap, but turned to me and murmured: "Think of all that going through his head—" as though Beethoven had just communicated to him some unutterable experience.

In the field of modern music, he was completely lost, and indeed it would be too much to expect him to pioneer in another medium, when he had already gone so far in clearing the jungle around new literature and thought.

In the same interview with Mr. Wollstein, he explains why he does not like opera: "It is too clumsy, inharmonious in those structural proportions necessary for a perfect whole. . . . Nevertheless, I have to go to Wagner for the perfect expression of German fancy, the imaginativeness of the Teuton." Certainly, Wagner is akin to Dreiser's own Teutonic sense of inescapable destiny and gloom.

Later, in the interview, he somewhat wistfully states that the only opera which completely satisfied him was *Pelleas and Melisande,* with Mary Garden! (Probably it was the voluptuous lady herself who enchanted him.)

For the Ballet, however, ah, here again the incongruity— Dreiser waxes eloquent. But he frankly breaks with any consideration of ballet as music. It is the movement which counts now, the Russian choreography:

"I got the greatest kick out of that," he tells Wollstein. "There you have mass movement, mass color, mass spirit, and the most stirring effect of concerted and unified action." He goes on to consider the many dancers, the wonderful way they are brought up and trained and treated, as a result of the new Soviet freedom and reverence for art!

In leaving the subject of music, I must try to explain that there was always a musical quality about Dreiser himself, if it was only the vibration of his extraordinary soft, low and harmonious voice, when he spoke. He was also capable of making sounds in his speech, between words, or to emphasize words, to envelop them in a deeper, sardonic, or affectionate meaning. There were *Ahh's* of surprise or *Baah's* of scorn, or sounds, sighs or purrs, too subtle to correspond to letters.

He had a way of humming, a sort of running accompaniment to happier thoughts and moods. A low, harmonious undercurrent which bore his restlessness smoothly along. Sometimes he would follow some old melody or refrain of the day; at other times, it seemed as if he were making an indistinguishable murmur, like the noise of bees on a summer afternoon, usually in a minor key.

I can remember particularly how Dreiser used to hum when he was riding along in a car, after a happy day in the country. His low voice would fit into the purr of the motor, or rise above it, in some favorite old musical comedy number or verse for which he knew the words. Sometimes it was the melancholy, *Lover, Come Back to Me:*

> "I remember every little thing you
>   used to say
> No wonder I'm so lonely. . . ."

Or the lines he had written himself, for his brother Paul Dresser's *On the Banks of the Wabash:*

> "Through the sycamores, the candle-lights are gleaming
> On the banks of the Wabash for away . . ."

And the night would have a wholeness and a beauty around his humble song.

Charles Fort

Dreiser always enjoyed talking to those who ventured into the field of psychic or cosmic phenomena. A valued friend of his was Charles Fort, author or compiler of that curious *Book of the Damned.* The *damned* were not people, but *facts,* happenings that science had banished or condemned to silence, because it could not explain them. They included everything from natural phenomena, such as a rain of live frogs over an African desert, to supernatural events of the haunted-house variety.

Fort's method was to spend hours in libraries all over the

world, looking for items about strange facts and occurrences, in old newspaper files or journals. He would collect them and string them together in his own fashion, arranging them without apparent art, yet with purpose of his own, creating mystery and climax; he really practised an involved form of *documentary art,* before this expression began to be popular.

One evening, Fort came to Dreiser's studio when I happened to be there. He was a low-set man, dark with a greasy complexion, scant black hair brushed over a round, dynamic head. His hands were fat and protruded from filthy shirtcuffs under a dark, nondescript suit. In spite of all this, there was something fascinating about him; he seemed utterly alive, carefree and all-knowing, as he talked. His mind was clear of any tradition or prejudice, reaching for knowledge as a native skin-diver grabs for fish. Indeed, he seemed like some subterranean creature, living in dim caverns, delving under the surface of ordinary knowledge, to bring up strange, questionable and incongruous treasure; unidentifiable facts, cosmic mistakes, ghastly beauties, like the *Samphire* of Powys' imagination.

Dreiser loved Fort for this curiosity, devilment and immense verve. He could get Fort talking, in a smooth and gleeful manner, although it was said that he was a veritable recluse and wouldn't see people for days at a time. He had a miserable apartment somewhere in the Hell's Kitchen section of New York. But he never settled anywhere for long. He would get restless, and go off on a trip to collect more strange *facts.*

The night I saw him in Dreiser's studio, Fort told us a story of what happened to him once, in London, his first home. He had grown tired of a routine job, and scraped enough money together to go down and buy a passage to South America. When he reported to the dock a few days later, he found that the steamship agency had made a mistake and sold him a ticket to South Africa! A ship was leaving for South America a few days later, and of course, the agency was willing to change his ticket, but he decided to take the first boat out. It made no difference to him, he said, as long as he got away. And as a matter of fact, he found a lot of new and curious stuff in the libraries of South Africa.

Dreiser roared with amusement over this story, and urged Fort to talk on, relishing his originality and the eerie universe he evoked with his odd investigations. This was the cosmic world into which Dreiser, too, loved to plunge, and to hear the two men talking together was an experience which also illuminated Dreiser's daring way of thinking.

Certainly Fort was one of the people who prodded Dreiser into serious scientific study. For though Fort made a point of flaunting science in his half-sarcastic reports on natural phenomena, he also knew a great deal about it. His brilliant anarchist-tempered mind had turned out a number of books which had gained him a special following, indeed a *Fortean Society* had been formed around his work and personality. After the *Book of the Damned,* which Liveright had published at Dreiser's insistence, in 1949, there followed *New Lands,* (Liveright, New York, 1923), *Lo,* published by Claude Kendall, New York, 1931, and *Wild Talents,* also published by Mr. Kendall, in the same year. All these volumes were crammed with sensational and often hair-raising occurrences. In Dreiser's copy of *Wild Talents,* he had underlined Fort's statement: "Upon the principles of quantum mechanics, one can make reasonable almost any miracle, such as entering a closed room, without penetrating a wall, or jumping from one place to another, without traversing the space in between." Again in the same book, Dreiser underlined: "Professor Einstein applies the principle of uncertainty not only to atomic affairs, but to such occurences as the opening and shutting of a shutter on a camera."

In *Wild Talents,* and also in *Lo,* there are numerous cases of what Fort calls *teleportations:* He believed "that there is a force, distributive of forms of life and other phenomena, that could switch an animal, say, from a jungle in Madagascar to a backyard in Nebraska." He quotes a story from *The New York Sun,* Nov. 12, 1931: "A certain Dr. Mathers had seen an animal acting strangely in his backyard, and found

it dead, the next day. It was an African *Lemur*—now stuffed
in the State University at Lincoln." No explanation was ever
found as to how it got there. This was simply one of thousands of cases, mostly expressed in the form of newspaper
clippings, which Fort had found and recorded. But most remarkable of all, to Dreiser, was Fort's way of surmising,
through some kind of instinct or intuition, what might be
the underlying *core* or *cause* of human life and actions. This
Fort had first put down in a remarkable manuscript named
X—which he had brought to Dreiser back in the days of his
10th Street studio. Let Dreiser tell of it in his own words:

> *Fort, in his book, saw certain rays, only he did not call
> them* X *or* Cosmic, *for* X *was the mysterious something
> from which these rays were emanating. But what these
> rays did, and wherein it was that their wonder and
> power lay, I will try to show. These rays were the ema-
> nation of something that was capable* through them *as
> a* medium *of creating us, you, me, all animals, plants,
> the earth and its fullness, its beauty and variety and
> strangeness, its joy and sorrow and terror as well as
> the ecstasy of this thing we call life in all its variety and
> scope. And* X *did this quite as we, by the means of light
> and photography, throw a moving picture on a screen,
> the sensitive chemicals of a photographic film and the
> light that causes that film first to receive an impression
> of something and later, to retransmit it as seemingly
> the very substance of reality. Only to* X, *the earth is
> the sensitive film and its speeding rays, the light of the
> modern film camera.*
>
> *Of course, all this was interwoven with comments on the
> history of man, or the dubiousness of his recorded knowl-
> edge, the unreliability of his so-called facts, together with
> much data sufficiently substantiated to seem to be well
> worth accepting, or, if not that, of investigating . . .*
>
> X *was an amazing book and at the time I thought to my-
> self, "Well, here at last is something new . . ."*

Dreiser goes on to tell how various publishers rejected the Fort manuscript, until finally Dreiser asked him to leave a copy with him:

"But no, he wouldn't do that. He took it away, and the next thing he told me was that he had destroyed it, and was writing The Book of the Damned *and that he would rather I would interest myself in that, which I did, only still believing that X was even more wonderful. . . ."*

We will see how the idea of Fort's *X* haunted Dreiser and was later brought into his own *Philosophy.* At this time, however, Dreiser had not begun his own more systematic research, and these ideas of Fort's were like strong drink to his curiosity.

The Nigerian Head Hunters

A memorable occasion in the big 57th Street studio was the party to welcome a group of Nigerian Head Hunters to this country. They were male dancers brought from Africa and discovered in Harlem by Caroline Dudley, herself a dancer and one of the three talented Dudley sisters, whom Dreiser had first known in Chicago. Dorothy Dudley, already mentioned as the author of *Dreiser and the Land of the Free,* was a frequent visitor to the studio, a dynamic, subtle, sensation-loving person. It was she who encouraged her sister Caroline, to celebrate the arrival of the dancers here.

The big room was filled with the usual contrasting personalities, the atmosphere already heady with smoke, drinks and spirited conversations, when the Nigerians suddenly appeared, issuing from the back regions of the apartment and running across the huge, dim studio toward the piano. They threw the room into a near-panic, with their cries, costumes and gleaming bodies.

They wore little more than grass or fur loin-cloths, weird masks or painted faces. The lean, taut nudity of them, the speed, noise, novelty of their dance was almost too much for the space given them. People pressed back against the walls, against each other, to leave more room, and to contain their own emotions.

The dancers' rhythm was wild, explosive, and they hurled words, shouts, shudders as they leapt and circled; the whole place was filled with the odors and passions of the jungle.

For once, something seemed strong enough for Dreiser. He was speechless, aglow. As the head hunters ran out, people tried to recover themselves in wild applause.

Some wanted the dancers to stay on, but they were spirited away as quickly as they had come. Caroline Dudley told us afterwards, that they had to be cared for like strange children, because some had come directly from their tribes and their behavior was unpredictable.

They were part of a small migration from Africa, at that time. Harlem had lured them, to dance in night-clubs, or take other jobs, but a number of them got into trouble, and were deported, again. Others stayed on, and became assimilated, so that actually there are a number of Negroes in Harlem who are first-generation Africans. Indeed, Dreiser had a Negro maid who married one of these Nigerians.

People who were in the studio that night did not forget that party. It was in a sense, one of the climaxes of all that happened there, the evenings of good music and literary conversation, notwithstanding. There were not many more parties after this, as the studio was given up the following year, and this occasion stood out in Dreiser's mind, as it did in the memories of others, as *The Night the Nigerian Head Hunters danced in the Studio,* a kind of symbol of the strong emotions that gathered around Dreiser.

Later, I teased Dreiser, asking why he did not follow these Nigerians to Harlem to find out more about their primitive dancing and love-making, since he was so fascinated by them. But he shrugged off the question. There was a limit to his curiosity about sex. Much as he was obsessed by it, at certain times, he never explored it for its own sake. There must always be a strong, personal element of romance and mystery about any situation in which he could become involved.

In every woman, Dreiser sought some special feminine

charm, some quality of mind or body, some emotional response made to him, alone. And here his great love of secrecy came into play. He wanted no talk about his emotional life, no confessions, from *his* side, and he enjoyed love most when there was no plan, and very little premeditation about his actions. The most desirable thing to him was a romance which he could keep in his mind, as a thing of beauty—to respond to it, in the urgency of the moment, was passion, creative fire. But he wanted both; illusion and reality.

One evening, I happened to be driving by a different section of the city in my car, and saw him lumbering gaily up the street with a cute little figure of a girl who fairly tripped along to keep up with him. I could not see her face, but she wore white cotton stockings, like a trained nurse or a nursemaid. He seemed happy, and hidden in such an anonymous mood that I never wanted to ask him about it. But that picture of him seemed typical of his devious, unfathomable ways.

II. A PLACE IN THE COUNTRY
—Mt. Kisco and Wood's Hole, 1929

Mt. Kisco—Iroki

With the earnings of *An American Tragedy* Dreiser, in 1927, fulfilled a long-nurtured dream of having a place of his own in the country. About four miles from Mt. Kisco, New York, he had bought a large stretch of land overlooking one of the Croton Reservoir lakes.

Coming along the dirt road from Mt. Kisco, a heavy stone fence on the left marked Dreiser's property. A solid wood gate, painted a bright blue, swung open and a downward trail, at that time hardly more than two ruts running through the grass, led to a stony hillock, crowned by a rustic bungalow of white birch logs. Originally a hunting lodge, Dreiser had added considerably to it. The wide porch commanded a fine view of the reservoir, about half a mile away. All around were rolling hills, unkempt meadows. To the left of the bungalow rose the long shoulder of a higher ridge, but the rest of the ground fell away toward a small pond. Here were groups of trees, a copse, and woods in the distance. Beyond the lake were rather bleak, pointed hills foretelling the Berkshires.

The first day we drove up there was a prematurely warm Sunday in May. We walked down to the pond which was lush with leaves and grasses. But Dreiser had had it dug deep enough for swimming and he suggested that we take a dip—

26

which we did—Helen and Teddy, my husband and I—in our underclothes!

Dreiser loved the water, as much as anyone I have ever known. Not so much to be on it, as in it, or near it, looking into water, to answer an inner mood. His books are full of the fascination he found for this element—which, the psychologists tell us, is a symbol of the subconscious. In *Dawn* he describes his boyhood walks in the country, when he thrilled to the sight of "certain aspects of the morning and evening sky. . . . small pools in the woods in which leaves and trees were reflected."

In *The Bulwark* manuscripts there were many early descriptions of Lever Creek, into which the young Solon liked to look and where he caught fish in a dip-net for the young Benecia. Dreiser wrote about this brook, flowing quietly through Solon's property, and at the end of the old Quaker's life, he sits by it again, brooding over the wonders of nature, and the Creative Force.

On that mild Sunday, Dreiser told us he was planning to make his pond still bigger and deeper, plant trees near it, and build a larger house just above it, where the ground was smoother and a lawn might be made.

In the meantime, the white-birch bungalow was adequate and delightful. In the center of the main room, there was a long, plank table, with benches on either side. As the weather grew warmer, Dreiser came here every Sunday, and as always, people gathered around. As many as twelve or fifteen might sit along the plank table, eating and drinking, and talking endlessly about life.

Here, as at the studio, Dreiser held open house; he loved the ferment and exchange of a gay crowd around him. In the country, there was an even more relaxed and free atmosphere. On week-ends there might be as many as six or seven cars parked at odd angles in the grass and, at the blue gate, more cars whose owners had hesitated to drive down the long rutted road through last year's uncut meadows.

The young Burton Rascoes used to come over from a nearby town, bringing their children. Konrad Bercovici and his fam-

ily would motor over from Ridgefield, Connecticut where they
had just settled on an old farm. Many drove out from New
York. I remember the large, red-haired writer, Ford Madox
Ford, who argued with Dreiser until the two waxed vehement,
yes, even here in the hills, over religion and the cosmos.

Here I first saw Dreiser indulge in one of his favorite tricks,
which consisted in bringing two friends together, who, he
knew, disagreed on some interesting topic. He would start
them off, arguing with each other, and then sit back to enjoy
the fray!

There were other evenings, too, full of peace and calm
beauty; then Dreiser would sit in a rocker on the porch, looking over the hills. When guests had gone or on week-days,
the place was like a sanctuary, the big blue gate swung closed.

Later, Dreiser built two cabins on this property. The first
was a genuine log cabin, constructed by his friend, Wharton
Esherick. Long and low, it was fitted under the brow of the
high hill to the left of the white-birch bungalow. It had a
heavy, masonry chimney at one end and the door opened at
the center of the other end, away from the valley. A few tall
trees acted as sentinels around the door. The windows were
very small, and the roof came down to within a few feet of
the ground. Dreiser loved this place and hoped to work in
it. John Cowper Powys, who had settled for a while, in a
small farm some miles from Dreiser watched the building
of this hut which was almost like something from his native
Welsh moors. He begged to spend the first night there, after
it was completed, and Helen tells of his performing a Celtic
house-warming rite in it. Dreiser did work in the cabin a few
times and spent some time camping out here, at various
periods, but he found that it was too damp to stay in for long,
especially in the summer when it was too hot for a fire.

So eventually Dreiser built a more prosaic little box of a
cabin, over the top of the highest hill on his land. It had one
room, a porch—and a magnificent view. Dry and airy, in the
hottest weather, it was rather like a look-out, for a fire warden. Actually, Dreiser never used it as much as he intended
for it took a good stiff walk to get up to it, and he did not want

to spend the money to have water brought to it, nor electric
light.

Then he began constructing the larger house, near the pool.
His decision to build had been precipitated by a fire which
broke out when he was not there, and burned the lovely white
birch bungalow to the ground. (Dreiser tried to sue a care-
taker who was supposedly responsible for a brush-fire which
had burned out of control, and so consumed the house. But
this was an unfortunate and unsuccessful attempt to console
himself for having lost the first place that had given him the
joy of having a *Dacha*, . . . Actually, he was never as happy
in the larger house, as we shall see.)

It was the land, the view, the thought of sinking roots—
if they were nothing more than the foundations of a new
house—into soil of his own, that gave Dreiser his greatest
satisfaction in connection with *Iroki*. There had been no place
in his life, hitherto, where he had been settled for any length
of time. As a boy, with his family, he had moved from one
shabby rented house to another, living in four different ad-
dresses at Terre Haute, where he was born, and then moving
on to other Indiana towns; Vincennes, Sullivan, Evansville,
Warsaw. Then followed the series of nondescript rooms in
Chicago, and the other cities of his newspaper days. Finally,
New York, with somewhat better lodgings, studios and apart-
ments. And at last, a home of his own, a big, sprawling place
in the country.

It was not the first piece of land that Dreiser had owned,
for he had bought a building lot in Glendale, California, when
he tried to settle there with Helen, and had bought others,
in Florida, near Fort Lauderdale, and later, in Santa Mon-
ica. . . . Some of these were investments which paid off well,
when they were sold; but in the beginning, each one had been
a dream of building in an ideal spot, for quiet, for work, and
then life had pulled Dreiser away again. Now here at Iroki,
the dream seemed to have come true.

Often, that spring, we drove out to Mt. Kisco, Dreiser,
Helen, my husband and I. Helen was a beautiful driver and

always looked well at the wheel. She reminded me of those *Concourts d'Élégance* which automobile salesmen and hotel managers put on in European resorts, where the elegance of the auto, plus the chic of the lady driving it, would win a prize, complete with ribbons and champagne, making, of course, excellent copy for photographers and the press.

Helen often wore big soft hats and gauntlet gloves, dress-maker sport-clothes in beiges, grays or whites. There was also Nick, the Russian Wolf-hound, who was Helen's constant companion for many years. He was a huge white curly-haired magnificent specimen, with a brown patch around one eye and a brown fleck on his side. He loved to ride in their open car, and followed Helen everywhere. I remember seeing them on 57th street one bright day, Helen in light clothes and Nick prancing elegantly on his leash, and everyone on the street turning to admire their beauty and style.

Wood's Hole, Nantucket—Dreiser and the Sea

During the following summer, of 1929, Dreiser spent some weeks at the sea-town of Wood's Hole, Massachusetts. Here his friend Calvin Bridges, an outstanding scientist, worked at the Marine Biological Laboratory and he had promised to show Dreiser some of his experiments.

Bridges was a bold lovable character, popular with his fellow scientists. He introduced Dreiser to a free, simple yet intellectual life of the most refreshing sort. Besides the growing fascination Dreiser was experiencing for scientific detail and discovery, he enjoyed the discussion and exchange of ideas each evening, around the table, or at informal meetings or picnics. Everywhere, the sea was a part of the picture, whether it was in the laboratory, or in the view of harbor or inlets, or just in the tangy, salt air of the port with its changing winds and tides, one was everywhere conscious of this marine atmosphere, and Dreiser loved it.

Not in the same way as he loved the ponds, the brooks, the *Banks of the Wabash*. But in a different way, his spirit responded to the bigness, the variableness of the sea.

When he had first come to Long Island Sound, in 1901, it

had been to share a cabin on a wild rock, near Noank, Connecticut, not far from here. He was with his friend Arthur Henry, and was later joined by his wife, and another girl. But this was not a happy period in his life. Coming from the Middle West he was not used to the sea and salt water. Everything seemed damp, and not clean. He brooded over the cruelty done to the fish that were caught, to the crabs that were used for bait. He was oversensitive because his whole struggle to live and to be a writer, seemed destined to failure.

But how much had happened since those days. He had become a world figure, crossed the ocean several times, grown to love the sea, and he had Helen, for his beautiful companion. He had accepted the scientific approach to life, whereby all things fitted into some vast pattern, and, although he was just as sensitive as ever to sufferings of man or beast, he did not make the problem of the universe as such a personal matter. Ideas were just as challenging—but they did not crush him. He was equal to playing with all of them—and did so, with such zest that he seemed to me a part of this whole seascape —a cosmic man rising out of all this beauty and freshness and mystery of nature, to question, and to claim his part in all of this—a very small part, to be sure—for at this period he said that he considered man "an infinitesimal individual." Dreiser was so gay, so irrepressible in his cosmic speculations that summer, that his mind seemed like a little, open boat riding the waves of that universe it knew not, swinging in the sun and summer wind, not weighted down but defying all conventional people and ideas, with its own brave, uncluttered construction.

I wish I could have jotted down some of the conversations I heard that summer, at Wood's Hole and at a beach on Nantucket Island about five hours away by boat where my husband and I had rented a cottage. I had had considerable correspondence with Dreiser about a piece of work I was doing for a *Gallery of Women* and he finally announced that he and Helen were coming over from Wood's Hole to visit us, one week-end in August.

Dreiser was in excellent humor. He loved our little house,

a typical resort cottage of the old-fashioned type, square living room around a red-brick fireplace, and above it four tiny bed-rooms, with dormer windows.

Above us, on a cliff carved by the sea, towered the huge red and white banded cylinder of the Sankaty Head light-house which could be seen by ocean liners, far away. A long flight of shaky wooden steps led to the beach below us. Most of the day we spent on this wide, white strip of sand, wearing our bathing suits, plunging into the water for a few tingling moments, and then sunning ourselves again, play-ing with bits of shell or stone as we talked, and looking off over the endless incoming blue waves. Helen and I decked our-selves with garlands of sea-weed and we took photos of each other in this happy, sun-kissed mood.

On Sunday, we were joined by Calvin Bridges and Cleves Kincaid, an old friend of my husband's, a playwright whose one great success, *Common Clay*, carried him through years of less successful writing—a witty and delightful character whom Dreiser immediately liked. He had a small thin body with scant reddish hair, not thoroughly covering his dome, and very fair skin of the sort that freckles and burns badly; because of this he wore a long raincoat, trailing over his bathing suit as he wandered about the beach, and a large, linen cap such as worn by the first motorists of linen-duster days. He thus presented an outlandish yet somehow dis-tinguished appearance, and my husband invented the name *Palgrave Seymour, the famous Botanist* by which Dreiser and all of us affectionately teased him. Indeed, he had that natural and somehow pathetic dignity which comedians like Charlie Chaplin or Eddie Cantor have rendered irre-sistibly appealing. Coupled with this, he was an excellent raconteur of stories both ludicrous and literary.

Bridges, on the other hand, was a larger, less delicate character. Almost tow-headed, he had deep scintillating blue eyes, a quick smile which threw his features into a con-tagious, country-boy grin. He was in love with life, crazy about women, and really brilliant and serious about his work.

With these men it was easy for Dreiser to plunge into

those far-reaching philosophical conversations which he loved, as he did the sea.

I remember how strange it seemed to me, at this time, that Dreiser, his fame secure, his personality triumphant, judged by worldly standards, should still seem so uncertain as to the meaning of life, so shaken by doubts as to the validity of human existence. My husband was also a person of deep feelings, great intelligence, and yet of pessimistic temperament; similarly, Cleves Kincaid did not hold forth any salutary theories of life. Bridges alone, of the three, had a definite, optimistic view: Science has the answer. Why look further? See how we are all victims of cause and effect, and then go ahead and enjoy life to the full; don't worry about reasons or explanations on a vague, philosophical plane: *Live* as fully as possible, in response to these stimuli of nature, whether you are studying them in the laboratory, or come upon them in life outside, particularly in the form of beautiful girls!

Dreiser was quite ready to agree to this program, and indeed, followed it himself. And yet, always, he was haunted and *pulled* by all the other possibilities—What if this was not all? And what of the *other* forces at work, those veiled, mysterious forces of darkness that he had believed in almost more than in the forces of Light; the things that you could not escape, even if you did not seek the good; the weird, the inexplicable, the evil, perhaps even the super-evil. . . . For did he not *see* faces at the foot of his bed, sometimes, evil faces such as he had described in *The Hand,* and also later, described to me? And what about the strange things he had seen happening at séances, the inexplicable messages of the Ouija Board?

Pooh! Learn more about science, and these things don't bother you, was the answer of Bridges, who had never had any such psychic experiences. Then would come another story about some girl, and his laugh, and so the conversations on the beach, and later, around the fireplace, got nowhere, but circled pleasurably to their quick temperaments.

Sometimes Helen and I would put in our "two cents" worth

of opinion, and here it was that Dreiser was always courteous, curious as to what we had to say, eager to encourage self-expression and fearless pursuit of whatever concepts we could offer. He had respect for the *urge* that is in every individual to express, to speculate and to *proceed,* even though it be in the direction of darkness, of still greater uncertainty. The motion onwards, the *obedience*—and here he became a supernaturalist again—to the superior or stronger Force which is driving you *anyway,* whether you want to obey it or not, this was all-important; this was response, to the Stimulus, behind the stimuli.

Whether we were on the beach or by the fire, there was always this heightened sense of living, because Dreiser was there, bearing up all the smaller personalities in his compassionate interest, making us gaze off into the very face of the cosmos as he did, restless and irrepressible in his desire for truth, as the ocean itself.

Fall and Winter, 1929-1930

In the fall of 1929 Dreiser returned to his 57th street studio. Immediately, he became involved in all sorts of conflicts, literary and personal. I did not work for him, as I was living in the country expecting a child, but Dreiser had a habit of sending out copies of his controversial articles, or letters, to a wide list of friends, as well as opponents; I was a recipient of a number of these barbed communications.

Most of them now, do not bear repetition, since they reflected matters of the day. Some were against censorship, against the Catholic Church, against the divorce laws of the State. Some defended his views on the Soviet society, and some showed an erratic, independent thinking; "He was not to be restricted in his speculations by Moscow, any more than by Boston"—and indeed, the Soviet press criticised him for his petit-bourgeois outlook and noted that "his value lay in the artistic portrayal of the decay of capitalism, rather than in an affirmation of alternatives." Quotations are from Robert Elias' *Theodore Dreiser,* Alfred Knopf, 1949.

Certainly, he was not afraid of hurting nor of being hurt

and some of his remarks seem unnecessarily belligerent and even petty today.

But this was the Dreiser who, scorned and rejected for so long, could now be heard, and make *polite society* smart with his denunciations. Now that he could feel his own strength, he loved to fight, in public as well as in his home, with friends as well as with foes, with women, with publishers, with churches, with the world. . . .

I had already seen him engaged in two arguments which had really shaken me although I had been only an observer and not the object of his anger. Helen once said to me: "Teddy loves to fight. I think that one reason he likes me is because I can always give him a good fight." That was true and that winter he seemed increasingly embattled.

Yet there was always the other side of him, that was brimming with a warm response to life, to women and children, seeing the lighter side of his daily struggle. His sense of humor was clumsy but delightful. More or less as a joke, I had sent him a questionnaire, with self-addressed envelope, so he would have no trouble in answering it. For in spite of all his other work, he liked to get letters from women and took trouble to answer them, in his small hand. Now he filled out my blanks promptly: (Dreiser's words in quotes) When may one expect the new book? "Which one?" (I meant, the *Gallery of Women,* but he was also working on another.)

Is there any Balm in Gilead? "Yep—the name has been changed to Vicks, 26 million bottles last year . . ."

Have you any helpful suggestions concerning life? "Yep. Turkish Baths. Cocktails, lewd, licentious tales, impudently told; drunkenness, witty, destructive comments about others. Stock rises. Kind words (when received). The hope of blessings to come. The charms of letter like yours. The knowledge that the Holy Father retains his health. Dough in plenty."   (Signed) "St. Theodore the Nubian."

In December my husband and I came to New York, where our child was born, in the Harbor Hospital. A few days later, Dreiser sent me the deluxe edition of *My City,* for which I had found illustrations; a handsome book, two feet tall, with an affectionate inscription. With it came a letter addressed to my new son: "Dear Hilary; Welcome to this best of all possible worlds . . ."

There followed a manuscript of great charm and rhythm, in Dreiser's inimitable letter-style, his small, rounded handwriting flowing along page after page. Full of humor and delicate affection, it was the other Dreiser, poet and chivalrous admirer of the weaker sex, and of the tender, unspoiled and remote. How lovely he could be with children, although he never had any of his own, how responsive to the poetry of awakening things. Later, in *The Bulwark*, this quality came into his work, but it was always in his attitude toward the very young. The letter has been published in *Collected Letters of Theodore Dreiser,* so I will not repeat it here.

Shortly after the New Year—1930—I saw Dreiser and found him depressed about business matters and other things. Late in 1929, the stock market had crashed and half of Dreiser's earnings on *An American Tragedy* had been swept away or greatly lowered in value. Some of his stocks, however—through lucky intuition—he had redeemed and changed into gold, which he kept in a small, roundish black bag, in a vault of his bank. Later, when gold was called in, he re-invested this money to advantage. However, he had lost a great deal, and was now involved in considerable expense because of his expanded way of living, at the studio and at Mt. Kisco.

Dreiser also admitted that the Russian Ballet project had fallen through. The reason seemed to be a mysterious block on the Soviet side. He heard later that persons involved had been suspected of disloyalty or profiteering, but whatever the cause, the whole thing was an unmitigated disappointment to Dreiser. Some of the money he had collected could be returned, but many investors in his Ballet stock had to take a loss. This put him in a very embarrassing position.

Another thing that troubled him was the various critici-

cisms that were being made of his *Gallery of Women,* which
had come out in November. Many were not good and he himself was dissatisfied yet belligerent about his work.

He was dynamic as ever, if somewhat more brusque than
than the winter before. He seemed to be eating and drinking
more. He had gained weight and, as usual in winter-time,
he was struggling with one of his bad, bronchial colds which
made him cough and spit into his handkerchief in what
might have seemed a most objectionable way, to one not
interested in his personality as a whole.

I did not feel the full impact of his distress, as I was occupied with my child and did not see him often. But I sensed
a fierceness and loneliness of mood in him which was almost
terrifying.

It was about this time that Kraft told me he had spent a
day with Dreiser which lengthened into an evening and then
a whole night, as they talked and brooded over drinks in
the big studio. Dreiser would not let Kraft leave; he was in
one of his blackest depressions:

"I can't live," he told Kraft, "I think I'm going to die."

He seemed overwhelmed with a sense of futility, of guilt.
Moods like this had come upon him before, at various times
in his life. Each time, his despair took on the special character of the circumstances which beset him, but also plunged
deeper, to some underlying level of disillusion and despondency in his very nature.

Now it was partly financial reverses, distress over his
Gallery of Women—which he knew included some very bad
stuff, yet trucks were going around the city with advertise-
ments about it plastered on their sides—and again, no one
knows what personal agonies.

For Dreiser sometimes experienced the soul-sickening
heaviness, the kind of disgust that Baudelaire and Oscar
Wilde and other artists and sensualists have reached, which
does not, strangely enough, differ very much from the pros-
trations of certain saints or mystics before their God. Only
in these high-powered, self-ridden artists there is no relief,
for they do not seek forgiveness or purification, as does the

saint, but only turn in the mud of their own senses like
wounded eels, until some stimulus from life itself jerks them
upward again.

These moods had given Dreiser a special understanding of
Oscar Wilde, his *De Profundis* written behind bars, and his
imprisonment in *Reading Gaol* haunted Dreiser, so much
so that he went to visit the place long after Wilde was dead.
I wonder if Dreiser had it in mind as a symbol, when he
wrote his prose-poem *Mood, The Prisoner:*

> *How well I have succeeded in concealing the ill that is*
> *   mine. . . .*
> *Nevertheless*
> *Chained in the deepest dungeon of my soul,*
> *It speaks.*
> *I can hear its sighs, its groans.*
> *And there, in spite of me*
> *At times I must go—*
> *I cannot avoid it—*
> *Into that darkness. . . .*

In March, Dreiser boarded a train and headed West. He
had been continually bothered by heavy colds, but this was
also an attempt to cure the restlessness that was in him. He
had travelled through Arizona and New Mexico briefly at an
earlier period, with Helen, but now he was determined to
go alone and get his fill of this wild and special country.

From a doctor-friend in Tucson, he rented a large car and
started off with several blankets and scant camping equipment, along the then deserted roads, running south, through
Indian reservations, toward the Mexican border. Each night,
he simply pulled the car off the road and lay down on the
ground near it, an old rifle beside him and a blanket pulled
well over his head.

During weeks of this strange camping, no animal harmed
him nor even disturbed his slumber. He saw as few people as
possible, going in to cheap roadside restaurants to eat. Only
then would he talk, to Indians or anyone who happened to be
there, asking them about themselves or the country he was

traversing. Then he would always find out some "interesting little facts," and go on, at home wherever he might be.

"It was something like this"—he said once, when we were driving through desert country, his last year in California. He made a sweep of his long hand, over a great plain, stretching as far as you could see without a break, except for dotted bushes of sage or lupine; with an occasional cactus. Then he continued:

"To sleep, I didn't take care to choose any particular place. The ground always seemed comfortable enough. What I loved was being out in the night and seeing the sky, with nothing but a blanket over me. You can't imagine how near the stars were, and how *many* stars.". . . And he said *stars* in that special diapason tone reserved for those things he loved.

It was a time of inviolable recuperation for him. But it was a wonder that he did not end up in the accident ward of some hospital or was not found lying dead beside a smashed car. For he told me that several times he was so lost in the landscape, or in his own thoughts and reveries, that he drove straight off the road! Indeed, it was this trip that made him decide to give up driving, except when absolutely necessary, because he found it so hard to remember what he was doing. He had never had a feeling for mechanics and always preferred to let others drive, when possible, so that he could give himself over to the contemplation of the scene he was passing, or follow his own inner train of thought.

However, this trip did not end as a hermit's pilgrimage. When Dreiser got to Texas, he suddenly plunged back into the world of art and ideas. He attended the Dallas Symphony Orchestra concert, and went to the Oak Cliff Little Theatre, where he saw *Jute*, a play by Kathleen Witherspoon, which greatly pleased him. Congratulating her on her work, and that of the Theatre, he said:

"Leave any part of the United States alone, and it will develop a native culture"—Even in those days, Dreiser bewailed the fact that American culture and artistic expression seemed to be falling into a pattern of sameness and commercialism, as dictated by Hollywood and the big advertisers.

A new controversy brought him back. Word had come to him that Irving Babbitt, professor and critic, was going to attack him, H. L. Mencken and Sinclair Lewis, in a *Humanist* manifesto; Carl Van Doren and Henry Seidel Canby were also lined up against him.

Dreiser lost no time in answering the on-coming attack. His reply was printed in *The Dallas Morning News*. He sent me the clipping and it shows Dreiser at his sarcastic best. It reflects his own struggle for self-expression, as against the prudish and insensitive critics who had attacked *Sister Carrie, The Genius,* and other writings and opinions of Dreiser's down through the years. It is curious to observe how censorship has broken down since those days; it would seem that many of our modern novelists employ vulgarity for its own sake. This Dreiser did not do, despite his *realism*. He was always deeply sincere, and delicate in revealing personal relationships.

I did not see Dreiser when he returned east, as I had gone away for the summer. I saw him briefly in the fall when I showed him a manuscript he had encouraged me to write. He gave me criticism and a short blurb which I used when my novel, *Borealis*, was published the following spring: "The honest analysis of character is here very well done. . . . The book carries one along. It is the smooth, enticing current of a moody, changeful, sensitive mind."

Grateful as I was to Dreiser, I felt that I had no part in his complicated life. I was determined to start my life over again, this time, in Switzerland where I then established residence, in order to obtain a divorce.

It was almost three years before I was to see Dreiser again. I treasured the clipping he had sent me, because it seemed to express the first Dreiser I had known—irrepressible, full of outlandish humor, pugnacious, and yet also brooding, profound, an avid lover of life and beauty and mystery. The following interview in the *Dallas Morning News,* May 6, 1930, captures some of his zest and spirit:

DREISER IRED AT CENSORING BY HUMANISTS

Unless I am greatly mistaken, humanism *is a phase of literary reform; we are to write not necessarily greater but more gentlemanly, or, should I say, ladylike books . . . In short, Dr. Babbitt and his confreres appear to be joining up with the Watch and Ward Society, the League of Catholic Writers, and Methodist Book Concern and Reed Smoot. . . .*

Life, in the case of the writer at least, and if the humanists *are to have their way, is to be approached in a* gentlemanly *spirit. His watch-word is to be*—It's not done. *He is to be alert to select what will not offend conservative thought, have a constructive, social conscience and do his duty by it . . .*

But, as I have repeatedly said, it is not any given society but life, nature, a universe, no less, with which he has to deal and so confronted, a social conscience is not always an exact guide. For there, and quite in the face of the aspirations of organized society, Dr. Babbitt and its other well-wishers, we find not only offensive but desperate and so most dramatic material which organized and quite polite society would rejoice to ignore, if it could. I call Dr. Babbitt's attention to all history, as well as to his morning newspaper.

Personally, I appear to be charged with being a realist. I accept the insult, but with reservations. For I fear I do not run true to type, do not march with any clan. Rather I see myself as a highly temperamental individual compelled to see life through the various veils or fogs of my own lacks, predilections and what you will, yet seeking honestly always to set down that which I imagine I see.

I am told by some that it agrees with what they see. By others not. But what I think I see is beauty and ugliness, mystery and some little clarity in minor things, tenderness and terrific brutality, ignorance, sodden and hopeless, and some admirable wisdom, malice and charity, honesty and dishonesty, aspiration and complete and discouraging insensitivity and indifference. Yet altogether contriving a gay, restless, and in the main, fascinating picture from which but a few of us, however great our ills and complaints, are prepared to step out. In fact, it is not less but more of this inexplicable and often more bitter than sweet brew that we desire—to seize the best of it and escape the worst.

In addition, it is not any petty scribe, but life itself which makes the often grim and terrible tales to which Dr. Babbitt and his humanists *object. His personal desire appears to be that the writer ignore phases of this greater reality in order, as he sees it, to give society a better impression of itself and nature. I disagree. No cult or school or theory or religion should be able to say to any serious observer of life,* thus far and no farther.

Truly enough, today in America the tendency is all toward a narrow, bigoted and mentally and so artistically stultifying censorship, but I cannot believe that it will succeed. In the long run, life itself nullifies all such bans. The censors pass but that which they sought to destroy, remains. Nothing of true value from Sappho to Wilde, from Juvenal to Swift, to Voltaire has really passed or will. The best Dr. Babbitt and his humanism *can expect is the usual American* hooey—Lo! *here and* Lo! *there, accorded every gaseous reform from prohibition, short skirts, Billy Sunday, Mother's Day, to Sunday theatre closing and anti-white slave law. I am, —with various bows and gestures*

—Theodore Dreiser

III. FIGHTER FOR HUMAN EQUITIES
—New York, 1933-34

It was not until the summer of 1933, that I saw Dreiser again. I had returned from Europe for a brief visit to my mother and wrote, asking if he had time to see me. Immediately, he summoned me with a note, reproaching me for my silence.

I found him in a small suite at the Ansonia Hotel at Broadway and 73rd Street. (This was one of those noble old hotels, built in the international style of The Gotham or St. Regis, in New York, The Grand Hotel in Paris, or the Astoria in Leningrad!)

As Dreiser rose from his desk to greet me, the room seemed too small for him. He towered over me, hearty and dynamic as ever, wearing a deep blue shirt, and bow-tie, his white hair trimmed close to his round, bomb-like brow; His eyes— those amazing, uneven eyes—blazing up and tender, scowling and laughing, scrutinized me as they had the first night I met him.

Yet, after talking with him for a while, there seemed to be something more solemn, more dedicated about him. He was burning with a zeal for improving the lot of his fellow men. Interested in politics as he had always been, ready to champion the cause of the oppressed, enthusiastic about Russia and the socialist experiment, he had seemed primarily a

writer, inspired by all this. But now he seemed more like a
political *worker* of some sort, one who has determined to
fight for his ideas not only with his pen, but in a bodily, personal way.

He told me about how he had gone to Harlan, Kentucky, to
expose the conditions among the miners there, formed a committee of prominent liberals to help the miners in their
desperate fight to form a union, risked arrest and prosecu-
tion, and become involved in endless dispute and publicity
over his book, *Tragic America* just issued. He was so busy,
he said, that he had hardly time to go out to his new house
in the country. However, he wanted me to see it, and invited
me to *Iroki* the following Sunday.

The great stretch of hillside was as unkempt as when I had
first seen it; the white birch bungalow was gone from its
rocky hill. But down nearer the pond, stood an extraordinary
house. It had the proportions of a huge, thatched hut, more
Russian than English-looking, certainly not like anything out
of America. From the ground, a stiff little stairway ran up
to a huge door, a half-story above the grass. In front of it a
space had been leveled for use as a lawn and lounging spot.
Here rose three or four giant stone mushrooms, which some
Russian friend had given Dreiser. They had a foreign, fairy-
tale character, as if some Puck or troll might pop up from
under them at any moment.

But it was the roof that gave the house so strange a look.
It was literally shingled with half-logs; stout, rough-sawn
pieces with bark on them, standing out in uncanny relief. It
was like a roof from a stage-set—the house of the witch in
Hansel and Gret'l. Later, this roof burnt off, and was replaced
by a stern and tidy slate one, but I shall always remember
the house as it was then, shaggy, fantastic, a little *unbeliev-
able,* as Dreiser himself!

But if the house was fanciful outside, it was even more
incongruous, inside. To the left of the door was a small, high
living room, with a huge fireplace running up to the ceiling;
on each side, were diagonal slits of windows, filled with
colored glass! This was certainly no chapel calling for stained

glass windows, and there was not much point to these artificial yellow filters for the country light. But that was only
one of the strange features. In the corners, were electrical
fixtures behind panes designed by Henry Varnum Poor, making columns of light. The walls were painted in bands of
gray and the wooden floor was painted orange, with borders
of red. Over the doors were life-sized plaster doves. A ladder-
steep stairway led to a balcony and bedroom under the high
gable of the roof, and here another pair of plaster doves was
perched.

To the right of the entrance door was the bath, originally
painted with gay scenes of Pompeian folly. (Alas, they had
to be painted over later when the house was rented!) There
was an attractive modern kitchen but it had no outer door,
so that the garbage had to be carried through the living-
room. Beyond this was a large, square room, originally intended for dining. The floor was black and the walls were
painted in blues and golds, in oriental style. There were
small, many-paned windows, but one big picture window
brought in the view of many trees, and the stretch to the
pond. Helen used this for her bedroom.

In a corner of the living room, a narrow, turning stair
led down to a huge studio, the length and breadth of the house.
It seemed half-cellar, half den. A big stone fireplace did
something to dispel a feeling of dampness or hardness, caused
by a tiled floor and masonry walls. The side toward the pond,
however, was cut away and a huge casement window, almost
level with the grass gave the full picture of the pond, the
trees, the ground falling away to the reservoir in the distance and the wooded hills beyond.

In this room were the huge chairs, the yellow Venetian
couch, the lavish nudes that had been in the 57th street
studio. Instead of the square rosewood desk—which Dreiser
had left in the city—there was a long, handsome table made
by Wharton Esherick, especially for this place. It was an
elegant, hand-sculptured version of the rustic plank table,
with crossed boards for legs, of beautiful grain and waxed
to perfection. There were bookcases in this room and other

attractive furnishings scattered about, rugs, chairs, colored bowls, Indian and Russian objects, dolls; these, with many paintings and several pieces of sculpture, gave the whole house a gay, artistic atmosphere.

I will never forget how handsome Nick, the Russian Borzoi looked in this house of wonders. That summer Helen's sister and mother were visiting her here, and they also had a Borzoi, from the same litter, snowy-white and rangy-limbed. To see them as they roamed over the fields, or lay in graceful poses around the house, was a delight.

Helen's sister, Myrtle, looked very much like her, and was near her in age. They had always been very close companions. Both had long faces and straight features; though Myrtle did not have Helen's beauty, her voice was perhaps, better. Both sang, and loved music, nature and animals, with a fresh, Western sincerity. Dreiser was glad to have Myrtle come to visit Helen, for he often felt that he could not give her all the company she craved. They had started off well, in the big new house, yet even before it was finished, Dreiser had lost interest in all those evenings and entertainments of the past, at the 57th street studio, and in the white birch bungalow. He was beginning to feel a financial pinch, and his life had taken on a new concentration. . . . Sometimes, the singing and talking was too much for him. He simply ducked out of the picture. . . . and Myrtle and her mother stayed on, because they knew Helen was lonely. Already, the big house presented a problem. It was unlucky from the start.

Sensing this, but feeling, as before, that I had no part in Dreiser's tumultuous life, I came to the Ansonia a few weeks later to say good-bye to him.

He had asked me what I had been doing in Switzerland, and I had told him that I had been trying to write another novel without much success, but that I had friends, and a new passion for mountain-climbing. Now he seemed almost angry that I was going back. He listened patiently while I described the thrills of mounting a great peak; the breath-taking beauty of a rock-and-snow landscape. Suddenly, he stopped me with a roar:

"So—you're going back to climb more mountains. Is *that* what you are going to do with yourself?"

"What should I do?"

"You can work for me."

"But I have an apartment in Switzerland, furniture—"

"Well, of all things—for a few pieces of furniture, you would go on wasting your life!"

For the second time, he had brought me to a realization that I was a parasite, doing nothing but amuse myself. This time, it made an indelible impression.

I took a room near the Ansonia, going home only for week-ends to see my son, who could stay with his grandmother.

At ten o'clock each morning, I was to report to Dreiser, to get my work for the day. The first morning, after giving me an article to copy, Dreiser took a book out of his case, along the right-hand wall:

"Here—that's part of your job. I want you to read it."

It was Veblen's *Theory of the Leisure Class!*

There followed a period of fantastic effort on a great variety of assignments. Dreiser still had his excellent secretary, Evelyn Light, but his correspondence was always more than one person could handle. Now that he had entered the political arena, he had hundreds of requests for statements, opinions, articles on economic subjects. Individuals all over the country wrote to him of situations that they felt should be investigated; labor conditions, health hazards, personal wrongs and injustices that should be righted. Each appeal reached Dreiser's attention, and he would try to answer, or have one of us answer, each serious letter. Similarly, with books or manuscripts sent him by young or struggling writers; he would try to glance through each one and send some encouraging word, if it was merited.

There were, of course, other letters of criticism and protest, and to these he gave less attention, but they took his time, nevertheless.

My chief duties were in connection with manuscripts or with Dreiser's editorial work on *The American Spectator*. To gain an adequate picture of this self-termed *literary news-*

paper, it would be necessary to run through the 14-odd issues with which Dreiser's name was connected. In retrospect, I fear that looking there for worth-while material would be highly depressing. Seldom has such a concoction been served up in the name of literature.

Its prospectus had stated that it sought "the type of critical reaction which ignores the conventionalist, the moralist, the religionist, and favors the unaccepted and the misunderstood as opposed to the accepted and understood." The editors were listed as George Jean Nathan, Ernest Boyd, Theodore Dreiser, James Branch Cabell, and Eugene O'Neill—certainly a promise of creative material.

Nathan was the *working* editor, as I now learned; the others, contributing or special section editors. Boyd, for instance, reviewed books. That fall, Sherwood Anderson's name was added to the roster, and he contributed *Walks around New York,* casual, literary pieces with more value than much of the other material.

The paper had vicious, little features: There was a box for the *"Worst Book of the Month,"* in which was once listed the grave and beautiful *Le Songe de Descartes* by Jacques Maritain. There was a monthly *"Servants of God"* item, reprinting some clipping about a religious character who had fallen into temptation, a certain parson leaving the ministry for a better business opportunity, or another shooting the watchman of a rival church! Some of them, indeed, were pitifully humorous.

Articles debunking this and that are not very funny to read, now. A piece by Nathan purporting to *debunk* Ambrose Bierce, by quoting his *Devil's Dictionary* can easily be turned against Nathan himself, against the too-facile and malicious humor of the *Spectator,* for such wit seldom stands the test of time.

Dreiser's contribution of lengthy pieces to this paper, was not enough to satisfy his sense of responsibility for the publication as a whole. He was deeply concerned as to what went into it, and Nathan rather resented this interest. Nathan felt quite capable of choosing the material and setting the tone for each issue, and he had nothing like the zeal for aiding humanity that animated Dreiser. As Kraft once put it, the whole thing was a "conversation piece," a collection of opinions not more serious than might be discussed, or thrown around, at a cocktail party.

Dreiser had wanted it to be a keen, literary instrument, capable of influencing a change-ripe society—if only through the medium of satire. Also, he wanted the *Spectator* to serve as a forum for original minds, and as a champion of free speech and human rights.

Consequently, many independent and controversial letters and articles poured in to *The American Spectator,* and also to Dreiser's mail-box. Many of these caused debate between Dreiser and Nathan. If they were not *clever,* or did not add to the brilliance of this literary conversation, according to Nathan, out and back they would go. Rejected writers sometimes complained to Dreiser personally. Of course, he agreed that the editors must keep a high standard for their limited space, but he also knew that some good "hot" stuff was being sent in and he was not even seeing it.

At the time I came to work for him, this situation had reached a climax. He decided that one of my jobs should be to look over the material that was coming in.

Naturally, Nathan did not like this idea, considering me a rank outsider, but he agreed to a compromise. I was to come into the office of the *Spectator* "on Mondays and Thursdays, in the afternoon," and look over the rejected stuff. If I agreed that it should be rejected, no comment was necessary, but I could take away anything which I thought Dreiser should see.

This I did for some eight weeks. I never caught a glimpse of Nathan; he seemed to make a point of being out when I came in. As for the "stuff" that I had to read over, it was mostly the unusable kind of writing that comes in to any publisher. In all that time, I hardly found anything that was worth showing Dreiser. Of course, it was a terrible waste of time to read all this bad material twice, for Nathan's readers had already been through it. I could not help wondering, as

Dreiser did, whether I was really seeing *all* the stuff that
Nathan turned down.

The matter was clarified one day by a peculiar coincidence,
which occurred under quite unbusiness-like circumstances.

That fall, Prohibition, the Federal law forbidding the sale
of alcoholic beverages of any sort, which had been put through
the legislature during the war of 1914, was finally repealed.

America had been through the experiment which had made
drinking—in private and in speak-easies—a national sport,
and led to the rise of gangsterism, not to mention all sorts
of lesser evils and hypocrisies. For those who lived through
this period, the return to a normal state of affairs, was
heralded by much excitement.

Dreiser had invited me to celebrate the occasion with him
and Helen and a few other friends, at the romantic old
Luchow's Restaurant on East 14th Street.

The high, dark-panelled room with its gaudy paintings
was warm with a spirit of carousal. Tables were crowded and
every one was talking animatedly. Dreiser's table was a
center of attention, as he launched forth on one of his favorite
themes.

Next to us, was a group of young men who were fascinated
by Dreiser, and sought to follow his conversation. Finally,
one of them got up and asked if they might be allowed to
listen to what he was saying, since they recognized him and
were greatly interested in his point of view.

Dreiser responded with his characteristic warmth toward
young people, especially those who had ideas to share; a shift
was made, the two tables brought together to make a long one,
and we found ourselves among a group of young composers.
(With them, was W.W. Norton, the publisher, a delightful
conversationalist, and amateur musician.)

After a stimulating exchange of ideas, a number of
drinks, and much laughter, Dreiser started to talk in a more
serious tone, about *The American Spectator*. At this, one of
the young composers, Lehman Engel, told us that he had been
indignant about a piece that Nathan had published on modern
music, and he and his fellow moderns had answered, attacking

it, and putting their own strong feelings about their work into an article called *The Cats and the Mouse*. This piece had been promptly returned to them with some dead-pan comment.

"*When* was that?" I asked, knowing that I had seen no such rejection in my two months' experience at the office.

"Last week, or the week before," they answered.

Dreiser was aroused, angry but delighted to discover this. "Send the article to my hotel," he said, and our celebration went on, an added filip of excitement given to this impromptu gathering of vital, creative minds.

Sure enough—when the piece arrived, it was a complete surprise to us, an excellent exposé of the difficulties of the American composer, a well-written protest against academic restraint, presenting Roy Harris, Aaron Copland, Roger Sessions, Walter Piston—all talents which have since proved themselves important.

Of course, Dreiser faced Nathan with this paper. Just what the results were I do not know. But the incident was one of many things that hastened Dreiser's departure from this increasingly superficial *literary newspaper*.

This was the time when Roosevelt was doing many fine things with his New Deal. He had also accorded official recognition to the Soviet Union, and Dreiser was elated over this. He had given me material to prepare for a number of articles on the subject, yet no comments about these important matters found space in the *American Spectator*. It was a paper designed to tear down, to laugh, to *debunk*, but not to build.

Particularly obnoxious was the attitude of the paper to Hitler and the rising menace of Fascism. The editors seemed to take it as a huge joke, or as material for clumsy comment. Nathan, himself a Jew, callously reported on a book called *Birthright* by Richard Maibaum, saying. "It seems that the Nazis don't altogether like the Jews, and the author is mighty sore about it . . ." True, nobody took Hitler seriously enough in those days, but the flip attitude of the *Spectator* toward anti-Semitism had already been seen in an "editorial Conference," published in September of that year, in which

Nathan, Dreiser, Cabell, Boyd and O'Neill made some of the most absurd remarks ever printed under the names of intelligent writers not only about Jews, but about art, religion, and life in general.

(It is to Dreiser's credit that he resigned from *The American Spectator*. With some verbal fire-works, he finally told the editors that he considered the whole thing, from his point of view, a waste of time.)

Dreiser and the Films

Dreiser had always seen his own work in terms of drama. His plots and characters are easily adaptable to stage or screen. This was because he always put drastic action into his stories, something that had happened in real life. To him, truth was always stranger, and stronger, than fiction. He proved the proverb many times, by taking a crime or tragedy from a newspaper clipping, and building a study of human character around it.

Dreiser could have been a dramatist himself, if he had consciously developed techniques of stage or screen. But it would have been at the expense of his lengthy delineations of the subtleties of character and the workings of the human heart.

When he sold the rights of *An American Tragedy*, to Paramount for the *then* unequaled sum of $155,000, he was tremendously elated, and took for granted that the film would parallel his book. He was doubly thrilled to know that the great Russian film director, Eisenstein, then engaged by Hollywood, had agreed to do the screen interpretation. This he read, and it met with his approval.

Some months later, however, Eisenstein's scenario was mysteriously dropped, and Dreiser was shown a shooting script that was clearly inferior. He was determined to fight for the integrity of his work. To calm him, Paramount offered to pay his way to Hollywood, with a script-writer of his own choosing, so that he might work out changes. Dreiser chose Hy Kraft, and the two set out. Kraft gives the story in *The Screen Writer*, (March, 1946). It seemed obvious that after they reached Hollywood, they were given the run-around. No meeting with script writers was arranged, and Dreiser was treated in a vague, off-hand manner, as some kind of literary curiosity, to be tolerated but not taken seriously:

"Dreiser's demands were minimal and hardly unreasonable," Kraft relates. "He wasn't too displeased with some rushes he was allowed to see. Editing and re-recording would have satisfied him. There were proposed changes in a portion of script still to be shot, which would have shifted the emphasis. But all of this was predicated on the approach to the picture as a whole . . . Dreiser felt that the beginning and end of the script fell far short of the thematic and dramatic possibilities so apparent in the novel. He had devoted almost half of his book to the early life of Clyde Griffiths. . . . without this reconstruction of the boy's childhood, the reader would not have understood the inevitable and tragic climax. . . .

"Dreiser did not demand the same proportionate share in the film . . . but he did insist that, in one way or another, the violent social, economic and moral influences affecting Clyde, be clearly damatized. Ultimately, if I remember correctly, a fragment of our scenes and words were used, but not enough of either, according to Dreiser.

"He was also convinced that the end was too puny, too weak, almost meaningless. He hoped for a sweeping, epic scene . . . He pointed to the death-scene in Pat Kearny's dramatization of the book—which played with great success on Broadway—and we submitted an extension of the scene . . . But Dreiser, like his characters, was caught in an unescapable web of conflicts and contracts. . . .

"Dreiser summarized his position as follows: 'I have a literary character to maintain and I contend that I have a mental equity in my product and in the character of my product. Even though they buy the right of reproduction they don't buy the right to change it into anything they please.'

"Dreiser went further than mere statement. He decided to test his stand in the courts. He sued for an injunction to restrain Paramount from releasing the picture; the court denied his motion.

"Though Dreiser lost legally, the evidence indicates an historic victory," concludes Kraft in his article, "Surely, the individual screen writer recognizes the aspiration of the novelist and approaches the screen play with greater thoughtfulness. . . ."

But whether or not this is true nowadays, Dreiser was the first writer to challenge Hollywood's power, even though he had received the largest amount ever paid an author, up to that date. Dreiser's experience with this film, did not embitter or discourage him. On the contrary, it made him dream of producing another great film drama, if possible, with independent means.

This film drama was first to be called *Revolt* and later, *Tobacco,* and was to deal with the plight of the Southern share-croppers who had revolted during the time of Theodore Roosevelt against the Duke tobacco trust. Dreiser had written a powerful story of individuals almost in slavery to their landlords who reaped the enormous profits to be had out of cigarettes. The film was to end with a great conflagration— the frustrated underpaid share-croppers setting fire to their masters' warehouses. This, Dreiser felt was a scene worthy of the power of the medium.

As with the Russian Ballet project, or with any new creative idea that obsessed him, Dreiser went around for several weeks that winter, talking, dreaming, acting out the new film. It must be said that both Kraft and Dreiser had worked on this idea from its inception. To get realistic detail, they had gone to the South together, to study the terrain and its visual possibilities.

Kraft told me how they had arrived at a small-town hotel late at night, after an exhausting train trip. He pleaded with Dreiser to retire, but no, Dreiser must see what sort of a place this was, at once.

After a prowl around the town, he returned in the highest spirits, arousing Kraft to tell him what he had found. Yes, conditions were just as bad, indeed worse, than they had expected. Such poverty and dilapidation!

Why, right down the street, he had seen an old woman,

sitting in a rocking chair on a wooden porch smoking a pipe. And she had invited him in; there were girls inside she said, and it would cost very little to enjoy their company.

This shocked Dreiser, upset him emotionally, as if it were the first time he had heard of such down-trodden women.

Dreiser and Kraft stayed for several weeks in this town and the surrounding country, talking to share-croppers, farmers and persons who knew about the working and living conditions of the section. He found the simple cabin where the slain leader of the share-croppers had been born; although it was like many others of the same ramshackle sort, he examined it minutely—*this* was the birthplace, and not another. It was damp winter weather, but Dreiser plodded around for hours in the tobacco fields; the very ground fascinated him and he crawled on his hands and knees along furrows, picturing how the leaves were grown. He had no conception of how impractical it would be to try to film outdoor material in this way, without proper lighting and the latest camera techniques. Unprofessional? But that's just how he wanted his picture to be. To Hell with professional cameramen and their directors and technical tricks . . . Did they ever get the effect of real *life*—tense, crude, human drama? Seldom—practically never.

He was sure that with his realistic, raw approach, he would create new possibilities for the film. This was in 1933 and very little good, documentary work had been done. Dreiser foresaw a new style of honest character portrayal, a true drama of the soil.

For a time, it seemed as if an independent producer was found, one who saw the promise of this film. But the tentative arrangements were not satisfactory to Dreiser. Another combination of producer and backer also fell through.

Dreiser and Kraft had worked on a first, powerful version of a drama, containing all of Dreiser's original ideas for love-story and plot. But the dialogue was too slow, too long for film techniques. Kraft said that Dreiser could not grasp how fast the medium was nor understand certain technical factors. So Kraft did his own version, which Dreiser felt

lacked his original force. I was given the two scripts to
check against each other, and it was a ticklish job, for I knew
as little about writing for the screen as Dreiser did. It was
easy to see that Dreiser's story was better from a literary
point of view.

I liked Kraft, as Dreiser always had, and tried to reconcile
their ideas, but bad feeling flared up between them, and each
had his own version copyrighted, in his own name, making
it impossible for either of them to sell the story without a
legal fight. However, all winter, Dreiser was hopeful of finding some ideal, daring producer who could bring this great
rural drama to light. He talked of it at times as if it were
his dearest brain-child. "Why, *someone* will see this," he
would exclaim. "*Imagine* that scene at the end!"

And he would speak of the terrible burning of the tobacco
barns as the drama reaches its climax. This film would be so
much more satisfying than just another article. He was involved in many of the social struggles of that time but this
would be symbolic of them all—a full, frontal attack, a
flaming work of art hurled against injustice.

Jean Lurçat

That year there was a meeting between Dreiser and the
French painter, Jean Lurçat, who was having an exhibition
in New York. Their conversation symbolized the concern of
creative people everywhere for bettering social conditions.
Lurçat was a man known not only for his modern canvasses
and the revival of the art of tapestry (for which he has since
become world famous) but also for his untiring efforts to
establish cultural centers and activities for workers of the
French Popular Front. With other leading French intellectuals, including Malraux, Aragon, and Picasso, he had
founded the *Maison de la Culture,* in Paris, where novel
experiments were being made in the *rapprochement* between
working people and artists, writers, sculptors, and other
intellectuals. For the first time, social laws had been passed
in France, which gave people a forty-hour week, with free
Sundays and summer vacations. After years of being over-

worked, the French suddenly found themselves with a problem of how to spend their leisure hours; the *problème des loisirs*. Sport groups organized exercise, excursions and youth hostels, and the artists tried to provide culture. . . . There was a new spirit in France, comparable to that which was springing up around our W.P.A. Arts Projects, and the New Deal. . . .

Dreiser was fascinated by all this. Lurçat also told him of the *Amis de l'URRS*, a French society for promoting friendship with Soviet Russia, which had over one million members. These and kindred subjects threw the two men into immediate rapport, though Dreiser spoke no French and Lurçat very little English. Acting as interpreter, I had only to repeat a sentence here, a phrase there, to help them express their unity of purpose, their love of mankind.

Lurçat, not as old as Dreiser, was almost bald, with handsome head and dark, knowing gaze. You could sense his instant liking for this American giant with his caveman face and eyes kindling with the gleam of those who are capable of living and fighting for others. As they grasped each other's hands to say goodbye, it was like a pledge of friendship, of their intent to go on fighting, always, for the cause in which they both believed.

Matthewson

A curious contrast in these days with Dreiser was the typing of a manuscript which I will never forget. One morning, he handed me a thick sheaf of his hand-written pages, among other shorter matters he wanted me to attend to. This typing he wanted by the next day, with two carbons.

I went to my room disheartened wondering how I could manage everything. Sometimes, in a few short minutes, he could load me up with work enough for three days.

An hour later, I was absorbed, entranced by the manuscript I had been given to type. It was so different from the political, combative kind of work we had been doing, that I was transported into another world—to the plane where Dreiser, the creative mystic, brooded over the fate of man.

The first paragraph is so beautiful, so evocative of Dreiser at his literary best; his subtlety, his skill, the way he could become involved in a long sentence and come out, whole and clear at the end, that I will quote it in full:

> *As against the vital, the successful, the avaricious, the brutal—those who see life as something to take by storm or to win against by subtlety or, what is worse, inequitable chance, I offer Matthewson. He was a journalist and, by temperament if not by scriptic achievement, a poet and writer of distinction—yet with reservations of his own. That slim and somewhat small and perhaps more disadvantageous still, clerkly figure! Those dark, mellow and entirely unacquisitive eyes. The fine, long and somewhat pointed oval head, with a seemingly loose growth of limp black hair. The unobtrusive nose, sensitive mouth, pale, rather bloodless hands and small, almost womanish feet.*

The whole sketch about this man, makes him seem as eerie as a character out of Poe or Baudelaire. Actually, he was a newspaper man whom Dreiser knew in his early days in St. Louis. This sketch was a sort of memorial dirge for him, almost a tone-poem of the defeat of a human life through supersensitivity. It was what Dreiser, I think, at times felt his own life might have been, had there not been that other side of his nature, the positive, materialistic, sensual side, loving the earth and violence.

Other quotations, supposedly scribbled by Matthewson himself on scraps of paper which lay beside him in his disordered room, showed the delicate and despairing mind that was his.

"Color and music are perhaps the two most valuable phases of life. But of these two, color is the indispensable one."

"A heavy heart and an empty stomach. Take away the heavy heart and the empty stomach is endurable. But with it—what is food?"

"The struggle to live without violence is a dream; to live by violence is aesthetic death."

"Religion is merely a dream of a life without brutality or torture."

"When desire is strong enough to become a prayer, it is likely to become a reality."

The story ends where Dreiser reports that Matthewson was found dead, peacefully curled up, as in sleep—"bringing drugs and drink to the aid of a philosophy or reaction which could not endure the reality it encountered." He finished with the line—repeated as Dreiser sometimes deliberately liked to do for that special emphasis which only repetition can produce:

"The struggle to live without violence is a dream; to live by violence is aesthetic death."

This was the first Dreiser I had known, the brooding, philosophic mind, partaking of the woes of humanity without the political violence, the constant fight that seemed to be in him. Now, in all the welter of action, he had been writing this. I felt humbled and swept with appreciation of him.

Long hours of the night, I worked to type this story, feeling that the transformation into type from his small, erratic, though often beautiful, handwriting was a sacred trust.

But the next morning, I had not finished it, and the typing was poor. I had a *skip* in my typewriter that showed up, especially in the carbons. I had failed in my trust.

Yet to type over some thirty-five pages unless my typewriter were first repaired seemed useless. In desperation, I went up to the mezzanine floor of the hotel, where a public stenographer was available. She copied my bad typing, while I finished the transcribing. I paid her myself. Dreiser would never know, as he was out that morning.

In the afternoon, I appeared with neat, perfect type-script and carbons, and he was very pleased. He was in a particularly mellow and deep mood. I, too, was still flooded with the joy of the story itself, the elation which comes from a newly created work of art.

He put away his new script and carbons, and holding out the original, looked down at me: "Here—Do you want this?

You can keep it—" He was looking at me with that intense gaze which had in it, unpredictably, a wild challenge.

"No—I don't particularly want it," I said. Either I was too stupid to realize the value of some fifty pages of handwritten manuscript of Dreiser's, or I was simply light-headed, with a kind of false pride, not wanting to seem grasping to him, wanting to show him that I was glad to work for him, just because he trusted me, and not for any reward. It was both stupidity and a kind of reckless, non-material emotion.

His eyes darkened, like skies before a storm. Without a word, he savagely tore the thick pile of papers and threw them into the waste-basket.

Conclusion of this Period, 1934

The work went on. I now felt closer to Dreiser than ever before. I knew his way of doing things, intensely, but without apparent rush. There was no petty nervousness about his gestures. Writers have mentioned his funny habit of folding and pleating his handkerchief into little squares. I saw him do this only when he was in a company of people, perhaps impatient because he could not get on with some work. At his desk, he never wasted time nor motion. Years before, he had given up smoking, because he felt it was belittling to have to spend time looking for matches and ashtrays.

He did not like to waste words in matters of no interest or small import yet he had a sense of fairness in handling all communications addressed personally to him, so that he would frequently dispose of dozens of letters in an hour by giving some sentence, some idea, which could be incorporated into a note which he would trust me to compose around his basic answer. This is where he had trained me to be useful, and I was often amazed at the original and thoughtful replies he could turn out, with little trouble. Of course, by this time he had had many years of experience with human beings. He understood them and loved them, perhaps more in their weakness than in their strength.

Letters to personal friends, or on subjects of grave concern, he preferred to write out first by hand, even if they were to be typed afterwards. For in those days, thoughts poured from his mind into his pen, almost as quickly as he could speak them out, in conversation, and dictation was a brake to him. His mind was so original, so unpredictable that it did not fall into the usual phrases and sentences, but was always surprising.

So it was, too, with his days. He seemed to be guided by an inner schedule, because he got a lot done, without much plan. He hated engagements that could break a mood of work.

At the end of an afternoon, if he wanted to go on working, dinner meant nothing to him. Sometimes, he would come to my room with some urgent material and we might go on 'til eight or nine o'clock, then go out for a bite to eat in some neighboring cafeteria, and work again, 'til after midnight. At other times, he might declare a holiday, at lunch time, and ask me to drive him out to the country, or we might join other friends for evenings of fascinating talk.

Helen divided her time between the Ansonia and *Iroki*. There were other women whom Dreiser met occasionally. I did not try to keep track of his life, nor do more than respond to the needs of his work, and to him, when he wanted my companionship. There was something so completely understood and understanding about our relationship, that we never wasted words about it. My friends knew that I was working peculiar hours, and did not have much time for them. It did not matter. It was only important that I could help Dreiser and that he trusted me. This big, gruff, brilliant, tender man had every variety of mood and nature a woman could want. He was to me, an incarnation of that very life-experience I had always sought. But more than this, he had taught me to work, and we were working for something bigger than ourselves. This had given my life a meaning, a sense of completion I had never had before.

Then suddenly, Destiny pulled another way.

Because of the thrilling urgency of our work, I seldom spent more than a short week-end in my family home, to be with my son, who was now five years old. I had brought a Swiss nurse with me when I returned the summer before, and I felt that she took excellent care of him. Besides, my own mother was there and loved him dearly. But it was always a wrench to leave the bright, sensitive child after the little walks, the few hours that I could be with him. One Sunday, I noticed that he had a bad cold, but left on Monday as usual. I phoned the next day, and he was worse—pneumonia.

I dropped everything to nurse him through a two-week fight for life. As soon as he was strong enough to be dressed the doctor ordered him carried to a train, and sunshine.

Of course, Dreiser understood that I had had to leave his work; He even grudgingly conceded that I take the boy South. But when I came to say good-bye to him at the Ansonia, I had made up my mind to leave him for good.

It was an icy, terrible winter day; we talked all afternoon in that city-gloom-coming-in-through-hotel-windows, evoking a sense of fatality.

Dreiser was deeply sympathetic about the boy's being sick: "But he's over it—any one can take care of him now. People don't give up jobs like that. Go South, if you must, and come back as soon as you can."

But something was gripping me—self-reproach. Plainly, I had neglected my child. This work was too absorbing. Dreiser's impact was too strong. It would always be so, if I were with him.

Dreiser did not give up so easily. He told me of another project which was taking form—a magazine which would really represent his views, and for which he had backing. He wanted me to be in on it from the start. He had already had several conferences about it. Alfred Bingham and A.J. Muste would collaborate with him, to bring about a new alignment of liberal forces dedicated to the free expression of the best, progressive ideas. But he would not do it, he said, if he could not count on me to help him with all the extra details.

I said something about coming back the following year, if my son were well and old enough for school. But now he became angry:

"No," he growled dully, his voice like distant thunder. "No —if you don't stay now, I'm through with you. Don't think you can come back. I've spent all this time training you, and you're going away just when you're getting useful."

But I said I must go. I had yielded completely to the gloom of that day.

Dreiser followed me out to the elevator as I left. The long, dull-carpetted corridors of the Ansonia seemed like endless tunnels of defeat. He trudged beside me, his heavy feet muffled by the rug. Only another moment we stood together, Dreiser glowering down at me, finding nothing to say for a good-bye.

IV. SEARCH FOR TRUTH
—scientific and philosophic research, 1936-38

In the winter of 1936, Dreiser was living at *Iroki*. When I first returned from Europe, I had been almost afraid to get in touch with him, but finally sent a note to Mt. Kisco, as I found he was no longer at the Ansonia. In a few days I received a cordial reply from Helen:

"T. is at work on a very difficult piece of work and here he gets the quiet necessary for this kind of concentration. We are living in the guest house for the real cold months and later, we will move back to the large house . . . T. works through the week here, but Sundays we are usually at home and on that day we usually have callers, one or two or more, whoever comes. We would be glad to see you any Sunday. . . . That seems to be the limit of our social activities for T. seems to have descended or ascended, or what you will—into one of his real working states."

The guest-house and garage had been added to the left of the large structure, so that they did not interfere with the view. They were of rough, gray texture, flat on top and edged with a border of the same kind of half-logs which made up the roof of the big, stone building but doors and windows were relieved by deep Russian-blue trim.

Inside the smaller house were the same, odd-angled windows, a fake fireplace and trick lighting, carrying out a diagonal motif. It was comfortably and colorfully furnished.

I found Dreiser behind a modest desk, the usual array of papers and reference books around him. But here were not his ordinary volumes, dictionaries, magazines, his favorite glossary of girls' names. There were books of science and cosmic lore. He was scrutinizing me with those deep, intense, baffling eyes. You could never quite tell which one was looking at you, because of a slight cast, yet for this very reason, they seemed turned-on more intensely. This was particularly disturbing if you did not know what mood he was in.

Although it was almost three years since I had seen Dreiser, he did not seem older, but more reserved, perhaps, on the defensive, like a horse with its ears down.

"Well, what are *you* up to?" He challenged, gruffly. Instantly I knew from his tone that he had forgiven me. There was the old, sardonic warmth. I could get him to talk. When he was angry or annoyed with people, he simply refused to say more than a few words. He could turn-off his interest like a light.

I asked him about all the books that were lying around, and soon he started to tell me that he was engaged in an entirely new project; it was something that involved research of the most exacting but fascinating kind.

He had given up all thought of bothering with editorial ventures. This was something that would really *knock people's eyes out,* as he expressed it.

Yes, this time, he was going to show people what they are —what we all are—an infinitesimal part of the most amazing universe—part of an utterly inescapable, cosmic life that is whirling us along in a process of which we are the creatures and through which we dance, like motes in a sunbeam—no more important, and no *less.*

For it was somehow important that we were motes, atoms, electrons, in this process. It meant that we were part of a whole. He was going to show that everything was a part of a whole, chemically, electrically and also philosophically.

He was writing a philosophy of life that would show the utter insignificance of man; that would prove, once and for all, that there was no such thing as *free will,* as he had indeed always believed, but now he could *demonstrate* it—finally and without a doubt—and yet he would also show that there was a kind of utter and terrible and healing beauty in the very fact that all life is One Process and One Thing.

This was the gist of what he said about his work, that day. I do not remember all his words. But I remember the shock and surprise it was to hear him, to glimpse his vision, and to see this new panorama stretching ahead of him.

As always, he could put such sweep and urgency into what interested him at the moment, that he could make it seem like the most important thing in the world.

Oh, yes, he was still concerned with politics, but now his quest was burning in him like a new fire which only work could put out. How long would it take him? Several years— perhaps longer. But then it would be really worthwhile. He wanted it to be his final contribution to humanity, as I understood him—a synthesis of what a writer-scientist-philosopher might finally say about life.

Alas, I saw that there was little I could do to help Dreiser at this time. I was anxious to do journalism along political lines, to join in some way, the fight against fascism, against the Nazi terror I had seen in Germany. I knew little about science or research—nor was I needed in that capacity, for Dreiser told me he now had a young college-girl secretary who was typing material and doing work with him, for which she was especially trained.

As I left, Dreiser gave me a copy of his *Moods, Philosophic and Emotional Cadenced and Declaimed,* which had come out in book form, the winter before (1935). Many of these I had seen, or typed for him. I plunged into reading them again, and found astonishing new ones, as well. Here was the key to his further desire for truth. Nothing had satisfied him.

Above all the love moods, the nature moods, the moods of defiance or despair, rise moods of cosmic speculation, staggering the imagination. Such is the poem *Ephemeron,* showing Dreiser's deep aspiration to understand, as well as his despond because of human limitations:

EPHEMERON

Tremendous bulks of raging elements
Suns with girths too vasty for conception
A billion light-years hence
Algol
With two dead monsters at his shoulders
Space
With a billion dead monsters
Ready to resolve themselves
Upon impact
Into vasty veils of fire
Stupendous bridals of the dead
that bring to birth
New suns
But how?
Why?

Ask me not how or why.

An eternity of time behind one
An eternity of time before one
An Ephemeron
In time and space
One's life
A thing of moisture and of heat
Between degrees of light and heat
One's broodings
Feeble and purblind
Poor fruit
Pathetic fruit
Ridiculous fruit
Of illimitable space
Illimitable strength
Illimitable wisdom

Betrayed
But not by the Gods of mine own invention
But by the lacks
That are not of me

Ask me not of whom.

This was the extent to which his restless spirit was trying
to reach. He was no longer satisfied to have become a leading

novelist, famous for his daring pictures of truth in human lives; nor was he satisfied to have produced some of the most subtle and lovely, blasphemous and mystical prose-poems that ever tested the validity of language to express cosmic awe.

He was launching out into a most curious and would-be practical attempt to explore and explain the secrets of the universe. He was searching for *facts*—in chemistry, in biology, in astronomy, in psychology—not only for themselves, but to be able to transmute them directly into philosophic truths, or particles of truth which, he hoped, would eventually make up answers, or some of the answers to the questions he had endlessly asked. How? Why? Perhaps, as he seemed to envision, there would be just One, great unified Answer. And with it, he would astound the world. It would be "so simple, so conclusive, so—well perhaps, *beautiful. . . .*" These last expressions were his, as he talked to me.

For this, nothing was too hard. So now this man of sixty-four was ready to study, to plod in and out of libraries, laboratories, and face facts and theories that many a younger scientist would fear to attack—and this, in a dozen different fields. It seemed at once a daring, magnificent, and crazy project!

Now it was the microscope at the Wood's Hole Marine Laboratory, or now the telescope at Mt. Wilson, that enflamed his imagination. He wanted to read every new book that came out along scientific lines if it touched on universal problems. The *Brownian Theory*—the latest book by Alexis Carrel—he could hardly wait to read them. Had these men discovered the truth before himself? He must understand all these things, press onward—the final word had not been said. But he longed, and in his longing, almost *prayed* to say it.

That spring, Dreiser worked on in the guest house, until he became involved in an emotional situation with Helen which led to one of their many separations. Helen went to California, and the big house was rented for a good sum.

Although Dreiser retained the guest house for his files and belongings, it was too near the other to give him privacy, so he moved to the two cabins that he had built on the long shoulder of ground which rose to the left of his place, as you drove in.

He lived in the lower one, the log cabin which Powys loved. It was delightfully quaint and roomy, with furnishings of the most primitive sort. Dreiser slept in a low, square bed and sometimes cooked simple meals over the fire. Except in the hottest weather, it was good to have a fire in the evenings, because of the dampness. He did his work in the higher, airier cabin on the top of the hill. Here was the little porch where he could sit and look off at the hills, as he loved to do.

There was no water in either cabin, so he went down to the guest-house for it, and got meals there, when he wanted to. His young secretary came every day in her car and besides their regular work, did errands for him, or simple cooking. In the evening, they would often drive out to eat. He loved this quiet life, and would have been perfectly content, had it not been for various problems which arose in connection with his tenants.

Just as things had seemed to go wrong when he lived in the big house, so now there were leaks, electrical troubles and breakages. The drainage system around the house was very bad. Every time it rained, dirt washed down the road into the garage, into the gutters and even into the big studio. The long drive from the gate which had been hardened and reinforced at great expense, now acted as a natural water-carrier. The houses stood directly a-thwart of the long slope that made up the property.

Silt also ran down and collected in the pond. About this, the tenants complained vigorously, since this natural swimming pool was supposedly one of the features for which they paid a high rent. Then Dreiser would have a gang of men come to drain the pond, as they would a cesspool, at considerable cost.

Dreiser was really beginning to worry about money, now. He had lost a long-drawn-out lawsuit with the Liveright heirs, and was obliged to pay back some $30,000 in advances, which he had long since spent. No money, or very little, was coming in from his old books, or occasional articles, and he saw no chance of finishing his *Philosophy* in the near future. A certain amount of cash was his only reserve and he kept constantly drawing on it; he had visions of ending his days in the poorhouse, when his mood was low.

Into the grounds, buildings, road and walls of *Iroki,* he had poured over $100,000 in the four years that he had owned it, and yet, though he tried a number of times, no bank would give him a mortgage on the big house. It was too unusual and impractical. The banks would send their best people out to see him; they were polite but adamant. Nor would they give him a loan on his earning capacity. His whole set-up and literary prospects (perhaps because of his political reputation) looked to them like a bad risk.

Dreiser had always had certain penurious little habits, dating back to his years of struggle with poverty, and these became conspicuous again. He gave embarrassingly small tips in restaurants, and he used the cheapest kind of paper for his work, even for manuscripts that he was going to send out. He would send his secretary to a distant five-and-dime to save a few cents, rather than buy better paper in the local stationery store.

However, in the higher brackets, he was more indifferent. Small sums worried him more than larger ones which he did not handle in cash. It must also be said that he could throw off financial troubles, at times, with the ease of a gambler, or a millionaire, if he was in a high, emotional mood. On the whole, he was in a happy state that summer. He would work all day in his upper cabin. Around six o'clock, he was usually ready for a little drive, dinner or a good time.

One late afternoon in August, I drove over to see Dreiser, with Josef, a German friend whom he knew. Dreiser had said he was moving back to the guest house, but everything there looked deserted. As we drove out again, over the long, rising road, I stopped at the tracks leading to the old cabin, wondering whether he was there.

The little place looked utterly right and harmonious, fitting into the hill and the wild grass—Here at least, he should have been able to find that peace of mind that was always evading him.

As I sat thinking of him, Dreiser suddenly emerged around the corner of the cabin and started down the long ruts through the grass. He was white-headed and lumbering like some Rip Van Winkle, powerful, primitive and lonely as these hills. Then, in a moment, a tiny fair-haired girl in a blue smock came out, following him. This was at the time that there had been a series of newspaper stories about an old Kentucky mountaineer who had married a twelve year old farm girl. This looked like just such a strange couple of back-country folk.

Then they saw us, and waved; the illusion was gone. This was the college girl who worked for him. We all went to the guest house and had something to eat and drink.

Dreiser talked about the gigantic task they were doing and what a help this girl was. "She's got a brilliant mind, simply brilliant," he said, as she was getting ice in the kitchen. It was obvious, too, from the way she talked, that she had a most disarming and natural charm.

Her hair was long and light and she had wide hazel eyes, brimming with humor and a kind of candid challenge. She was small, slim as an elf, and clever as a man.

But as we talked, I noticed how cynical she was, and how, for all their scientific study, they seemed to have come no nearer to finding any meaning for life. Dreiser had convinced her that there was no such thing as free will.

We spoke of someone who had died—"The after-life?" Pooh, there was no such thing—at least, we know nothing, and we are nothing, except this chance temporary combination of atoms and electrons, and when we are dead—*Whew*— *Gone*—*Finis*—Dreiser said the words with horrible finality, and a dire sweep of his long hand.

I tried to tell him that his own works proved that he believed in the supernatural—in something beyond life. But that day he was at the extreme pole of his doubts, angry as a cornered bear. Both he and this tiny girl turned on me with such a devastating line of scientific arguments, that I was all but crushed. I remember him standing over me, threateningly, and in a sinister, black tone repeating the word, *Nothing, nothing, NOTHING*—as if I were a silly bird, flying in the face of all his serious work and reason, squawking against knowledge of which I had no right to speak.

But our argument was violent only over our drinks. We settled down to a delightful evening, and it was not until after midnight that my friend and I departed.

A few weeks later I received a humorous note from B., his little secretary, inviting me and Josef to come back again before Dreiser closed the house:

"People are shooting birds, rabbits and one thing and another all around here. I have to go for the mail in a bullet-proof car and vest. I live in momentary expectation of being taken for a rabbit. D. expects to be taken for a deer. If we can only find some antlers, everything will be fixed . . ."

That evening, we went down to the old cabin and built a huge fire there. We cooked sausages and coffee for our supper, and the flames leapt up, throwing the rough log structure into high relief.

We did not argue about eternal truths. The simple little place seemed answer enough for our comfort that night, and Dreiser talked beautifully about the unity of nature, and all living things. It was then that I heard him tell the story of the snake, which he told again, in *The Bulwark*. As I remember his words they were something like this:

"One day, I saw a large snake in the high grass near the house, and I got out my gun, and shot it. It was a beautiful creature, a puff-adder of a variety common around here. Someone who saw it assured me it was not dangerous in the least. A few days later, I saw the same kind of snake near the same place. I thought it must be the first snake's mate, and felt sorry for it. I stood watching it, noticing its beautiful markings. Then it started to move off, and I spoke to it. I said I thought it was beautiful and I was sorry that I had killed its mate."

"It stopped, and I took a few steps toward it, telling it not to be afraid; that I was not going to harm it. Then slowly it turned and came toward me, passing right across the toe of my shoe—and disappeared into the grass on the other side."

Dreiser in New York, 1937

When Dreiser finally closed the guest-house and the cabins at *Iroki,* he took a tiny, two-room apartment at the *Park Plaza,* a small residential hotel off Central Park West, on 77th Street, in New York. The Hotel was nice enough, looking over a small park area, but Dreiser's room was on an inner court, an air shaft. He barely had room for his papers and himself, but this was part of his poverty complex.

For a time, Helen appeared from California, to try to get Dreiser to return with her, but he did not wish to be interrupted in his tremendous *Philosophy* project. Helen stayed awhile, but left again. Dreiser was utterly absorbed in his research which, everyday, seemed to carry him further, and nearer to the Truth. Occasionally, when he had more to do than he could manage, and did not want to take B. away from a special task she was doing, he would summon me, and I would help out for a few days. I liked B. and we got along very well together. I was away for a part of the winter, but toward spring, I dropped in frequently, and often Dreiser pressed me into service for a few hours. It was a way he had with friends, whether they were employed by him or not. He inspired volunteers, and I was only too glad to be able to have a small share in his life and work. In this way, I kept in close touch with him, over a long period. I knew the fascinating material with which he was trying to shape his book, or rather, his thought. For he was far from deciding what form a book might take.

Of the hundreds of notes, illustrations and philosophic comments that Dreiser compiled and wrote, it is impossible to speak briefly. An absorbing, rich and many-colored note-book must someday be edited out of this material.

The variety of the subjects gathered, and some of the ideas

that were going through Dreiser's mind at the time are evident from pages which I typed for him.

One was to be classed under the head of *The Emotions.* It was his reaction to a book on experiments which had been conducted in England describing the effect of color on emotions. It showed how certain cross-roads had been painted in various hues, inspiring motorists with fear or caution. Then Dreiser wrote:

> *To reduce the numbers of suicides from Blackfriars Bridge, the City of London painted that gloomy old structure a bright green. Suicides declined by more than one third. Did the* green *alter the mind or mood of some of the disheartened? Or was it the* absence of black, *traditionally associated with tragedy and death? One thing is sure. Green registers itself as green. You do not "think,"* this is green. *The greeness pervades you for the moment and is only displaced or modified by registrations of other things, people sounds, recollections aroused by green.*

> *You could not possibly "think" this is yellow. It is too definitely a physical reaction and to call it* thought *is nonsense, unless you accept that thought is a chemical and physical reaction and registration, and once impressed or registered that registration is automatically associated with earlier registrations of other greens, as well as colors that contrast with green, or moods and deeds affected by green. The whole process is physical.*

Or the following (which really answers early questions of his *own*):

> *Many people are accustomed to argue thus: 'If all things follow from the unalterable laws of the universe and the universe or its laws by which we are here, are* good, *how is it that so many imperfections have arisen in nature—corruption, for instance, of things until they stink; deformity exciting pity or disgust, confusion, cruelty, crime, etc.'?*

But the perfection of things in the universe is not to be judged by their effects, pleasant and unpleasant, on man. *Decaying meat is not pleasant to smell or behold, but as the inevitable chemical result of changes in the equations which make protoplasmic life possible and more, as the unescapable reaction of one element to another, under given matter-energy conditions, it becomes agreeable and even awe-inspiring—the more so, since it involves a mystery of action which is not only universal but entirely beyond the range of the human mind.*

Nor are such things—murder, cruelty, or beauty, more or less perfect in nature because they delight or offend the human senses or because they are beneficial or prejudicial to human nature.

Cold Spring Harbor—Summer 1937

It was unthinkable that Dreiser should spend the summer in his little suite on the air shaft. He had rented the big house and even the cabins at Mt. Kisco. An opportunity presented itself, which he was glad to accept.

His old friend Calvin Bridges now worked at the Marine Biological Laboratory at Cold Spring Harbor, Long Island. He arranged for Dreiser to get a room in the cottages usually reserved for scientists.

Bridges of course, was, interested in Dreiser's unorthodox search, and had given him material on the *Drosiphila,* or fruit fly. This insect has unusually large genes for its size and is both prolific and short-lived, and thus ideal for a study of genetics or heredity. Bridges and a group working with him had received a Nobel prize for their research achievements.

The simple, almost monastic, atmosphere of the colony at Cold Spring Harbor appealed to Dreiser. Its rather sequestered location was cool and refreshing during the heat of that summer. It consisted of a group of cottages and long low laboratories—white wooden buildings—at a turn of the road running along the North Shore of Long Island Sound. A long cove ran into the property, and there were open tanks for breeding various kinds of fish, along grassy banks. Just behind the houses, heavy greenery and woods grew down to the road. It was a much quieter and more rustic atmosphere than that at Wood's Hole. Dreiser wrote to me:

> *It is so charming over here. These people! These scientists! How sincere! How self-sacrificing! How completely respectable! After the scramble for inanities and trivialities—the money standard of values—to come here and find them ideally set aside. Two dollars for a room or tent. Seven to eight dollars a week for food. An eight o'clock bell calling to breakfast. A long day's work—a six o'clock bell for dinner. And such simple fare! A lovely, clean, courteous world of thought. And for what reward —I am reverent. I am deeply respectful.*

The scientists themselves had first looked upon Dreiser as somewhat of an intruder in their quiet field. B. had also been given a room there, so that their work continued, but no one knew what it was about. Dreiser was, as usual close-mouthed and secretive about himself.

Then a mussel-bake was announced. Bridges insisted that Dreiser and B. must go. About twenty men and women in several row-boats started away from the beach in the late afternoon and reached a beautiful point of land, where they pulled up their boats, and all joined in a search for those hard, blue mussels which grow by rocks below the tide level.

By sun-down, baskets of them had been collected and a huge bonfire by which to steam them, in sea water, was lighted on the wild, open beach.

Around the meal was that mellow and meaningful conversation which springs up when intelligent and unpretentious people are relaxed and harmonious together.

Dreiser delighted everyone with his remarks and responsiveness to the scene. There were songs, in which he joined, and a good feeling of fellowship as they rowed home.

After that, Dreiser was beloved by all, a treasured member of the little community. He, too, experienced a growing sense of peace and truth in this atmosphere of science.

He began to see that the beauty he had always worshipped

in women, in art, was also here, in the things he saw under the microscope, and in the laboratory. There was beauty and design in all created things—what care, what precision had gone into the formation of the smallest organism! It was at this time that his concept of the *oneness* of life was evolving into the concept of a *Creator,* although he said nothing about it. Yet it was here that he came out of the laboratory one afternoon, having looked a long time through the microscope, and suddenly noticed a little bunch of yellow flowers, growing along the path. He stooped over them. Here was the same *design,* the same beautiful detail that he had been observing in the tiny forms under the glass. What care, what love—had created these things. Not only some great intelligence, but a careful, loving Artist . . .

It was then, he said, that he began to experience a different feeling about the universe—but it was only seven years later that he related this story to me.

Dreiser at 11th Street—Winter, 1937-1938

After his summer at Cold Spring Harbor Dreiser's little room at the Park Plaza seemed even smaller. It was out of the question for him to move out to Mt. Kisco in the winter. For some weeks he stayed on working in his dark room on the air-shaft; it was no better than the dreary chain of hall-bedrooms and boarding houses he had inhabited in the worst days of his poverty.

He did not complain about his own comfort, but he literally did not have room for his work, his files and other things. B. and I finally persuaded him that an old-fashioned apartment in the *Village* would be less expensive than a bigger room in this hotel, and that he *must* move.

As chance would have it, B. found him an apartment in the very house where he had once lived with his sister Mame. B. agreed to a $75 a month rent, but when Dreiser came down, he talked the landlord into accepting $70. It was the second floor front of one of the old red brick Rhinelander houses on 11th Street, built in the New Orleans style, with wide porches and fine iron-work railings. Alas, these were since torn down.

Dreiser told me about how he had brought his brother Rome, here after he had found him living like a tramp in Chicago. Rome then lived with Mame, while Dreiser paid his board. Rome was gentle as an old dog, but his mind was softened by drink and age, and he would wander down Eleventh Street with a bucket in his hand, looking for the railroad yards where he had worked in earlier years.

The landlord was a character who intrigued Dreiser. He looked like a handsome society man, grown old and down-at-the-heel. His basement office was always lit by a strong, unprotected bulb and was literally tunneled with old boxes, papers, stacks of books and furniture. Its shades were never down, and the sight of it was troubling to Dreiser, as he passed:

"What *is* Mr. Lamb going to do with all that mess?" He would say, and groan. His own things were never quite in the state that he would have liked to have them. He had a strong sense of order, especially when it was kept by others—and sometimes when I tidied up his things, he would repeat the words *Order-Beauty, Beauty-Order*—as if the two were synonymous.

B. was sick the day Dreiser had to move, and I helped him load my old car with papers and files. His clothes were contained in one suitcase and a few boxes tied with string. He had no false pride about carrying queer bundles, and never made any pretense of being prosperous, when he was not.

At the last load, he turned over to me a stack of old magazines which had accumulated, including the English *Blackwood's* and the Russian *International Literature*. He was still getting plenty of personal mail, though not nearly as much as three years before.

Now he wanted me to make sure that the Post Office had his new address. He was always interested in his mail, though he could not begin to read all the printed matter, bulletins, reports, that came in. But letters always excited his imagination. Perhaps in the next mail, there would be an offer from

a publisher, an agent, a film company—or just some charming, feminine message of affection. Alas, the latter were more
frequent than the former!

The new apartment on 11th Street consisted of a living
room of good size, with a fireplace, and French doors opening out to the handsome New Orleans balcony. There was a
small bed-room, also on the balcony, and a fair-sized kitchen
with refrigerator and counter. The latter was used less for
cooking than for a bar!

That year, Dreiser had a particular fondness for buttered
drinks, not only hot rums, but he would add a bit of butter
to the rim of an *old-fashioned* whiskey, even though it was
cold. He also invented a cocktail which was part grenadine
and part vodka. He would beat up a white of egg for the first
drinks, but after that, he just added more vodka, as the
drink went down!

However, he never drank more liquor than he could handle.
Drinks enough to affect the average person badly would give
him no more than a pleasant glow, or steam up his emotions
if he were arguing about something. He might have a hang-
over the next day. But this was easily cured by his favorite
remedy—Bromo-Seltzer, with a dash of spirits of ammonia!
A doctor had told him once that he wouldn't last long if he
took such a combination. But that didn't bother him. Like
Rasputin, he believed in the infallibility of his own strength
and energy.

Dreiser loved color and we had procured for him two
gouaches of Jean Lurçat, in warm orange, reds and blues.
We lent him a burnt-orange silk Persian prayer-rug for the
floor. We wanted him to feel comfort and beauty around him.

He chose another drawing from a group I had by Louis
Adolphe Soutter, then a little-known genius, in spirit like a
combination of Baudelaire and Roualt! This was the head of
a woman, life-sized, with extraordinary hair, dark strands
with a swirling, tragic quality that suggested the torments
and delights that might be offered by some young witch.
Dreiser loved this, because to him woman was always a witch

or a troll of whom he could never be sure. He liked reading
his own inconsistencies into women of his choice and could
more easily forgive erratic conduct than a boring conformity
to convention, as he saw it, or a restraining hand upon himself.

His primary purpose that winter was to complete his scientific reading and notes, and now he had begun to study books
on psychology by Jung, Menninger and others. However, he
was faced by the ever-desperate need to make money. By
this time, he had spent some seven or eight hundred dollars on
scientific books alone, although he took volumes out of libraries whenever possible, marked them lightly for copying, and
then had B. erase his pencilling before she took them back.

He wrote several hasty articles, but could not sell most of
those he sent out. He was not willing to take time from his
Philosophy, to do a better job. He expected that editors would
be glad to get his stuff, anyway. "That's good enough for
them," he would say if we balked at some uneven piece.

Then, he tried developing a new kind of article, out of his
scientific findings, challenging old beliefs and putting start-
ling, new ideas in their place. But these did not fit into any
whole, for his own theories were not brought to a conclusion,
and no short piece could give an adequate impression of what
he was doing. The work was still too scattered, disparate, immense.

Some one put him up to trying radio programs. He held
an interview with Helen Menken, the actress and she was
glad to have him do some sketches for her use, on the air.

He met Gertrude Lawrence and wanted to write a play for
her. She was acting on Broadway at the time, and let him
call on her in her dressing-room after the performance—
quite like the days with his brother Paul—and he enjoyed
her immensely. But here again, plans fell through because
he did not want to spend time away from his main project.

A New Magazine Venture—Direction.

Dreiser was not indifferent to the storm that was arising in
Europe. If he had seemed to withdraw from the political

struggle, it was partly because President Roosevelt had inaugurated the New Deal, and social conditions had begun to improve on the home front. However, he always read the newspaper, and had a passionate interest in the fate of man as it daily unrolled in the press.

When I had first returned from Europe, he was most interested in hearing that creative people everywhere were becoming involved in the struggle against fascism. In Paris, I had been to meetings organized by Picasso, Jean Lurçat and others, to help the people of Republican Spain, and to bring to the attention of the world, the civil war raging around Madrid. The new dictator, Franco, was receiving help from Mussolini and Hitler, and the intellectuals of Europe were doing all they could to arouse an indifferent public. In America, only certain journalists and liberals seemed to know what was going on.

To inform the public and organize resistance to Hitler and all that he represented, several vigorous groups were formed, notably The League Against War and Fascism, The North American Committee to Aid Spanish Democracy, and the League of American Writers.

Later, in the McCarthy era, it was claimed that these were "Communist Front" organizations and that those who joined them were "Communists" or "Fellow-travellers." Even people whose names could not be connected with "left-wing" groups, were almost humorously classified as "premature anti-fascists"—if they had taken any stand against the menace of World War II before Pearl Harbor! But Dreiser, as well as hundreds of us who joined these groups, never felt that we were "dominated" by Communists nor by anything except our own hearts and consciences.

Dreiser had always avoided joining any political parties because he wished to fight for "the equities," his favorite word for social justice, "without a delaying quarrel over a name." This quotation in a letter from Dreiser to me, will be discussed in a later chapter, but I would point out here that Dreiser gladly lent his name and prestige to the League of American Writers. One has only to look at the distinguished

list of League members in those days to see that it represented a true popular front of our best American authors.

I had brought back material from outstanding writers
of the Popular Front in France and had inside information
from Germany as well. There, my own cousin had been
thrown into jail for being a friend of anti-Nazis, although
he was an American citizen. I had articles from Heinrich
Mann and later, from Thomas Mann. With all this in reserve,
I had hoped I could interest Dreiser in starting a magazine
such as he had envisioned when leaving *The American
Spectator,* but one which would also be international in scope.

"No—you missed the boat on that one," he had said, meaning that I had gone away just when he needed me for a new
magazine venture and now he was too busy with his scientific
research.

But Dreiser was sympathetic toward the idea of my trying
such a venture, and said he would contribute, though he
did not want his name put down as an editor. B. was also
anxious to help, as her mind was always teeming with ideas,
many of them daring and original. A number of young
writers like John Hyde Preston, Thomas C. Cochran, Edwin
Seaver and later, Richard Wright consented to be co-editors.
We plunged into print in December, 1937 under the title
Direction, with Dreiser's picture on the leading page, and a
quotation from his files:

> *As the antique order of an old house becomes the dis-
> orderly decay of a newer age, so with changing ideas.
> The refreshing tides of the seasons, years, generations
> succeed each other not without sadness and despair and
> suffering for what was, but mainly with welcome and
> gladness for the vitality and promise of what will be. To
> some it is necessary to find out these new* directions,
> (my emphasis) *build new forms, be the van of circum-
> stance; and to some is necessary blindness and the steril-
> ity of age and decay.*

> *This balance is a part of the universe of which our puny
> ideas, theories and proclamations are only a reflection,*

but a necessity, or so it seems. The seeming of what is
new is only possible through the seeming of the old.
The eager delight of a fall wind takes its rise from the
ennui of summer heat. And who does not thrill to the
arrival of what is untried and promising power and de-
light?

Dreiser's next contribution was an idea of B.'s that a
spontaneous conversation between two equal minds on topics
of the day would make good reading. B. would take down
what was said, in short-hand.

We approached John Dos Passos, who had already contributed a short story to our first issue, and he consented to
come to the 11th street apartment. Conversation flowed easily
—the result was a lengthy piece published in the second
issue. (*Direction*-Feb. 1938) Some comments on the affairs
of the day are still valid, but on the whole, the idea did not
turn out as well as it should have, due to lack of editing on
my part. I was too afraid to cut or change anything these
famous authors had said. In another conversation about
Spain, which was recorded, but not published, Dreiser and
Dos Passos said something as significant today as it was
then:

My absolute conviction, said Dreiser, is that there is
now an economic and financial understanding between
financiers of all countries where there is wealth, and that
they are all for the fascist form of government, as op-
posed to the democratic or communistic. They want to
Fascisize the world, put the poor dope *at the bottom and*
a select few at the top. In other words, the next Caesar
will be a financial Caesar.

Do you think there is any chance of that in this country?

Dos Passos answered: "Yes, all kinds of chances, in this
country . . ."

and he went on to enumerate some of our fascist-minded
business men and companies, some of whom have since been

exposed by books such as *Under Cover*. Indeed the John Birch Society of today seems dominated by just such mentalities.

From this time on, Dreiser frequently sent me pamphlets, reports, letters or information that had come in to him, which we could use in the magazine, and so we felt encouraged and stimulated by his interest.

The Shack—*Summer, 1938*

Dreiser loved the sea as much as ever that summer, 1938, and enjoyed coming out to a ramshackle beach cabin I had rented near my family home in Connecticut. It was off Noroton Bay on Pratt's Island. We used it mainly for week-ends, but as summer approached, Dreiser asked if he might work there during the week.

The Shack, as we called it, had a South Sea Island appearance, standing on stilts above a curved stretch of sand. The roof jutted out over an ample porch. Its weather-beaten shingles were the same tone as the rocks that ran out into the water at the right end of the beach, near the front steps. A few trees leaned over the roof at the other side. Then the beach swung out, some hundred yards away, into a long reef, at low tide extending far into the Sound.

Long Island could be seen, some ten miles across the water. The lights of Bayville twinkled at night. Oyster Bay and Cold Spring Harbor were not much farther down the opposite shore. On clear days, sailboats would appear like birds upon this wide stretch. The marine landscape was always changing. Submerged reefs and rocks showed their heads when the tide was down, and there was always its ebb and flow to watch and meditate upon.

Inside *The Shack*, a tent-like roof was studded with dark nails, giving a rich texture to the old shingles. There was a square iron stove and an exposed stove-pipe which heated the place on chilly days. A big yellow table and porch chairs were the main furnishings. A partition, going half way up to the roof, screened off a small bed-room; behind this was another tiny room, and the kitchen and wash-room were equipped with cold running water—luxury enough for Dreiser.

Here he brought several huge boxes of files and papers. B. brought her typewriter, so that their work continued as usual. During the week, Dreiser plugged along quite steadily, taking time out only for an occasional dip or sunbath.

On week-ends, the picture changed. I would come down with my son, or sometimes with Josef, my German friend who had been to Mt. Kisco and whom Dreiser liked very much. He was a big, powerfully built Bavarian, an expert swimmer and skier and the sort of person who could spend hours quite happily without saying a word.

Dreiser liked such basic unpretentious people and always believed he could learn something from them. Josef would go off in an old gray rowboat and fish for hours off the reefs. When he got back, Dreiser would want to know how the fish were running, what kinds he had caught, and the secrets of currents and fishing holes Josef had discovered. He was the best cook of the four, and made Bavarian dishes which delighted Dreiser and which we would wash down, on warm evenings, with plenty of cold beer.

Other weekends, Dreiser invited friends from New York, among them Edgar Lee Masters who was then living at the venerable Chelsea Hotel, in a rather bad state of health. He would come and sit for hours in a rocker on the porch, while Dreiser moved about in his scant, bright-blue bathing trunks, going in and out of the water several times a day, but finally settling in a chair beside Edgar, looking off over the ever-changing scene of blue and white and gray.

Both of these natural poets loved such hours of revery. Masters would sometimes tell a story in his inimitable, quiet, rather teasing manner. Or they would exchange reminiscences of New York, Indiana, Chicago. They poked fun at each other on every possible occasion, particularly on the subject of women. They had shared some pretty rocky days in Chicago when they were both involved in agonizing love dramas!

Once, a group of scientist friends from Cold Spring Harbor came over on the Oyster Bay Ferry to spend the day with

Dreiser, and for hours he was plunged into that kind of specu-
lative and far-reaching conversation which was nearest to
his heart and mind in those days.

A Party with Howard Scott, Technocrat

On one particular Sunday there was a big gathering at *The
Shack*. It was a rustic open-house such as Dreiser used to
have at the white-birch bungalow. I don't remember all the
people who came, but they included Dorothy Dudley Harvey
and her husband, Hubert and Marguerite Davis, Kenneth
Hayes Miller, John Hyde Preston with his first wife, Barbara;
Olin Downes, the music critic and delightful writer, and Art
Young, grand old radical cartoonist, who brought Gilbert
Wilson the painter.

At first, Dreiser did not take kindly to the gentle, seclusive
Gilbert Wilson though the latter was from his own Indiana,
and had made a portrait of Dreiser to include in his Antioch
College mural of Hoosier characters. But when he learned
that Wilson was devoting himself completely to Art Young
that summer, his attitude changed. I had gone to fetch them
both at Danbury, where Young was spending his last days in
a boarding house in back of the old Green Hotel. It was
obvious that he was failing in health and mind, though he
still had his amazing mirthful personality.

(Dreiser could not help feeling his superiority when he
saw men of his own generation showing their years so much
more than he did his. This was also true when he was with
Masters. He was especially proud of his own strong yellow
teeth when Edgar had finally lost all of his!)

After this gay throng had sunned themselves, talked and
imbibed freely for some hours, a smart gray car drove up
behind *The Shack*, and a tall, imposing man of military carriage sprang out. He was followed by another, younger man,
both of them wearing identical gray whipcord suits. On the
door of their car and in their button-holes was the S-like
symbol of *technocracy*, dividing a circle into red and gray.
This was Howard Scott and one of his lieutenants. They explained that they were late, because they had been put off

the Merritt Parkway—just opened that week. On account of this symbol their car was considered a commercial vehicle!

But their theory of a Utopian state run by technocrats was far from commercial. Indeed, it was dangerously ideological. They had schemes for taking over the means of production and technical resources of the country which smacked of fascism rather than of socialism. In this modern mechanistic world, they maintained, no one was fit to hold power except a trained aristocracy of technicians.

They talked with precision and moved with precision around the sands and the shambling house and made us all acutely conscious of the fact that we were not as mentally *on our toes,* as they were!

Dreiser was amused by this super-efficiency of Scott's, and he had always been a little jealous of Scott's easy and dominating way with women. Yet he was genuinely fond of him.

There was a story that in 1915, when they were both living it the Village, in shabby circumstances, Scott happened to walk in on Dreiser in His rooming house, and found him nearly dying of pneumonia. Although he scarcely knew Dreiser at the time, he took care of him, brought him medicines and literally nursed him back to health. Dreiser never forgot it.

By nightfall, the party had become a typical Dreiser festival. Every one was over-stimulated with liquor and daring conversation. Dorothy Dudley was arguing violently and brilliantly with Scott, in her extraordinary, husky-cooing voice.

Dreiser, as usual, liked to get people started on some controversial subject and then sit back and watch them, like a spectator at a cockfight. Now he kept stirring things up around Scott, who was himself a brilliant speaker. John Hyde Preston was a whole-hearted liberal who detected Scott's potentially fascist mentality, and it infuriated him. So Dreiser kept prodding him on.

He himself was more interested in talking to Barbara, Preston's wife, who was a beautiful woman with natural vivacity and a charming way of tossing her curly hair while she spoke. She also had great mental charm, and Dreiser later exchanged several letters with her.

The party was in a whirl of excitement, when suddenly someone announced the hour. There was barely time for some of our guests to make the last train back to town. Dorothy Dudley drove off with Scott, still arguing spiritedly.

Such were the interludes between days of quiet work. Sometimes, I would take papers I was editing to *The Shack*, to ask a word of advice from Dreiser or just to share the creative atmosphere around him. Occasionally, we would find ourselves alone for an hour or so, without friends, without rush. Then, borne in by the tide, would come that sense of oneness, completeness, because there was a universal love that we could share, asking no place in lives already crowded, but always there, underneath the surface.

Thoreau Introduction—Call to Spain

Late in the summer, Dreiser received an interesting proposition to select, and write an introduction to a Thoreau Anthology. The publishers, Longmans Green, were bringing out a series entitled *Living Thoughts of the Past presented by great Minds of the Present*. Authors were chosen because of their kinship with masters of the past, so Thomas Mann had been asked to present Schopenhauer, and André Gide, Montaigne.

Dreiser was to select only enough work to make a small, readable volume, and his introduction was to be an interpretation of Thoreau in terms of the modern world. Although the subject interested him, he did not welcome any distraction to his own study. However, the cash advance offered was something which he could not well refuse. As he was debating in his own mind, how he would manage this with minimum interruption, a still more urgent matter disrupted his life.

He was called to Spain!

The plight of the Spanish Loyalists had grown desperate. Liberals and thinking people everywhere were horrified to see the so-called democratic countries stand by, while Mus-solini and Hitler tried out their modern methods of war-fare on the million or more Spanish Republican soldiers who were left, crowded around Barcelona, after a two-year loosing fight against the dictatorship of Franco. . . . The tragedy need not be described here; it will always be in the gallery of the world's great injustices.

But at this time, it seemed as if something might be done to arouse public opinion by bringing out a clear picture of what was going on. And so the League of American Writers, which included some of the leading, creative minds of the day, had asked Dreiser—old newspaper man and political warrior that he was—to go and get such a picture.

He could hardly refuse. The situation in Spain was very real to him. But it meant publicity, speech-making, political struggle, all physically and mentally exacting—and emotional heart-break awaited him, too, when he would see the Spanish people. Was there to be no peace for him, to work on his *Philosophy?*

He did not complain. In a few days, he was ready to leave. I can only remember him groaning, *O, my*—as he tried to get his papers in proper order, to be transported to New York—uncertain as to how or where he would live, upon his return.

The last evening in *The Shack* was a strange scene of preparation. A bright electric bulb, bared of its shade in the urgency of packing, lit up the angular tent of the room. Dreiser's bags and boxes stood out in clumsy relief. There were strangers in *The Shack;* a reporter was already inter-viewing him, about his departure; another man was awaiting to arrange some business matters for him. Each were in neat city clothes while Dreiser still wore a rumpled blue shirt and beach slacks. Little B. was calmly and efficiently clearing away papers and letters, letting me help. Both of us were silent, a little fearful of what this trip might mean to Dreiser.

Finally, when the men left, we tried to make him eat and rest. But there were more letters he wanted to dictate, and someone in Paris he wanted us to contact. So he went forth into a valiant, hopeless battle, with all his ragged strength, this man then sixty-seven who had stormed his way through life, never sparing himself, gloriously careless of his health and of his future.

V. DREISER VISITS FRANCE AND SPAIN, 1938
—Move to California—Notes on Life

Dreiser's first assignment on his sudden trip to Europe was to speak at a *Conference Against the Bombing of Open Cities* held in Paris, July 28th of that fateful year, 1938. Here he was representing *The American League against War and Fascism,* another liberal alignment of the day.

Presiding were Lord Cecil of England and Georges Bonnet, then Finance Minister of France. At a luncheon preceding his scheduled address, Dreiser realized from the conversations around him that the Conference, far from being an attempt to aid Loyalist Spain against her agressors, *the bombers of open towns,* had all the earmarks of a strategic move to win support for England's policy of neutrality. His own views on the subject were coldly received.

Although he was supposed to be one of the first speakers that afternoon, he was informed by a sympathetic French writer that his speech had been withdrawn from the program. Nevertheless, he mounted the platform and sat there, with such dignity and resolve, that finally it became impossible for the chairman to ignore him any longer, and he was called upon to speak.

This speech was a model of the patience and wisdom which Dreiser could exercise when he chose. Instead of lashing out at these callous diplomats, he pleaded with them, on the high

ground of irrefutable principles of humanitarian good-will
and *equity*.

For as he explained to me later, he still believed these men
might do something for Spain. He knew it was useless to
antagonize them, reactionary as they were, but he hoped that
their emotions and their sense of fair-play might be touched,
their common humanity influenced a little, in behalf of the
defenseless Loyalists.

The speech was called *Equity between Nations,* and was
hailed and given full space in the Paris newspapers. However,
it received no recognition from the assembly, nor was he
asked to speak again.

Other distinguished intellectuals and Spaniards, who had
come from far, were given no chance to speak nor tell of
what they had experienced in the horror of civil strife. Outstanding among those ignored was *La Pasionaria,* who came
as a Loyalist envoy and became famous throughout democratic circles. Dreiser was greatly impressed by her testimony when he met her, privately.

Throughout the proceedings, there was nothing but indifference when Spain was mentioned. No one protested the
pitiless, year-long bombing of Madrid, the desecration of
Guernica and other towns boastfully discussed by Nazis as experiments in the new techniques of dive-bombing—and this
was a *Conference Against the Bombing of Open Cities!*

Then Dreiser crossed the French border and drove over
the mountains toward Barcelona in an old-vintage limousine,
of the kind that were used as official cars, buses, ambulances—
anything needed by the besieged Loyalists.

His first impression was of the charm of Spain, the soft
light, the good air, the little farms. Yet immediately he sensed
an impending doom, hard to define. Perhaps it was in a flight
of birds that startled both him and the driver, as if an air
raid were coming.

Everything was infected with fear. In all the villages they
drove through, the central squares or market places were

cut across by trenches into which people could throw themselves at the sound of planes.

The terror of war, shared in a million variations by peoples over a great part of the inhabited globe during the Second World War and before it, may seem out of date, now. But this was Dreiser's war experience. Walls shattered, a village cut in half, with people going about their business, cooking supper in the ruin of their kitchen. An old woman watching over her dead, in a dream of misery—these Dreiser described later, but many things he could not describe.

In Barcelona, he lived in one of those typically luxurious *Grand Hotels,* made up of echoing corridors and huge rooms. Part of the kitchen had been blown away, but the vast, half-deserted dining-room was open for business, a few waiters still serving on silver platters. A meal might be one bun and the black juice they called coffee, or a sort of pap, made out of vegetable matter and fried to look like meat.

Red velvet hangings and furnishings were still in evidence, but there was hardly a pane of glass left in any window, and no sheets on the beds. All available linens, towels, etc. had been turned in for bandages. There was no soap to be had in the whole of Barcelona. After a few days, Dreiser developed an itch on his cheek and neck. At the drug-store he was given some watery solution which did not help in the slightest. He was told that all antiseptics and ointments were needed for the wounded and that over a third of the inhabitants of the city were suffering from the *itch,* without any way of treating it.

The clothes of the people struck deep at his emotions, their tied-together shoes, their patched backs. In the morning he would see little groups setting out with sacks, to forage in the surrounding country; in the evening they could be seen coming back, perhaps with a few sticks of wood, a cabbage, or a few turnips, or with nothing at all. At that time there were an estimated twelve million Loyalists living on territory that had formerly supported about two million people. They were slowly starving. But on the whole, they were uncomplaining.

Dreiser had inspected the air-raid shelters cut under the city; some few were equipped with water and lights. Certain people spent half the day in such shelters; others did not seek them even when there was a raid.

After Dreiser had been there several days, the sirens started screeching and some people ran out of the hotel to the shelters, but others did not, nor did he. "You simply felt, *what's the use*," he said, later. "If they're going to get you, they're going to get you,"—and he stayed in the hotel during several raids, once being badly shaken by an explosion a block away. But he also lived through days when planes came over the city again and again, not to drop bombs but to terrorize.

He spoke with both Del Vayo and Negrin, and found them "more like intellectuals than like political leaders." They dressed in civilian clothes and discussed the situation realistically, without pretense. They told him that they had, at various moments, considered giving in to save the people more suffering, but that each time, they had been convinced that the people themselves would not give up; they would simply find new leaders, and go on.

When he left Barcelona after two weeks, Dreiser promised Del Vayo that he would try to get the French Foreign Minister, Georges Bonnet, to permit a few more automobiles to cross the border. The power-plant near Barcelona had been blown up so that there were no more street cars. Horses and donkeys had disappeared. Transportation was perhaps the most desperate need of all.

In Paris, Bonnet received Dreiser and said he would see what could be done. But nothing *was* done by official France, as far as Dreiser knew, to let more cars across that tragic border.

More encouraging was Dreiser's reception by the writers, artists and intellectuals of Paris. He spoke freely to many individuals, and addressed audiences warmly sympathetic to the Loyalist cause. However, there was little that French sympathizers could do, except to receive the defeated flood of refugees who later made their way across the Pyrenees.

Dreiser's mission was to return to America, with his story. He stopped only briefly in England. (It was only there, that his *itch*, treated by a Paris doctor, began to disappear.) For a few days, he visited his old friend John Cowper Powys, who had returned to his native Wales.

Then he sailed for New York.

Return from Spain—Aftermath

It was a hot, early September day when Dreiser's ship came up the Hudson. Reporters had already met him when the boat stopped in Boston, and big-headline stories appeared in the New York papers as he stepped ashore.

He took a taxi to the George Washington Hotel on 23rd and Lexington Avenue where his backers had engaged a suite for him. I was one of the first to meet him there, for rumors had come to me of a plan to undermine what he had to say.

He seemed tremendously strong, looking very well and charged with the electricity of his will-to-fight for the people of Barcelona. He took command of the situation like a general arriving on new territory. He was appreciative but a bit scornful of my warning, very sure of what he wanted to say and do.

He gave a number of interviews, wrote three major articles which had been ordered by the *New York Times* and made several speaking engagements.

The League of American Writers organized a dinner for Dreiser on September 15 (1938) at the Hotel St. Moritz on 59th Street where he made his first public speech about Spain. It was a moving occasion. He painted the picture of the Spain he had seen, and told of the cynical attitude he had found at the Conference in Paris.

When Dreiser talked well, he talked extremely well; like a great actor, taking you into his confidence. You were not bored by an ordinary speech, you were listening to an eloquent heart. He spoke with passionately hushed voice about the people of Barcelona, the fear, the itch, the starvation, the bravery, and he ended with the words: "Such spirit as there is in Spain seems to me—" with a pause and sweep of that long hand "—well, *beautiful.*"

When Dreiser used the word *beautiful* in this way, it expressed to him some ultimate of human experience, nobility, depth. Strange artist that he was, *beauty* meant to him the final quality, beyond the power of words to describe or specify, that he found most desirable, most true, most nearly approximating the spiritual secret of living.

Hy Kraft told me once that it was when Dreiser came back from Kentucky after his famous trip to defend the miners of Harlan County, that he first talked extemporaneously before groups of people. Before that, he had written speeches such as the one he delivered in Paris on the *Equity of Nations* (published in *Direction,* Sept. 1938). He had always avoided public speaking, if possible. But after he had been with the miners, something relaxed in him, some connection was made between his feelings and his tongue, such as is found in great orators, so that he could speak strongly, transmuting his thoughts directly into words.

In the fall of 1938 he spoke on a number of occasions, some of them gatherings arranged by The North American Committee to Aid Spanish Democracy. And he had never seemed more eloquent, his words more moving, than when he talked of his experience in Spain. His articles also gave him satisfaction, for he knew they reached many. But he still hoped to do something more specific, more effective, to aid the people he had seen. In this hope he wrote to the White House, requesting an interview with the President.

It was soon forthcoming for shortly the President invited Dreiser to a meeting aboard his yacht in the Hudson River. They cruised pleasantly along, and Dreiser had plenty of time to tell Roosevelt about Spain. The President asked many questions and was deeply moved by Dreiser's report. However, he said he could do nothing to lift the embargo on food stuffs without more pressure from public opinion behind him. He said that he himself was convinced that the Loyalist cause was just and that its defeat would be a blow for democracy all over the world, and yet he could not act, unless. . . .

He finally said that if Dreiser would form a committee consisting of outstanding people of all professions, and representing at least the three major religions, Jewish, Catholic and Protestant—and if such a committee would urge him to lift the embargo, he would be glad to do so.

But the President was quite frank about what he considered his responsibility to the people he represented. He felt that he could not—no matter how much he might want it—do something of his own accord, unless he felt that a majority of the people were in agreement with him.

This was certainly the opposite of dictatorship, and yet, what is a leader to do, if he is worthy of the name and sees justice and right where the majority of the people have not yet seen it? Dreiser pondered over this—how long should a President hang back, when all the world might applaud a decisive move on his part?

However Dreiser came away with a good impression of Roosevelt's charm and forcefulness, in spite of the physical disability which Dreiser found much greater than he had imagined. Immediately, he set about trying to form the suggested Committee.

One of the first supporters that Dreiser found for his prospective committee to aid Spain, was Rufus Jones, the venerable leader of modern Quakerdom, and head of the Friends Service Committee. This man was an amazing personality. As tall and heavy as Dreiser, he had the same kind of vibrancy that gave his presence an impact and his voice a deep tone that was both commanding and genial. His big homely face was disarmingly plain, yet he had written some of the leading books on mystical religion and the Quaker faith. Indeed, it was through him that Dreiser later began to get the light on Quaker ways that enabled him to finish *The Bulwark.*

The Friends Service Committee had already sent several boat-loads of food and medical supplies to Spain, but had been allowed to do so only because they gave aid to the Fascist side as well. Dreiser was impressed with the extent of their effort, and they were willing to do much more. "That's what I call Christianity," he said, a number of times.

Other religious leaders were sympathetic but few were willing to lend their names. Again, among the leading newspaper editors, Dreiser found approval of his committee on the part of individuals, but publishers were not willing to give the names of their papers to back it. No, they were like the President at that point, afraid to get too far ahead of their subscribers!

I remember Dreiser coming back from a long discussion with publisher Joseph Patterson of the New York *Daily News,* who liked to call himself a socialist and had held out some hope of support, in a first interview. It was an abnormally hot day for September and Dreiser was exasperated. He simply growled: "No—Patterson won't do anything—*Nothing—*" That night he wouldn't eat, wouldn't talk. He was sick in mind and body for the people of Barcelona.

The next weeks were full of disappointments and set-backs for Dreiser's committee. He found the support of many liberal leaders, whose public attitudes were already known, but the other sort of successful citizens that he needed, the conservative, entrenched businessmen, or the respectable philanthropists, for the most part preferred to keep silent about their opinions, or even if they expressed sympathy, would not lend their names.

No one who did not know Dreiser would believe how sensitive he was, and how much he suffered from such personal encounters with people whose minds did not function as his, who simply did not understand the validity of *compassion for one's fellowmen* without regard to one's personal interest. Some days, he seemed like a lone, old gladiator.

Ironically enough, Roosevelt himself organized such a Committee, late in December of 1938, and Dreiser wrote to him, Jan. 5, 1939:

*That you should have applied the mechanism of the plan
suggested so accurately and effectively, and particularly
in the face of the stalemate that any ordinary citizen
was certain to encounter, makes still more clear to me
the enormous value of a great executive in the Presiden-
tial chair. . . .*

*I am deeply grateful to you. You did what I so much
would have liked to do for you.*

But it was too late to save the Loyalist cause. In January,
Barcelona fell to Franco. But even before that, Fascism had
gained a tremendous victory.

On September 21, 1938, came the news that the Nazis were
invading Czecho-Slovakia. Dreiser heard it over a radio
croaking with static, for at the same moment, the Eastern
seaboard was being shaken by its worst hurricane. Dreiser
felt the mood of disaster. The physical violence of the storm
was almost a relief, to lift the burden he felt for Spain, and
the cause of Democracy.

After the hurricane

After the hurricane, we drove out to see what had become
of *The Shack*. It lay sprawled like an enormous bird, with its
back broken, its rafters like pinions, half buried in the sand.

Dreiser gave one of those *groan-sighs: "Aah,* What a pity"
—But then came a sweep of his long hand "—Change!" Though
he had loved the little place it fascinated him to see what
the storm had done. The whole level of the ground had been
heaved up, so that the nose of the row-boat stuck out of the
sand like some piece of an old wreck. It was lucky that all
Dreiser's papers had been taken away before his trip.

The cottage next door had been rented by Erskine Caldwell
who was about to marry Margaret Bourke-White. This house,
more substantial and set further back from the beach, had
not suffered badly, but their car was stuck in the sand, and
this brought us all into conversation.

This casual encounter led to a small dinner party at my
family home, some weeks later. John Hyde Preston was also

there. Dreiser was rather gruff that evening, as he sometimes could be. He started arguing with John about some housing project, embarrassing us all by the violence of his speech. Later, he calmed down and questioned Erskine Caldwell and Margaret Bourke-White about their experiences in photographing and recording the American scene. They had been sent by *Life* magazine to see what was being done by the New Deal in depression areas. *You have seen their faces*— published by Duell Sloan and Pearce—was the result.

Dreiser was much impressed by the electric personality of Margaret Bourke-White. "She's beautiful, of course, anyone can see that, but she's smart," he commented afterwards, "keen and clever and smart as a whip." He said it almost as a reproach. As if he could not quite keep up with her. He was tired that evening and angry at me, as if I had tricked him into this little dinner, when he had expected to spend a quiet week-end. He was very tired.

Caldwell said later: "I have never known a more stalwart, oak-like man. It was his nature to be kindly and sympathetic, but at the same time it was next to impossible to sway him with argument. Either one agreed with him and became his boon companion, or else one refuted him and became an outcast. Only a strong-minded, purposeful man could write the books that he did."

One exceptionally clear, fall day Dreiser had an experience which refreshed him, and which John Hyde Preston could never forget. John's sense of beauty and communication with nature was as strong as Dreiser's, and when he came down to the shore, he loved to row far out into the Sound. On this particular afternoon He was out rowing when suddenly, he beheld a mirage. Looking south, he saw the skyscrapers of New York, magnified by some freak projection of the fall light, and standing in the middle of the water. He raced back to the shore to get Dreiser, and they rowed out, fearing that the vision would be gone. But there is was—the magic city standing in the middle of the Sound!

Dreiser gazed and gazed. John did not dare to speak to

him, so intense was his mood. Both men were dressed only in bathing trunks, and the autumn sun was going down. John said later:

"When, after a quarter of an hour, I suggested we go back, he raised one hand and said, '*Wait, wait*' like a man wakened from a dream. He sat there, with mouth open, motionless as a Buddha, until sunset stole the vision from the sky."

The fall bleakened toward November. Dreiser began to be troubled by his chronic bronchial cough. He could not afford to stay on at the George Washington Hotel, now that his work for Spain was over. He was eager to return to the *Philosophy,* but first, there was the task of completing his selection of the writings of Thoreau, and doing the introduction.

While Dreiser had been away, B. had done a *beautiful job* —in Dreiser's words—of sorting, copying and breaking down the Thoreau material he wished to present. But now B. had become involved in emotional, personal problems which made it impossible for her to continue working with him.

The many *Philosophy* notes were stacked away, and there was no point in opening them up in a hotel room. Calvin Bridges had gone to work at the California Institute of Technology in Pasadena, and Dreiser knew other scientists who could help him with the final stages of his investigations and who were connected with California universities or with the Mt. Wilson Observatory, near Los Angeles. Here, he reasoned, he might find the peace and quiet in which to bring his work to conclusion.

But most of all, it was Helen who drew him back toward California. She had been living there for over two years, at that period, and kept urging him to join her; he had promised that eventually he would come out. Every time that they were separated, there was always something which brought them together again. Helen knew him so well, and would take him on his own terms, he knew. To Dreiser, who was most impractical about the small details of living, she was a wonderful balance. She ran a house well, drove beautifully, was a charming hostess when Dreiser wanted to see his

friends, and also respected his need for quiet when he was
working. Temperamentally, they were in many ways alike,
self-willed, passionate, capable of great emotional flights,
subject to fits of temper—(They could get into fights worthy
of London fishmongers!) They also shared a warm, spontaneous response to beauty, to interesting people, to those in
distress. Helen was especially generous and outgoing toward
others. She was dedicated to the cause of social justice, as
Dreiser was. And she was also dedicated to him. Her own
book, *My Life with Dreiser,* tells of the great struggle she
had had to control her own womanly jealousies, and accept
him as the strange partner that he was. With great courage
and self-sacrifice she had clung to him and made her life with
him, whenever she could.

Now Dreiser knew that he could count on her to make him
a new home in California. He had put the house at Mt. Kisco
in her name, but she was willing to sell it, if he would come
to Hollywood. She had always preferred to live in the West.
Together, they would choose a new house, and begin again.

So once more, the dramatic, disparate furniture was moved.
Everything was packed and cleared out of *Iroki* by professional movers; and sent, with books, paintings, files and
papers, to Hollywood.

Dreiser's Philosophy, *or* Notes on Life.

Dreiser wrote his introduction to the *Living Thoughts of
Thoreau* at the time of his own most concentrated thinking
about his life's *philosophy.* It therefore may well be the key
to much that he would have said had it been his destiny to
finish his unique project.

> *When I think of philosophy and philosophers as they
> range through the centuries from earliest Greece to this
> hour, I am impressed with the fact that all are men of
> genius, temperamentally and deeply moved, like poets,
> by the phenomena of life by which they find themselves
> surrounded. And in that sense, and in that sense only,
> that is, temperamentally, wrestling with the why as well*

as the how *of it all. For we know of course that science in its technical or practical approach toward the phenomena of existence has long since abandoned almost every hope of an answer to the* why *of things, and has concentrated on the* how *of what it sees going on about us. . . .*

Then, in language like that of some of his *Notes on Life,* he cautiously approaches his idea of a *creative force.* It is interesting that he does not use this expression in his Thoreau introduction, nor the word *Creator,* which he uses in later writings; I believe he was saving it for his own *Philosophy,* and preferred to employ various equivalents here.

The philosopher and dreamer or poet, while profiting by science and on occasion being identical with the scientist, has never ceased to concern himself with the thought of, or as I see it, he has unceasingly reacted to, the mystery of the why. *For there is, of course, this matter-energy which fills all space. There are these various laws by which the different forms of matter-energy are regulated, or by which they describe their inherent nature and therefore to which they voluntarily conform. In other words, they are either regulated by something (God is one word often used to describe that something, also Spirit, Brahma, Divine Essence or Force) or being all in all in space and time, they are* collectively, *the equivalent of this imaginary something. And whether self-regulatory or not, they still conform to laws which are the equivalent of self-regulation and hence of the essence or spirit otherwise assumed to inhabit or inform them.*

Through what they are and do, they express its uttermost character and being. And by us, as reacting evocations of the same, they can only be spoken of as the universe. And only such laws and actions as have been scientifically verified can be ascribed to them. All else must be shunned or ignored. (Shades of Fort's Damned

Facts!—M.T.) *For nowadays, the scientists insist that philosophical generalizations must be founded on scientific results. All talk of any supreme regulating, and hence, legal or directing force or spirit is* out. *There is no known God or Spirit. He cannot be scientifically described* in toto, *if even in part. . . .*

Yet side by side with all this, in all branches of science, is constant and non-changing reference to creative thought or deduction via increased nervous sensitivity to already long-existing data, as though man, an evocation of this non-understandable universe of matter-enery-space-time, could individually and mentally be creative, whereas that from which he derives could in no wise be.

Then, into this consideration of the universe, Dreiser weaves another concept, which had haunted him since the days of his coming upon the remarkable manuscript of Charles Fort's *X*, described in the first chapter of this book. Fort's idea is further developed by Dreiser, who could use illustrations from television, which did not exist in Fort's day.

For all its knowledge of how, *science cannot say* why. *And furthermore, it starts nervously at the faintest suggestion that man, powered as a chemical and physical contrivance of exterior forces, in responding to and synthesizing these in-pouring and down-pouring stimuli, may be nothing more than a radio or television device and that the same may be true with animals, insects, vegetation. In short, as a television station distributes voices, colors, forms, motions, and ideas or thoughts, via sounds and gestures—so some extra-planetary forces may be broadcasting man and human life to this planet.*

That, of course, carries to a logical conclusion the vast mass of data which tends to demonstrate that man is a cosmic implement or tool. *But to that point, our scientific mechanist refuses to proceed. He has not, as yet, he says, assembled sufficient data to warrant so esoteric a deduc-*

tion. We must wait. None-the-less, the idealist believes in cosmic law—and the mindlike processes which accompany it—in the engineering or technical genius which accompanies the construction, operation, continuance and dissolution of everything on this planet. He assumes that this could be the work of some superior force in the matter-energy-space-time continuum, something for instance that inhabits and directs that which everywhere appears as directed matter-energy; something in other words, that plans what matter-energy does and is to do. Alas, that's the rub. For that would be a God, name it as we choose.

So, after some five pages of magnificently challenging thought, Dreiser comes to the examination of Thoreau and places him, of course, among these philosophers and poets, as well as among the scientists of his day. Dreiser says:

The rich, if retiring and ascetic mood of this man has more and more come to be understood for what it is, a really important, highly poetic contribution to the metaphysical ultimates of philosophy, as well as to the data of science.

This is the contribution which Dreiser himself could make, in his own way with the commentaries and observations he has left us, on the vast data he assembled. It is perhaps best, because of the very nature of such writings, that they be random, unlimited by the framework of an intellectual philosophy. Because they go far deeper than the intellect in their glimpses of truth and intimations of the divine, partaking of the quality of spiritual writings, and of the highest art. Both Dreiser and Thoreau were enthralled by nature, and the implications of the wonder of the universe. So Dreiser says of this kindred spirit:

Thoreau reached the very definite conclusion, easily to be illustrated by a thousand passages from his writings, that underlying all is a universal, artistic, constructive Genius.

The whole presentation of Thoreau by Dreiser reveals much that is fascinating in the minds of both men, but it is Dreiser whom we are considering here. One other passage from his *Introduction* again throws light on his own work:

> *I am free to say that of all my philosophic and scientific reading of recent years from Democritus to Einstein, these scattered notes of Thoreau impress me as being more illuminative, not of the practical results or profits of science—(which have in our time so led to an increasingly complicated mass of material as well as to mental or ideational structures, with their accompanying compulsions to greater physical as well as to so-called 'mental' dexterities, that they well-nigh befuddle if not wreck the man-mechanism which has to deal with them)—but of the implications of scientific results or cosmology.*

Here again, Dreiser expresses his own purpose, probably without realizing it, in writing his philosophy; it was not his pretention, untrained as he was, to add anything to scientific knowledge, but rather to interpret it, in human terms, to understand, and help others to understand something of the vastness, the essential One-ness, and staggering beauty of cosmic life.

And inside of Dreiser's parenthesis, in his over-long sentence above, is a clue to the difficulty he found in concluding his study. He had taken on too much work, too many details, probing into formulas and facts far beyond the comprehension of the average layman. What Thoreau had avoided, with his scorn of civilization and intellectuality, Dreiser deliberately sought out. He felt he must cover the whole ground of modern thought, in order to speak with authority about his own deepest convictions. Fascinated by all the new discoveries of science, psychology, and even occult experiment, he was writing a hundred years later than Thoreau, and the world of knowledge was growing more complex. There were ever more approaches to the *One Truth*, and he must look at it from every side.

Eventually, Dreiser would probably have discarded much

of his material, as he did in the writing of his novels. It was his way to over-produce, as Nature did herself—wasting thousands of acorns to produce one oak. (This was one of Dreiser's favorite examples.) But his main theme was growing ever clearer, and I believe that someday it will emerge from his *Notes*.

Recently, in looking over Dreiser's scientific-philosophic files in the collection of his manuscripts at the University of Pennsylvania, my earlier impressions of their originality and literary quality, are confirmed. I do not think that a study of Dreiser is complete without taking cognizance of these notes, and the amount of time that he had spent collecting his source material.

These *Notes on Life,* as Dreiser tilted them, pending development of his thesis, arrived at the University in 87 packages. About two-thirds of the typed manuscript consists of quotations from scientists, doctors, specialists in various fields of research and scientific thought. About a third of the material is original writing and commentary by Dreiser himself, on the various subjects he had chosen.

The late Dr. Sidney Horowitz undertook to sort these notes, and put them into separate files, preparing to edit them for publication. Unfortunately he did not live to complete his project.

However, the original outlines which Dreiser made include some forty-nine challenging and provocative subjects. Only to delve into them is a stimulating experience. They also arouse memories of what Dreiser used to say in conversation on some of these vast and tantalizing topics. The outlines start with a list of *Mechanisms,* such as: *Mechanism called the Universe; Mechanism called Life; Mechanism called Mind; Mechanism called Man;* and so forth. Then come a series of *Factors: Factor called Time; Factor called Chance;* etc. There are a number of *Myths,* such as the *Myth of Individuality* (already published in the *American Mercury*), and *Myth of a Perfect Social Order.* Others are listed alone, as *Emotions, Color* (quoted in Chapter IV of this book),

The Salve called Religion, the Hidden God. Finally, there
are *Problems: The Problem of Progress; The Problem of
Death;* The section on *Death* is particularly interesting, bringing in many of Dreiser's experiences and vast speculations,
and containing his extraordinary manner of writing, both
detailed and vast, in which small facts emerge into his tremendous concepts and sweeps of imagination.

When there was first talk of publishing these notes, John
Cowper Powys sent an introduction to be used as an homage
to his old friend. Probably no one understood him better. I
would like to quote this warm and brilliant analysis of Dreiser's essential greatness and "cosmic" personality, but this
does not seem fair in view of the fact that it should first be
published as a prelude to these *Notes on Life,* which I would
hope to see edited in the near future.

For the same reason, it seems unfair to give a longer pre-
view of Dreiser's *Notes* or *Philosophy,* here. I will only say
that there is much speculation about *God, Creative Agents,*
the *Care* that goes into all created things. There is intima-
tion of immortality and great joy, that comes out of some
of these glimpses of a life-behind-life—the sort of joy which
Dreiser speaks of, as being "innate in energy itself" in a
baby's delight in movement, in the spontaneous expressions
of rhythms, or more complicated music. There is much beautiful writing. Here are the themes which ran through Dreiser's life, becoming clearer toward its end, as reflected in
The Bulwark, and, I hope, in this book. But in these notes,
the themes are done in splendid variation. They are thrown,
as it were, upon the sounding-board of the physical universe
and echo back in astounding richness; the theme of the essential unity of all things, and the theme of love.

VI. UNDISCIPLINED ORATOR
—Dreiser lectures in New York, 1941

Dreiser had been living in California for more than two years when he was asked to write a book and to lecture in the east, at the beginning of March, 1941. He had been trying to concentrate on his *Philosophy*, but the threat of World War II also weighed heavily on his mind. He wrote me that he was glad of this opportunity to return to New York for a brief period.

As a fore-runner of his trip Dreiser had sent me an article from California, published in the literary magazine of the League of American Writers called *The Clipper*, December, 1940, and announced as a chapter from his new book, *America is Worth Saving*. I was surprised to see that he had again entered the political scene, for he had written several times from Hollywood mentioning only his work on his *Philosophy* and two scripts for the movies.

But the chapter, *What is Democracy*, had a calm, reflective tone. It gave a picture of man progressing slowly through the ages, toward an economic system which will meet his needs, discarding old tribal customs as he must now discard the "competitive system based on scarcity." He explains that "the advance of democracy is no more than the advance of knowledge . . . In order for there *not* to be plenty for all in our era, there must be ignorance on the part of most."

There is a scientific flavor, almost a smell of the laboratory, about his illustrations. Obviously they were drawn from his scientific notes:

> *Nature didn't choose to hand the primary organism very much of anything, but she gave it remarkable persistence. The amoeba couldn't evolve until the earth was cool enough to provide moisture, but at that point, there was a working mechanism trying to live in—for it—new surroundings. The amoeba has hunger and can, via a 'phantom canal' push out energy, like a foot, and move in the direction where food lies. Also away from opposition or danger. To this 'phantom canal' there are no walls and yet the amoeba travels quite straight in the direction it desires, taking what it finds, if it finds anything, if not, trying another direction. It can surround something, enfold it, chemically absorb it.*

> *What is this immaterialized energy? That we still don't know, but I call it genius of the highest order.*

> *Perhaps more important for us is the question: Why doesn't it—this genius, creative genius of Nature— create the perfect mechanism right away and skip all the long and painful eons of evolution?*

> *The only answer I can see is that it doesn't want to. Struggle, growth, change, contrast, along with pleasure and pain, are some of the laws of its being—its desire to put on this show called by us* Life: *and because of this desire on its part, and by and through these laws, it supplies us with whatever of pleasure or pain, it or we know. Plainly, it lives on adventure. So too with man.*

Then he went on to show that the civilized world is moving slowly on its venture to a better society. Here were long vistas, leading back to the biological beginnings of life, and stretching ahead to greater possibilities, fulfillment. Had he, I wondered, put his *Philosophy* and scientific knowledge to use in the political fight?

But as it turned out, the new book had few of these scientific excursions. It had one burning purpose, to keep America out of war.

This was a curious period in history. England had refused to help Loyalist Spain, and betrayed the democratic Czechoslovakia into the hands of the Nazis. It was common knowledge—for Dreiser had much inside information on the subject—that certain English financiers, as well as certain French and American factions, had been backing Hitler all the way, supporting Nazism in all its horrors because of its avowed anti-communist policy. Then, the Russo-German non-aggression pact had changed the situation. Fearful of Hitler's further advance, England had at last gone to the defense of Poland. Now England and France wished to involve America. And this was what Dreiser protested. For as long as Russia was neutral, he felt that the United States had nothing to gain from being drawn into another European war. Indeed, public opinion was divided in America, and many sought to keep the peace, for widely different reasons, witness the short-lived *America First Committee.*

Dreiser, independent as ever, made speeches, wrote pamphlets and hastily compiled his book, *America is Worth Saving.* In February, he received an invitation to speak on several occasions, for the *American Council on Soviet Relations.* The Soviet Union had not yet been attacked by Hitler, and was also hoping for peace.

Dreiser arrived in New York on the morning of February 28, 1941. I had been asked to be his secretary for the short time he would be there, and I met him at the Grand Central Station. He came lumbering out from the train platform, taller, slower than the crowd, his slouch hat pulled down over his intense gaze, the shy, almost diffident smile.

He was greeted by Thomas Harris, affable clergyman and editor, and Corliss Lamont, keen idealist and Secretary of the American Council. We escorted Dreiser to his room at the Commodore Hotel, where the first speaking engagement was to be held.

Dreiser was dynamic as ever, not much older in appearance, his head still round and solid-looking like a heavy object coming at you through space. He was full of tumult, argument, very much on the offensive about his book, his opinions.

When we were alone, I asked him what had happened to the *Philosophy*.

"Oh, that's coming along," he replied evasively. "This other book had to be done—you can't imagine what a lot of time I had to put into it."

I asked him if he had a good secretary. "No," he said. "They have a wonderful system out there in Hollywood. You just pick up the phone and tell one of those agencies you want a secretary and they'll send one right over, by the hour. It's much simpler than being tied down to one all the time. Of course, I had special help on *America is Worth Saving*. Helen helps me, too. And there's another girl, Elizabeth, who is doing movie work with me."

With his strange, secretive ways, I could understand this, but could not help feeling dismayed about the fruition of his many tasks, without a regular secretary, to help keep order.

He seemed less careful than usual about the work at hand and anxious to get things done in a hurry. He was obviously driving himself, whereas before he had always seemed to act with inexhaustible energy.

That afternoon, he received a press conference, six or seven reporters such as were always on hand nowadays when Dreiser arrived in the city. They were picked men from their papers, and gave him great stimulus. He ordered ice and whiskey for all, and for about an hour lively conversation ensued. Indeed, the conference almost developed into a drinking bout, Dreiser getting very excited and talking in his most cavernous crescendos, about the political evils of the world, and also endulging in a new type of staccato humor, punctuating his statements with sarcastic *dears* and *darlings*.

A private interview with Robert Van Gelder, then of *The New York Times*, published March 16, 1941, gives an idea of Dreiser's mood and language during some of these talks: "Don't you know your current history, Darling?" He exclaimed to Mr. Gelder at one point. Gelder asked him about the difficulties that beset a person of his strong opinions, and Dreiser answered:

Rows everywhere—Once in a while you'll find someone who agrees with you. More often, not at all. A conversation will start on a train and soon a row will start, some arguing on your side, some against. And intolerance! Some of them want to put you off the train!

When Gelder asked Dreiser about his writing, he reports that Dreiser was reluctant to say anything about it, holding forth as follows:

At a time like this, when a man can't afford even to sit down in peace, when the whole world is at a crisis—No, Darling, that's not the time to discuss literature. That is a hell of a subject for you to be plugging at now. Why don't you try to catch up with the world? Do you think this system is so good it can't be better? Have you even seen Russia? No! And you want to talk about books . . .

Later, Dreiser added:

I'll write a book of philosophy and then probably another novel. My autobiography? There's plenty of time for that. . . . But now there's no time for private affairs, for matters of only personal importance. Son, don't you see the world is burning?

At that moment again, as with Spain, Dreiser was possessed by a whole desire to serve, to help the cause of *humanity*— not only of Russia, but of the whole world, sensing us to be, as indeed we were, on the edge of a terrible holocaust which flamed into five years of global war. He saw it all coming, and felt the tragedy and shame of our human lot. And he was willing to do anything he could to stem the tide of destruction, with his art, with his word, with the full strength of his body and will.

He seemed as paradoxical as when I had first met him, able to raise his mind to the highest philosophic planes—as in the first remarkable chapter of his *America is Worth Saving,* called *The World Moves*—Yet never more violent in speech and action, dangerously emotional and flaunting opposition with almost diabolic glee.

This was the state and the tempo in which he approached his first big engagement, the luncheon at the Commodore.

Commodore Luncheon, March, 1941

The morning of the big luncheon arranged at the Commodore by the American Council on Soviet Relations Dreiser was rushed from breakfast 'til noon. Autographed copies of his book were to be sold and between writing his name in some fifty volumes, he saw five or six different visitors, among them his most recent publisher, Richard Storrs Childs. This tall, quiet, daring young man had started Modern Age books on his own money and idealism.

As the lunch hour approached, we tried to keep away further callers, so that Dreiser might have some rest. He was already tired, not hungry, but longing to refresh himself with a shot of whiskey; however, he wisely refrained in view of the task ahead. But no rest was possible.

As he was about to go down to the dining-hall, his old celebrity-hunting friend, Alma Clayburgh arrived, bringing André Maurois and his wife. Alma had ordered a table, but Maurois had just learned that the luncheon was being given by The Council, and not merely in honor of Dreiser, as he had supposed. He was greatly perturbed and fearful lest his name should be mentioned as a guest on such an occasion, and yet he could not resist the temptation to meet Dreiser, before he took his departure.

In these strained circumstances, the meeting between Dreiser and Maurois could hardly be described as cordial. Alma managed some kind of conversation while Mme. Maurois drew me aside, and said severely that not a word of publicity should be given about their appearance here. She said that Russia was a great enemy of their country—France—and they had come to the luncheon not suspecting that it had anything to do with the Soviet Union. I assured her that her husband's name would not be mentioned, indeed, the speakers' names alone would take up all the space in our releases. They finally took their departure.

"Did you ever!" was Dreiser's only comment as he prepared, somewhat nervously, to go down. That nervousness of his was very quiet, only apparent as a sort of rasp in the ordinarily harmonious way he had about him. He had no notes of any kind, but he never needed them nowadays, when he spoke from his heart, and about matters which had just occupied months of his attention.

He took his place near the center of the long speakers' table. Dr. John A. Kingsbury was presiding; at his right, sat Muriel Draper, and next to her, Dreiser. There was a long period of waiting for him, as the meal was served. Finally, the speakers were announced: Thomas Harris, Jessica Smith, Richard Wright and Dr. Harry F. Ward, of Union Theological Seminary. All spoke at some length, before a collection appeal was made. Dreiser, being the honored and elder speaker, was kept for the last.

Poor Dreiser! He sat facing the crowd, and had done so for almost three hours. He had felt too nervous to eat but in order to make his exposed position at least tolerable, he had begun to order drinks, highballs, one after the other. Muriel Draper told me about it afterwards. She had become worried, but did not know how to stop him. He had seemed calm enough, and chatted with her, when he could do so without seeming rude to the speakers. Then followed the appeal; first, one hundred dollar contributions were solicited, then fifties, then twenty-fives. Finally, young girls in evening dresses passed around between the tables.

Alas, the climax of the afternoon was long since passed, when Dreiser was called upon. He felt that everyone in the room was as tired and bored as he. It would take a mighty effort to overcome this, to put up a good fight for the cause. He drained his glass and rose to his feet.

There followed a most curious literary event. I have always regretted that I did not put down as nearly as possible, what he said. After he had spoken a few moments, it was obvious that he was in a highly emotional state. At first he did speak about Russia, about the importance of our relations with her. But then he got off into an intense, burning discussion of the whole question of poverty and human suffering.

Now he began to let that theme which always lay at the bottom of his work—pity, compassion, indignation for injustice—play itself through him, and pour itself out, in words of rambling power.

He kept on and on, and most of what he said, if coldly considered, was sentimental, repetitious and not to the point of furthering American-Soviet relations.

Yet, on a wider plane, it was just that. For look what man has done to man mostly because of economic injustices which do not exist in Russia. If the Russian system had certain flaws, they were not relevant here. He was painting a picture of the raw poverty that has stirred our greatest novelists from Dickens, Balzac, Dostoievsky, on down.

And through his vibrant, sometimes sobbing voice came unforgettable details, descriptions of how he had stood in the London slums and watched people pick over a second-hand clothes cart, looking for a shirt perhaps a little less ragged or warmer than the one they were wearing, or for one shoe which could substitute for one which was quite worn through —and this in a country with more millionaires than we had. Again, he described mining towns he had visited, in England, and also in Kentucky, people listless, half-rotted from foul working conditions, bad air, dust.

It was obvious that Dreiser must be stopped. This was almost a scandal, a defeat for the dignity of the occasion. Handed a note saying that his time was up, he burst out:

"Some would like to stop me from saying these things—but I will not stop. I must tell you what I have seen with my own eyes"—and on went his moving, drunken dirge for the underprivileged of the earth.

It was like a revival meeting, at which some evangelist pleads with sinners to turn to God. If he could only go on a little longer, all *must* be convinced of these great evils, and resolve to remedy them—all must be made to feel this urgency, this sweep of destiny—tonight, tonight—everything must be made clear and the truth prevail. . . .

A number of times people burst out clapping at some dramatic remark, hoping that this would bring Dreiser to a stop. I think it was in the midst of such applause that Dr. Kingsbury was finally able to draw him from the platform. He was shaking, sweaty, and certainly drunk, not only with alcohol, but with the force of his own compassion.

Afterwards Dreiser was glum about this whole incident. He made no apologies; that was not his way. But he was frightfully depressed and the next day, did not care to read the newspaper accounts of the luncheon, although I assured him they were better than expected. *The New York Times* and *Herald Tribune* gave most generous and dignified notices, mentioning only that "Dreiser had to be stopped after forty minutes because the grand ballroom was needed for another gathering."

The Sunday Mirror was less kind, and came out with a malicious but rather funny reportage under the heading *Dreiser weeps for U.S. without Pal Joey* referring to Josef Stalin—describing his speech as punctuated with oaths and tears, as indeed it had been!

Meeting at New School for Social Research

The following day—I believe it was on a Sunday evening—Dreiser spoke at a members' meeting of the League of American Writers. The small auditorium of the New School for Social Research was packed with the many writers and their friends, who had turned out to hear their most distinguished member. Rows of seats in this hall rose rather steeply and the audience was brought around the stage, as for an intimate play.

Dreiser felt in good contact with his listeners. He addressed them in a quiet, subdued voice, which nevertheless carried plenty of power. He assumed that those there understood his point of view, even though they might not agree with him on all points. They were here because they cared about their fellow men. He felt very much a part of them, and said some beautiful things, encouraging particularly the young writers for the part they were taking in the struggle for social justice.

Richard Wright, just rising into fame as our most outstanding Negro novelist, remembered that meeting with particular joy, as did many others. Here, as during that evening at Luchow's restaurant with the young composers, Dreiser showed his love of young people, young talent which could blaze the trail of the future. He felt happy with them, as if they were his spiritual children, in the cause of truth and integrity in their art.

There was entertainment that night by two boys who had come from the Highlander Folk School in Tennessee, one of the first, progressive schools in the South, which helped both "poor whites" and Negroes to get an education. One boy was stocky and self-assured, a hearty farm-type. The other, a thin, gawky figure with a shock of yellow hair, was a real backwoods minstrel. They accompanied themselves with a guitar and rendered with inimitable tang, songs of the hills, of the chain-gangs, of the Deep South.

This was at the time that the New Deal had just begun to alleviate conditions of poverty all over the country. There had been a policy of asking farmers to "plough under" every fourth furrow of their fields, since they were not able to sell all their produce on the open market, and the government did not seem able to handle surplusses. Many economists had of course, criticized this method of actually creating a scarcity, when there did not need to be one, and many families were starving. So the expression "Plough" the fourth furrow "under"—had strong significance.

Now these boys sang a particularly mordant piece, deriding the country's drift toward war. Each verse ended with an almost rolicking, defiance:

"Plough the fourth boy under—"

The room was wild with enthusiasm. Here was a kind of American spirit, genuine and homespun as mountain cloth or corn bread, and revolutionary to the core. Dreiser was struck in a way which made his whole body respond with laughter and sardonic glee:

"Those kind of Americans" he exclaimed, "are *not* going to be ploughed under!"

Meeting in Newark

The following Tuesday, Dreiser spoke at a mass meting in Newark, New Jersey. It was his last engagement for The American Council on Soviet Relations.

The hall looked like an old-time opera house, ornate but shabby, with stiff, folding seats. It was packed with a rather rough-looking audience. On the platform were only a few people, among them Anna Louise Strong the sensitive, candid writer on Soviet life, whose powerful book on the building of the Dnieper Dam, *Wild River*, was then in preparation. She spoke first, creating a warm, human atmosphere.

Then, Dreiser began.

In all the years I had heard him speak, publicly and privately, I had never heard him give out the best of himself, as simply and magnificently, as he did to these working people from the mills, factories and shipyards of New Jersey.

He had made no more preparation for this than for his luncheon address but, sobered by that experience, he talked quietly, straight to the point. I took rough notes as he spoke, hoping to write them up into an article. This was never done, however, and it was difficult to capture what Dreiser said because his mind never fell into the usual patterns of dictated material. His sentences were always short, and made colorful by gestures, that range of vibrant tones he could give to his expressions to make them strong; sarcastic, sorrowful, meditative or compassionate. Only the bone-structure of what he said is here, as nearly as I could catch his words. It came to life then in the manner of his original presentation. He started with bits of historical detail which he felt make it natural for American people to be drawn to Russians:

Americans had great sympathy for the Russian people under the Czars. Tolstoy, their spokesman, gave up writ-

ing novels, to propagandize. Dostoievsky prophesied that out of Russia would come the White Christ, *who would save the entire world. He thought* love *would soften the hearts of the people toward the peasants. He did not live to see the Revolution. Lenin was the* White Christ, *in my opinion.*

Russia is now using the power of machinery not for the profit of industry, but for the use of people. Our industrialists think that great wealth distinguishes them, will make them go down in history—lousy, crazy, idea . . .

I knew Woolworth well; the multimillionaire of the 5 and 10 cent stores. He got great delight out of playing the organ with those cut-out paper rolls inserted in a mechanism,—fancied himself as some kind of musician because he could play these rolls, turning stops off and on. He built a huge house on Long Island, and the Woolworth Building (for many years our tallest sky-scraper) as his claim to fame. Yet he said to me "When you are sixty, they don't want you any more." But still, he wouldn't do anything useful with his money . . .

Thomas Edison of electric bulb fame, was just the opposite. He was interested not in money, but in inventions. *The rich could really distinguish themselves if they wanted to, by helping the millions out of work, by backing social programs, but no—for the most part, they still believe their money will distinguish them.*

To get back to Russia—Before the Revolution, Andrew White, our ambassador, was very much upset about conditions there. Americans were sympathetic to the Revolution, until propaganda started.

Last war—(The first World War) was a trade war. England was determined to keep economic supremacy— We fought in it and paid for it. Then Russia had her Ten Days that Shook the World. *Although we had just finished a war supposedly* for Democracy—*England organized opposition. Russia began to give her people land, freedom, 176 million of them—*

Then suddenly, in this country, the feeling changed. We helped Kolchak and others—anyone who would destroy the Soviet Revolution. But hungry and miserable as the Russian people were, they drove those swine out of there—(applause)

England and French Financiers and Wall Street were first to build up Hitler. England put in Rivera as dictator in Spain. The Spaniards drove him out; then England and Hitler helped put Franco back. We did nothing to help the Loyalists in Spain. We did everything to make Hitler strong to fight Russia. Then Hitler figured out that if England and France needed to build him up, they couldn't be so strong themselves—

Mencken said, when the English King gave up the Throne, it was the greatest news since the Resurrection. I say that the ten days that shook the world was the greatest news since the Sermon on the Mount.

After all is said, it is the People who run the world . . . Or should. Ford, and all our big corporations, are nothing without the people . . . (applause)

Look at Bermuda, where natives run after a penny, England, where a girl will sell herself for twenty-five cents. . . .

Our newspapers are kept, just as a whore is kept, by the big corporations—

Here Dreiser began talking too fast for me to get more than the high-lights of his climax:

Why don't we save this country—

We must be serious about it. We are up against the toughest gang, the big-business gang that wants to hold back these 130 million Americans from their true destiny—by trying to put fear into their hearts. Think about this. Don't go away from here and forget the fact.

Throw out fear!

Realize what they are trying to do and remember that when you want to stop them, YOU CAN DO IT!

He lifted his long hand, with a gesture of challenge— and shambled off the stage, to thunderous applause.

New York wind-up
Dreiser had not many days left to be in New York. Now that his name had been in the papers, many people tried to get in touch with him. He was invited by Vito Marcantonio to take part in a Conference of the International Labor Defense and the League of American Writers urged him to stay until their Congress in June. But he was determined to get back to his work in California.

Occasionally, Dreiser was conscious that people were trying to catch a glimpse of him as he strode through the Commodore lobby. He kept his slouch hat down, and seldom gave any one a chance to speak to him. Once, an elderly, dark, haggard man in a shabby overcoat accosted us hesitantly, as we passed.

"See what he wants" said Dreiser, ducking into the elevator.

"I'm so glad I saw him," said the old man, gratefully. "I've waited around to see if he would autograph this book."

Upstairs, Dreiser took the book in his hand, with surprise:

"Damned if he hasn't got a *very* first edition of *Sister Carrie*—Don't think I have one myself. It must be worth forty dollars." He looked at the worn volume, tenderly. "I'm glad to autograph it, really."

Then, suddenly, his mood changed. Perhaps he resented letting the book go. But he had already signed. "There— take it to him quick, now, and don't stand talking to him. He's probably a dealer!"

Dreiser had been asked to make a statement honoring

William Foster, then Vice-President of the Communist Party, on his sixtieth birthday. It was one of those documents presented to him by various organizations, to which he was willing to put his signature, although he did not write it himself. He was often careless about such matters, if they were to aid some cause he believed in. This was a two-page message, and Dreiser made only two changes; "To Foster, I owe much," was altered to: "To him, I owe very much." And between two paragraphs, he inserted: "To me, he is a Saint, —my first and only contact with one."

Signing the statement had given Dreiser the desire to see Foster again. The two had been together in San Francisco during the worst days of the Hoover depression. Foster happened to be in New York, and was glad to come to Dreiser's hotel. The two big-bodied men sat on a small couch in Dreiser's suite, and chatted affectionately together. Foster had a sweetness and a gentleness surprising in a man of his daring and persistence in the social struggle. Toward the end of their conversation, Dreiser took Foster's hand, and held it, as they sat there. He had a genuine love and admiration for Foster which he had never felt for Browder or any other left-wing leaders.

The last days of Dreiser's stay were darkened by his failure to get any advance on his book of *Philosophy*. Putnam was now supposed to be his publisher, and he showed Earle Balch of that firm the outlines of his project, as well as a few chapters which were finished. But Balch could not see the commercial possibilities of such a vast, heterogeneous work as Dreiser planned to produce. It was quite obvious to anyone talking to Dreiser in those days, that he was too impatient, too full of storm and argument to think dispassionately on any subject, particularly not in the cool world of scientific investigation.

Balch urged Dreiser to return to novel writing. He promised him a large advance if he would submit only part of a novel, the beginning of *The Bulwark* for instance, which had already been scheduled for publication in 1917—or any other.

Dreiser needed the money so badly that he reluctantly agreed to do this.

Now he was going back to California in a mood half angry and depressed. Why couldn't Balch see the importance of his *Philosophy?* He hadn't brought it far enough along. War . . . Yes, it was the threat of war that had upset him, upset his work. Well, he couldn't have done less. Once back in Hollywood, he could get some chapters of *The Bulwark* together as quickly as possible, and then return to his beloved *Philosophy.* Somehow, he would manage both.

Thus, he left New York, going by way of Philadelphia, to see Wharton Esherick, and then on to join Helen—and Elizabeth—in the West.

Tribute to Sherwood Anderson

In the meantime, Dreiser had had the sad task of writing a final tribute to his old friend, the gentle, heavy-browed Sherwood Anderson. Dreiser did not feel equal to attending his funeral, but Stanley Young, himself a distinguished playwright and novelist of a later generation, undertook the trip, having with him, Dreiser's lines. These were later published in *The Clipper,* in Hollywood, and in *Direction* we published Stanley Young's account of the gathering in the "tucked-away town" in South-West Virginia.

> *It was what people call a fine day, the whole greening land airy with the life and promise of the new season, yet not a day for burial, not a day to let go of a friend.*

> *The town was flooded with people, literary notables from Chicago and New York. . . . There were masses of flowers, fancy, heavy-scented wreaths and common bouquets picked fresh in the morning and brought in by the hill folk.*

> *The home funeral service was as simple and unpretentious as the man whose death called it forth. Two ministers read from the Scriptures, a hymn was sung by a local choir off in some remote room of the house. Paul*

*Rosenfeld, in a shaking voice, read his own fine tribute
to the man lying a few feet away in the coffin. I read
Dreiser's generous tribute, believing I would never get
through it. . . .*

Then Stanley Young read Dreiser's words which were
weighted with his love for Anderson:

*Whenever I think of him, I think of that wondrous line
out of* The Ancient Mariner, *"He prayeth best who
loveth best, all things, both great and small." And so
sometimes the things he wrote as well as the not too
many things he said, to me personally had the value of a
poetic prayer for the happiness and well-being of everything, guided as each thing plainly is, by an enormous
wisdom—if seemingly not always imbued with mercy—
that none-the-less, "passeth all understanding. . . ."*

*To me, amidst all the strain of living and working, he
was a comforting figure—never in any sense a slave to
money, or that seeming necessity to so many—show and
pretense. He was what he was and accepted himself in
just that sense—"I am what I am—Take me or leave me
for what I am to you."*

This was Dreiser's own attitude about himself—and yet
he could hardly be said to be a *comforting figure.* For all his
great simplicty, he had not found peace of mind nor a sure
issue out of *all the strain of living and working.*

VII. DREISER'S LAST VISIT TO NEW YORK
—May, 1944

In May, 1944, Dreiser made his last visit to New York.

The American Academy of Arts and Letters had notified him that he was to receive their Award of Merit Medal, together with a thousand dollars in cash, and Walter Damrosch, venerable Dean of the institution invited him to attend their annual Ceremonial in New York, and accept his prize in person.

The conservative Academy had completely ignored Dreiser up until this time, but he was not a person to harbor resentments, and he was very grateful to have this money, as his financial situation was worse than ever. He was also glad of another chance to come to New York, which he still thought of as *My City*.

Both Dreiser and Helen had written me of his coming, and I had procured a room for him at the Commodore.

Now I saw him striding across Grand Central Station, and was shocked by his altered appearance. He seemed thinner, fiercer, like an aging, hungry lion.

Yet when we reached his room, he threw himself into an armchair, and pulled me to his side, with his old, vibrant quality. Curiously enough, the first moments of our conversation were unexpectedly revealing. We had always had that way of bantering on the edge of serious subjects, and fell

126

into it naturally again. I said something half-facetious about thanking God for bringing him here.

Suddenly, he gave me that penetrating look that he could turn on, like a search-light: "Well, I believe in God, now—" he said, "—a Creative Force," he added, with a wave of his long hand at a gray space between sky-scrapers. Then he started to talk in that detailed way he used when anything truly interested him:

"You know that summer I was down at Cold Spring Harbor—One afternoon after I had been working all day in the laboratory, I came out in the sunshine, and there along the path" (he made a gesture of lowness) "were some little, yellow flowers. I stooped over them. Here was the same beauty, the same *design,* the same exquisite detail that I had been seeing all day in the tiny organisms under the microscope. Suddenly, it was plain to me that there must be a divine, creative Intelligence behind all this—Not just a blind force, but a great Artist, who made all these things with such love and care.... After that, I began to feel differently about the universe. I saw not only the intelligence, but the love and care that goes into all created things . . ."

I asked him whether he had written about this, put it in his *Philosophy:*

"I wrote a piece called *My Creator,*" he answered vaguely. "It's somewhere in my files."

The following days brought a flood of demands, invitations, callers. One of the first was a lovely, dark-eyed chic young woman, Margaret Carson, who was doing publicity for the Academy. Dreiser was immediately responsive to her charm, and accepted her suggestions for interviews and social engagements. By the time she left, there was established between them that *rapport* which Dreiser created so easily with women who interested him:

"My, that was a smart girl," he said admiringly after she left. "It's really these women who should run the world nowadays. The men ought to retire!"

Another caller was Richard Duffy, faithful friend who had first known Dreiser when he was writing *Sister Carrie.* He was an extremely able, discerning man of mellow temperament. They had kept in touch with each other through the years and Duffy was one of the men for whom Dreiser had real affection. He came now, quiet and somewhat red-faced, looking like an English barrister in dark clothes and derby hat.

They talked a long while, and Dreiser confessed that he was in a low financial state, and wanted to find a publisher who would undertake to reprint his books, and give him an advance for this, immediately. For Dreiser now owned the rights to his own works, and even had most of the plates stored in a warehouse. He was always being asked for books long out of print, and fast disappearing from second-hand book-stores. Duffy was at once fired with a desire to help, and went off, promising to work on this proposition. (It was always interesting to see how Dreiser inspired people to enlist in his personal campaigns, because of his own, warm, dynamic nature.)

In a few days, Duffy came back with a fine project for re-issuing Dreiser's major works. But now began a disheartening struggle to find a publisher.

With Putnam, he had come to a strange dead-lock. Since leaving New York on his previous visit, he had sent in some thirty chapters of *The Bulwark,* and had received a three thousand dollar advance. He could hardly expect more before finishing the novel. But Balch was far from pleased with the repetitious, new Introduction he had been shown. Nor could Balch promise to reprint his earlier works. The country was now at war; there were serious paper shortages and publishers were curtailing their lists rather than adding to them.

Dreiser enjoyed lunching with Balch; they were joined by Jo Davidson, the sculptor, and sat over a meal and drinks at the Century Club until four o'clock, arguing about Dreiser's favorite subject, *Free Will* . . . an occasion from which Dreiser returned a bit the worse for liquor.

He was in a dangerous and curious state much of the time, those days. He did not feel well. "I don't know what's the matter with me" he would say, "I guess a little whiskey will fix me up," and he would get out his bottle of inexpensive rye and take a nip, without bothering to get a glass. If later, he fixed himself a drink with ice and water, he would consider this his first for the day, not counting the nips! It was quite easy to steer him away from drinking, with some urgent work at hand ... But as soon as he was tired, or bored or discouraged, he would give one of those heavy sighs; "O *Lord*, something must be wrong with me—I wish I could find a good tonic" and he would start looking around for his whiskey. He also relied on aspirins and pheno-barbital, if he had a headache. (Luckily, he had given up the Bromo-Seltzer and Spirits of Ammonia combination, he took at 11th street!) Then there was a large bottle of vitamins which he took without moderation. He could pop one or two into his mouth and gulp them down without water, before you saw what he was doing. He simply could not seem to realize that as he was now over seventy, it was only natural that he did not have the same energy as in younger days.

Yet, in conversation, or work, he was as keen and creative as ever. His mind had never been more full of fantasy and charm as he talked to me, about *The Bulwark* and certain minor characters, the children of Solon, and the beauty of the country-side where they lived. Often, he hummed, and there was a certain little minor tune that ran through his head, for days:

"*O Roven, doven, dary o'day.*"... An old English folk-song.

His need for beauty and quiet had grown stronger than ever. He was easily bored by details, hating restraint. It was hard to make him keep track of time and places. When he had appointments he liked to have me walk with him, wherever he was going, and usually he would take a taxi back to the hotel. Sometimes, he came back earlier than expected. "Oh, that was enough of that"—he would say, evasively.

He had lunch with a number of publishers and agents of his acquaintance—Charles Scribner, Jacques Chambrun, William Lengel, to mention only a few. But no contract, no money, was forth-coming. Chambrun wanted him to write more short stories. Ah, yes, that was a thing he used to love to do—But he had written so many—Was there nothing to be reaped from the old stuff? Hadn't it been good enough? So he would come back, discouraged and a little on the offensive.

As the day of the Ceremonial approached, a gruff letter came from Mencken in Baltimore, refusing to come up to New York, as Dreiser had suggested, and reproving him for accepting gifts from the hand of the Academy that had scorned him so long.

"Old Menck—" grumbled Dreiser, affectionately. Things were not as they had been in the old days, for either of them.

The Ceremonial

To one who has never witnessed the annual *Ceremonial* of the Academy of Arts and Letters, it is difficult to convey its *pomp and circumstance* without seeming to exaggerate. The audience was gathered in a semi-circle facing the classic decor of a broad stage. Then, to the strains of a slow, orchestral march the members of this august body, clad in black collegiate gowns, paced majestically across the boards to their places. The whole atmosphere was truly Academic, archaic, almost, and guaranteed to impress the ordered heart. But it also put unconventional souls under somewhat of a strain.

Dreiser and Edgar Lee Masters, who had been honored by the Academy a few years earlier, took seats assigned to them in the second row, just below the rostrum. The first part of the program was allotted to music and a number of fine, young composers were presented with prizes.

Then came the literary awards.

Willa Cather, noted New England novelist, was the first to receive her prize, after a warm and well-deserved eulogy, by Arthur Train, to which she responded graciously by a rather long prepared speech. Then Samuel McClure also received a complimentary introduction by Arthur Train, and likewise replied, with a careful message.

Dreiser had also been notified that he would be expected

to speak, and was asked what general subject he would like to treat. He decided to avoid all political questions, and speak briefly on a subject close to his heart, the creation of a Federal Bureau of Fine Arts, or a Secretary of the Arts, to be included in the President's Cabinet. He thought this would be a subject which this irreproachable Academy might well take up. At least he felt that his suggestions might be a challenge, even a contribution to such a gathering. We had prepared a brief paper, and sent it in, but Dreiser was immediately informed that this was a *controversial* subject and could not be brought before this group without due consultation with its members, for which there was, of course, no time.

This amused rather than annoyed Dreiser, and he did not know whether he would say something about it anyway or simply respond to whatever was said to him, with the best grace possible.

Finally Professor Chauncey B. Tinker arose to make a speech introducing Dreiser. It was a curious, cold discourse, granting that Dreiser was a *naturalist,* a good one, a pioneer in the history of American letters. However, obviously knowing nothing about Dreiser's scientific and philosophic interests, his years of search, since the writing of *An American Tragedy,* he labelled him a materialist, a cynic, and a number of other heavy and ambiguous things

There was warm applause, however, as Dreiser lumbered up onto the stage; people roused themselves, and leaned forward to hear what he had to say.

Dreiser stood there, his presence all the more intense, because of his silence. He had a curious way of turning into himself, when he wanted to get away from some conversation or some person. Certainly, there was not very much to respond to in Tinker's speech. He hesitated a moment; if he had been a smaller man, the term *mousy* might be used to describe his attitude. But Dreiser's gesture was like that of a lion, turning away from his spectators at the end of his cage, a physically restrained but in-going gesture, suggesting a kind of triumph of its own, by its very resignation and rhythm. It was in this manner that he bowed very solemnly to Dr. Damrosch and to the assembly, took his prize, said *"Thank you"* and walked off, without another word.

At the elaborate tea served on the terraces after the Ceremonial few dignitaries of the Academy came to find Dreiser, but he was surrounded by personal friends, including the magnificent Paul Robeson who had also received an award for his current performance of *Othello* on Broadway.

Finally, escorting Edgar Lee Masters, and followed by the painter Kenneth Hayes Miller, another delightful old friend, Dreiser got into a taxi. He was in a low mood, despite the festivities and the May sunshine.

Arriving at his lodgings, Masters begged Dreiser to come in awhile, and he did so. In the company of a few others, drinks were served, and the spirits of all began to mount. Soon Edgar Lee and Theodore were teasing each other at the top of their form. Suddenly, I realized that it was time for Dreiser to go home and get into his tuxedo, for the dinner which Dr. Damrosch was giving for the Award winners. Dreiser rebelled: "Get me out of it, if you can."

At the Damrosch residence, a maid answered and relayed the message to her master: It would be difficult for Dreiser to get there. No special protest was made and he did not go.

Another evening was spent with the *Spoon River* poet and his second wife Ellen in his spacious, book-filled room at the Old Chelsea Hotel. He was just recovering from a serious collapse, and moved with difficulty. The day at the Ceremonial had been a hard one for him. But on this occasion as he sat with Theodore, in two stiff early-American type chairs, some of their old gaiety and verve came back, and the warm friendship of so many years did not need to be expressed in any profound language. They looked into each others' faces and saw change there, and times past, the great emotions about people, about life itself, shared and understood. The many things they had said to each other and in their books, needed no further display, but the essence of them was there as they talked, and in their eyes was fine, flashing irony, deep love.

On an evening shortly before he left New York, Dreiser might have been seen escorting Masters into the mahogany recesses of old Luchow's on 14th Street. This had always been one of Dreiser's favorite haunts; here he had celebrated the demise of Prohibition with the young composers, and this was a fitting place for a dinner of farewell.

The headwaiter remembered Dreiser and gave him a special table in an alcove near the orchestra. Both Masters and Dreiser felt tired at the end of the day, but a few drinks revived them, and they began teasing each other about the fatigue that each said was the result of the other's misspent life. They had never learned to behave themselves, they admitted, and now it was too late.

Then Masters took a letter out of his pocket which had just come from John Cowper Powys, in Wales. He had loved Masters as he loved Dreiser, with his fierce, complicated nature which had found no rest in America, though he had loved America just as he loved these writers of its very soil. The letter was written in random sentences, aslant across the page, or in the margins, as Powys liked to write. He was working on a book about Dostoievsky and translating Rabelais into his native Welsh! There was one line ending: "—you and Dreiser, we three who are closer than lovers with exactly the same amount of reverence and affection."

How long since they had been together—these three? A toast to Jack!

The arrival of beer and sausages touched off other subjects. Dreiser complained that the orchestra did not play romantic music as in older days whereupon the waiter spoke to the head violinist, and Dreiser was soon being charmed by gypsy airs.

A sports-writer who happened to be eating there that night, recognized Dreiser and later in his column, wrote up his impression of him with a warmth uncommon to the *Journal-American*, a simple testimony to the wealth of human feeling that Dreiser, as well as Masters, and especially the two together, managed to produce.

Dorothy Dudley Harvey

Another enjoyable evening for Dreiser was a dinner at the home of Dorothy Dudley Harvey, who had written the penetrating biographical book about Dreiser *Forgotten Frontiers,* reissued under the title *Dreiser, and The Land of the Free.* Here were her husband, Harry Harvey, Anne Harvey, her lovely painter-daughter and Georges Duthuit, French writer and critic. The apartment on 92nd Street combined the charm of a French interior with a dramatic view of the East River. Over wines and *Blanquette de Veau,* the conversation drifted to things French.

Dreiser, enamored of Balzac and other writers of the 19th century, was skeptical as to the contribution of 20th century France to our society, when compared to the power of thought she had generated earlier, and through the French Revolution. Georges Duthuit was eloquent in France's defense. The argument waxed fierce, as it often did with Dreiser. Finally, Duthuit, always the suave Frenchman, said humorously:

"Well, you must admit that France has given the western world sumptuousness, art, the aesthetic luxuries of life."

"But what does that amount to?" roared Dreiser.

"But what is more important," countered the imperturbable Frenchman.

Then suddenly, with one of those complete about-face moves of which he was capable, Dreiser's voice dropped to a rich purr. The socialist was also the sybarite; "Well—I guess you win"—he laughed.

Later in the evening Anne Harvey enchanted Dreiser with tales of the strange French writer, Barbey d'Aurevilly; Dreiser's mind was always open to the fantastic, and to the charm of woman.

Another night, Earl Wilson and Margaret Carson called to take Dreiser night-clubbing as part of their publicity for the Academy. He insisted that I come along, as usual, though I had not been invited. First, they took him to a low-lighted, small place known for its sophisticated songs. Then to the inner sanctum of The Stork Club, on 53rd Street.

As we went in to the room reserved for celebrities—and

people famous for their money—a dark, handsome man stood up to greet Dreiser.

"I'm glad to shake hands with you, Dreiser, I've always loved your work."

It was Moss Hart, the theatrical producer, who had always been a Dreiser fan. His obvious sincerity pleased Dreiser, his handsome head reminding him of Horace Liveright, at his best.

At a small table, with drinks produced, Earl Wilson tried hard to make Drieser say daring things about the beautiful girls of Hollywood, and quoted him in his column the next day, when he spoke about *Helling around* with the *salty old gentleman*. He managed to get in a few remarks about Dreiser's *blasting the rich* and uttering the word *revolution* in the sacrosanct Cub Room. As he discussed his old friends of the British Ruling Class, Dreiser broke off: "*Sweet*, Don't talk to me about England . . ."

On his way out of the Club, a well-known Publisher, caught Dreiser under the lighted canopy, in the midst of a battle for taxis. "Hello—Hello Dreiser"—There was hand-shaking and back-slapping.

The next day, Dreiser remembered him: "Say, that fellow was very friendly. Maybe he would reprint my books. I hate going to offices. Ask him to come around and have a drink."

On the phone, the publisher said he was too busy to come to the Hotel but Dreiser could come to his office. "But he's busy, too" I protested. "It's harder for him to get around—Tomorrow, perhaps?

"Tomorrow's my radio day—can't make it" came the short reply.

Radio Broadcasts—To Europe and Germany

To Dreiser, the most satisfying work he was able to accomplish on that visit was the making of two recordings for broadcast to Europe. This was about ten days before the fateful D-Day on which American troops were to invade the coast of Normandy. Thousands in Europe awaited the word, huddled by their secret radios. The Office of War Information had chosen Dreiser as one of the international figures whose voice could assure the people of the Nazi-occupied countries that their deliverance was near.

Dreiser thought of them, as he prepared his script most carefully. Then early one morning, he went up to the huge offices of the O.W.I. on 57th Street. (Just a few doors away from his old 57th Street studio!) His big bulk was quiet, almost reverent, in the white-coffered broadcasting rooms, his tone low, confidential. He read his message twice in rehearsal, coached by the keen, broad-browed Dorothea Beckman. Then he spoke it into the microphone, his voice full of concern and love for the people he hoped to reach. It broke only once, in what turned out to be a most effective pause.

A few days later, he made a second recording, to be used to address the German people when Hitler's borders were reached. This was a warmly personal appeal. For Dreiser conceived the idea of describing how his own father, born in Mayen-am-Moselle, left Germany to escape the tyranny of militarism under Bismark. He told how, with another immigrant Carl Fischer, who later became head of the music Publishing house of that name, he worked his way westward, peddling small articles, and finally settled in Indiana. Thus establishing himself as part-German, he called upon the German people to stamp out Nazism, affirming his faith that they could still produce great statesmen, scientists, citizens, who could help in the international task of establishing justice in the world. He ended with the challenge:

"Just as a try-out, let's have a few hundred years of the brotherhood of man!"

During those last days in New York, Dreiser wrote an article for *Soviet Russia Today*, entitled *The Russian Advance*, a most original piece, and he had a new idea for a short story. We kept urging him to go on writing, and not bother about reprints. So many creative ideas still surged through his head. But he tried once more to find a publisher, through Frank Crowninshield. This dean of New York aesthetes had long been a friend and admirer of Dreiser's, and as an editor of *Vogue*, and the beautiful, deceased *Vanity Fair*, was a factor in the literary life of the city. He called a number of publishers whom he knew personally, but without result. Maurice Hindus reported that Dreiser's books were in great demand in Russia, but that did not seem relevant, here. Wartime shortages of paper were most frequently given as an excuse. (Ironically enough, as soon as Dreiser died, his books were reprinted, although the war was barely over, and paper shortages still existed!)

Dreiser had his picture taken by Lotte Jacobi, distinguished exiled German artist, who invited him to sit for her. In her intimate studio apartment Dreiser felt relaxed and the studies she took of him that day are among the best ever made of his haunting, searching satyr face.

In the back of the apartment, we scarcely noticed a romantic, sad-looking elderly man, who had just become Lotte Jacobi's second husband. The next day, when "a boy" was announced with proofs of the photographs, this man appeared, very humbly presenting the envelope, and asking if he should wait, or go. Then we learned that this was Erich Reiss, who had been one of the outstanding publishers of Berlin in the days before Hitler. He had published many American authors, including Dreiser, and was anxious to see him, because of great admiration for his art, but hardly dared to raise his voice. His spirit had been strangely crushed by terrible experiences under the Nazis. But when care was taken to draw him out, he was an extraordinary soul, with smooth, sculptured face, far-seeing eyes, and a brooding, Beethoven-like profundity and delicacy which Dreiser remarked on, and did not forget.

Farewell Party

Many friends had asked to say good-bye to Dreiser, and he decided to invite them to the hotel, on Friday, June 2nd. The Commodore gave him a comfortable suite; there were flowers, canapés and cocktails.

Among those who came were Dorothy Norman, Richard Wright, George Seldes, Kenneth Hayes Miller, Dorothy Dudley Harvey, with Georges Duthuit, the Russian Counsel,

Kisselev, Edwin Seaver, Isidor Schneider, Robert Elias, Lotte
Jacobi with Erich Reiss, William and Sophie Gropper, Paul
Rand, Fred Ramsey, Ralph Fabri, Hubert and Marguerite
Davis, Helena Simkhovitch and Hilary Harris. Paul Robeson
was expected but could not get there.

The little gathering was warm and animated. Dreiser
asked George Seldes many questions about his sensational
news sheet, *In Fact.*

Dorothy Norman talked to him about the Academy Award,
and he told her about his aborted speech, on a Secretary of the
Arts. She wrote a strong piece about this in her column for
The New York Post, saying: "It warms one's heart to see
Dreiser so young in spirit . . . He has never lost his passionate
interest in all movements, all work that reaches out to enrich
life."

With Richard Wright, Dreiser spoke long about Chicago.
They agreed that it had been a stimulating school for them
both, because of the realistic vision of life that flourished
there, the youth and rawness of the city. It had not greatly
changed since Dreiser's day, because it moved so fast that
there was no time for traditional attitudes to form and
harden. Wright said later:

"When I talked to Dreiser, I was never conscious that I was
in the presence of a writer. The small, vicious habits of
writers never clung to him. He did not discuss his latest book,
nor the book he was about to write. Listening to his simple,
direct descriptions, you felt he was above all, a man, sensitive, creative, intensely interested in everything—bigger
than a writer. He could melt his mood into that of those surrounding him. . . . If you asked him a question, he would say
a little something in reply; and later, a little more, and perhaps later, still more—as if any idea was enough to start
some deep, emotional, psychological movement in him."

As the little party drew to a glowing finish, a telephone call
took Dreiser back to his room. His sister, *Mame,* had died at
her home in Astoria. He had been out to see her there, and
knew she was near death. It should not have been a shock,

but it was a shock. Dreiser stretched out a while, in his darkened room, before he returned to bid his guests good-bye.

Mame

Dreiser's sister Mame was Mary Frances Brenan. She was a few years older than Theodore. He had always been very fond of her, and greatly impressed when she began to "go out," and succeed in life, as he relates in his own autobiography.

She had married well, and lived in New York, when Dreiser was still struggling with poverty. Later when he began to succeed, she went through a difficult period (when living on 11th Street) and he had helped her. They had led long, parallel lives and never been completely out of touch.

Dreiser knew that Mame was sick, and on one of the first free days of his visit, we had driven out to the little house in Astoria where she had settled after her husband died. Finding she was in the hospital, preparing for a last-chance operation, we went there. She lay on her bed in a small ward, very calm and handsome, pale, with gray-white hair piled thickly on her pillow. With a weary dignity, she reached out and took her brother's hand:

"Just think, Theodore," she said slowly, "We can't even make a little blade of grass grow, without God." For many years, she had been a believer in Christian Science. She had been a source of great strength and help to Helen, during her days in New York, as Helen relates in her own book, *My Life with Dreiser.*

A few days later, Mame was taken back to her home, where Dreiser saw her once more. She was being cared for by another sister, Syl, or Silvia, who had been married for many years to a Japanese, but was now also a widow. She was a full-fledged Christian Science Practioner. While not as handsome as Mame, who looked like Dreiser because of her high, bombed forehead and commanding presence, Syl resembled him, because of the rather lumpy jowls that age had given them.

Here also lived Frank, a skinny, whitish, scatter-brained

sort of man who had attached himself to these strong women, like a homeless dog. Dreiser did not have much use for him, but he was no doubt some help to the aging sisters. So now Dreiser sat with this strange menage, sat and talked with Syl and Frank because Mame was already slipping into a dream.

A few days later Dreiser stood beside her casket at a Long Island funeral parlor. She was startlingly beautiful as she lay there, this big woman with features more classic than his, but with his noble brow, and the same, curiously long, expressive hands. I could not help making the direct comparison as he stood beside her. In the room, too, the younger, gayer brother Ed had the same, Dreiser hands.

A young minister in a black robe, read the usual funeral service.

"I am the Resurrection and the Life—He that believeth in me, though he were dead, yet shall he live."

"What beautiful words," said Dreiser, afterwards, "He reminded me of Alyosha Karamazov." Dreiser was thinking of the priest in Dostoievsky's great novel.

Mt. Kisco—Last Visit

A bright surprise for Dreiser was word that his place at Mt. Kisco had finally been sold.

We drove out to see it one spring afternoon. The house stood sturdy and original as ever but minus the log roof. Slate tiles gave it a neater, Norman appearance. The stone mushrooms leaned at odd angles in the uncut grass.

What struck us most was that the trees had grown so much that you could hardly see the reservoir. Dreiser did not have the key, but somehow we managed to get through a window on the stairs leading down to the studio. The big room looked damp and desolate without the furniture. Standing there, Dreiser recalled that he had once hidden under the big studio window, when he had heard someone outside, whom he did not want to see. It was an author, whose poems he had not wanted to endorse. Meanwhile this man, assuming Dreiser was not there, proceeded to show friends around the place, criticising it and Dreiser, who could do nothing but remain in his cramped position for a long time, listening to what a second-rate poet thought of him and his work!

We wandered up over the screened passage to the guest house. Here a bird—a beautiful thing with irridescent feathers—had flown against the screen so hard that its head had gone through the mesh. Dreiser took it out and laid it gently on the ground.

We did not try to get into the guest-house, but went around in front of the studio, and stretched out on the grass, facing the little pond. The May sunshine lay all around, with its feeling of hope and stillness. Dreiser was not sentimental. He was not thinking as I, *what an ill-fated house this had been.* A tremendous wave of nostalgia came over me, as I looked at the wild hills, the cabins he had loved so much, the empty house.

"Don't you feel sad to leave it?" I asked.

"No," he said slowly, enjoying only the quiet of the moment, "Change, change—that's the essence of life" . . .

Conversations with Elias—Last Days in New York

Dreiser was visited several times by Robert Elias, during these final days in New York. Then a young Professor of English, Elias had first come to Dreiser as a student when he had chosen Dreiser's work for his Masters Degree Thesis. This paper was so pleasing to Dreiser that he gave Elias permission to start collecting material for a biography. Dreiser liked him because he was keen, intellectual and sensitive, yet without any pretension or aggressiveness. Slim, nice-looking, a good tennis player, Elias had a quickness and lightness of manner which did not let his questions weigh on Dreiser or annoy him, as interviewers often did. He found Elias easy to talk to. Now Elias had come up from the University of Pennsylvania for the Ceremonial, and stayed on to check with Dreiser on certain earlier phases of his life.

One afternoon in his hotel room, Dreiser was seized by a mood of remembrance so vivid that tears choked him. He told of the night when he had been in such despair over his work, his life, that he walked down a street of Brooklyn

to the waterfront, intending to slip into the river. He thought
of how he had been saved from drowning by his brother
Paul, when he was a boy, along the banks of the Wabash.
And how when he had begun to lose consciousness, the sensa-
tion had not been horrible. . . .

With these thoughts in mind, he reached a long dock,
where a barge was tied, the kind of barge with a small cabin
at one end for a guardian. Despondently, Dreiser moved on,
in the dark, toward the water. Then a voice called out: "Want
to take a ride up to Albany tomorrow?" Dreiser was so surprised, that he turned around. A man had appeared in the
door of the barge-cabin and they started to talk about this
unusual proposal. This man's barge was going to be towed,
along with other barges, up the Hudson, and he could take
Dreiser along. "I thought you looked as if you wanted to get
away from your wife," he said.

Dreiser laughed; his mood of despair was broken.

Dreiser talked on in this reminiscent mood until almost
four o'clock. He had had no lunch, and we finally persuaded
him to come down to Thompson's cafeteria for a bite to eat.
He had breakfast in this place every morning, for it adjoined
the hotel, and he disliked spending more than necessary on
utilitarian meals.

It was a dead hour in the cafeteria. Not far from us in
a corner, across empty tables, sat a woman, pale, bruised,
really miserable-looking. And with her was a dark, brutal
man; you could sense he was an imposter of some sort. He
kept going away, and coming back, and she seemed terrified
of him.

We had brought Dreiser down here to cheer him and make
him relax over a pleasant meal. And now he could not take
his eyes off this woman. We did not know whether to speak
to her or not. We tried to smile at her, to give her a chance
to ask us for help, if she wished. But she only shrank back
as if more afraid. So we did not speak. We did nothing. Yet
we felt like spectators of some haunting tragedy.

Back in Dreiser's room, we tried once more to cheer him

and to talk about his work. The afternoon had turned gray, with thunderstorm rumblings. How could we defeat this mood of depression? Only through work. Fame no longer meant anything to him, but work, for its own sake, meant as much as ever. There was so much creative thought in him still. Yet sometimes he needed encouragement, rhythm, if only the clicking of a typewriter, to prod him, to get him started. During those weeks, he had found he could work with me, as of old; the articles, broadcasts and other bits of writing, had gone well. And we had talked about all his unfinished business, the book of *Philosophy, The Bulwark.* I was not sure that I could help him with the scientific material, but with the novel, it was mainly a question of reading through the older material, and helping him to get it in order. Now both Elias and I urged him to finish *The Bulwark,* and not to delay it any longer. Dreiser turned to me:

"If you will come to California and help me, I think I can do it."

I promised to come, if Helen approved, and if Dreiser himself did not change his mind, after returning to Hollywood.

Departure

The following day, June 5, 1944, Dreiser left New York. He had a lower berth on the 4:20 to Chicago, and the West. He was beseiged by last minute calls. He checked over the article he had just finished, *The Russian Advance,* and some things were left undone.

There was a last minute struggle to close a huge, black contraption of some resistant material unlike leather, in size half-way between a suitcase and a trunk. This was despatched to the baggage car. In his hand, he carried a small, duffle bag and over his arm, a light, brownish tweed overcoat; a soft brown hat and cream-colored scarf completed his travel equipment.

Because of war-time difficulties in obtaining food on trains, we had procured a loaf of bread, a large square of cheese and some fruit which were stored in a paper bag.

"I hate to go," he said, when he found his car, and we

stood waiting for the conductor to wave him on board. "But this time, New York was almost too much for me. Next time, I'll stay down-town and not tell anyone where I am."

The last glimpse I had of him was through the glass of the platform door, as the train moved slowly out. He stood in an old pose, his legs braced like a sailor's, his arms akimbo, half-smiling, half-scowling, intense.

A week later, a letter arrived from Dreiser describing his trip across the country as a slow one, his "fifteen car train crowded with soldiers, their wives or girls . . . Their noise and blether and drinking was enough to drive me mad. . . ."

He said it was impossible for him to concentrate on anything during that time, although he had been thinking of our plan for me to come to California. One line of his letter struck me as significantly revealing, as he thanked me for my help to "one like myself who is slipping so thoughtlessly into the closing years. . . ."

A second letter from Dreiser after he had settled in Hollywood again, repeated that he was "still confronted by *The Bulwark* and the *Book of Philosophy,* also by the, to me, so desirable thought of working toward the completion of both with and through you. For all the details of each book are so clear in my mind that I could easily outline the successive chapters or structure and once that was done, paint in the various scenes—their respective colors and emotional qualities. For with you—your sensitive response to the realities and unrealities—to address, all would come to me clearly enough . . ."

Having by this time decided that I could break ties in the East, I wrote to Helen, asking her opinion of my coming to California, saying that above all, I wanted harmony in life, and would not come, unless she approved.

Helen responded with her characteristic warmth, saying, however, that it was almost impossible to find places to live because of War-time conditions in Los Angeles and difficult to get along without a car. She concluded "I don't know if I have helped you in any way, but I do know that I wanted to. If you come to California, you'll be welcome."

This letter encouraged me to make further plans for a trip West. My fourteen-year-old son was looking forward to the experience of going to school in Hollywood. We obtained gasoline for our move from the local rationing board, and with our faithful German shepherd dog, in an old convertible, prepared to cross the country.

A final prod was a letter from Dreiser enclosing a money order for our expenses and saying:

"How I would like trying this proposed period with you, even though you did not—eventually—consider it successful. For I think it would be. . . . For one thing, I think I could dictate certain short stories that I am sure would come out better for the mere telling of them to you . . . For you do not know, I am sure, with what desire, what sense of impending work and achievement I look forward to these coming months."

Part II

VIII. THE CLOSING YEARS

—the writing of "The Bulwark," California, 1944-45

Dreiser's House and way of living

We drove up to Dreiser's house at 1015 North King's Road, Hollywood, on a burning August afternoon. The white stucco house with its deep orange awnings and tattered banana palms, with flower-beds around their feet, stood beside a low-terraced entrance. The house was one-storied, except for a square tower-room which rose beside a Moorish-style archway, leading to a matching, stucco garage. Through the arch, more palm fronds and flowering shrubs and trees suggested a wide garden beyond.

When we rang the doorbell, the sound of a melodious double-chime was heard; the heavy door opened a crack, to reveal one Dreiser eye.

"Well, eighty years later," he growled, in that way he had of using his voice to stress an emotion.

The house felt deliciously cool as we stepped in. Dreiser was dressed in white slacks and shirt, with a blue bow tie. He stood looking down, just as I had first seen him sixteen years earlier, a figure tall, surprising, scrutinizing me with that impenetrable gaze of his, force bound in a man, flashing out, defying destruction.

We explained that we were late, because we had stopped

to see his birthplace at Terre Haute, Indiana, and followed the *Banks of the Wabash,* far down.

Then Helen greeted us, with her old forthright charm. Though I had not seen her for some years, I found little change in her appearance. She was dressed in a summery blouse and skirt, a little heavier, perhaps, her hair a lighter, reddish shade. She wore it as before, long and soft around her face. There were the same, fine features, the level brow, the full spontaneous laugh, ending in a warm chuckle, as we started to talk about old times.

Here, in the long, white living-room, was the same furniture that had been in the big studio at 57th Street and then at *Iroki,* the handsome gold Venetian couch, the high, ducal chair, the grand piano, and one of the heavily painted, reddish nudes. The long, sleek table that Wharton Esherick had made for the Mt. Kisco house stood in the center of the room, loaded with books and photographs. In front of a Provincial-style fireplace were several comfortable big armchairs and a low, round table. Everywhere, were familiar framed drawings, photos and caricatures of Dreiser, and the lovely, large photograph of Helen in her long white hostess dress, standing with Nick, beside the pond at *Iroki.* And on one side of the fireplace, on a low chest, stood the life-sized plaster head of John Cowper Powys.

At the far end of this room, was an L-shaped wing with Dreiser's bedroom, bath and study. The first room was furnished in light, modern wood, its twin beds covered with yellow chenille spreads, and the sun coming in over them from a side terrace. Near the windows Dreiser had a rocker and a card table, where he sometimes sat and worked.

At the end of the "L," was his study. Here was the square, rosewood desk, in the center of the room. The low edge of the former piano-box made a backstop for the many letters and papers piled against it. Here were his various bottles of ink and paste, and boxes of clips and pins—(He still had the incurable habit of *pinning* papers together, even when he had clips at hand!) And towering over the clips, was his little good-luck Indian, clad in his bit of blue blanket, with real, black hair, and stern face.

All around, were bookcases with dictionaries, and many scientific books and magazines. Under the windows was a low couch piled with papers, magazines, and manuscripts; the whole room seemed alive with information and ideas, but it also had a cluttered feeling, not a restful place to work.

On the left side of the room, a door opened into the garden which had become his favorite place. Here was the profusion of palm fronds and poinsettias which could be seen through the archway. Stepping down, you passed under a magnificent Bougainvillea which almost covered the study roof.

Now Dreiser showed us his garden which comprised about an acre of leveled, luxuriantly green grass. On the lawn was an old shoulder-high rose tree and beyond a place to lounge under spreading avocado trees. Beyond the shade was a little pool, unevenly shaped, around which many kinds of small flowers, anenomes, African daisies and blue azuretum, were growing. In the water floated lilies above broad pads and below, goldfish gleamed and were gone, in the shadow.

Helen took special pride in keeping this pool clean and lovely, changing the flowers from time to time. Beyond, the grass stretched to a wall about fifty feet away and here were more flower-beds, red blossoms against the light stones, and to the right, two lemon trees were blossoming and bearing big, juicy fruit, at the same time.

Helen's own room was in the tower, a charming, feminine place, with boudoir and full, white curtains, and the life-sized portrait of her by Fabri, in her favorite hostess gown of flowing white, Nick, the Russian wolf-hound at her feet.

In any direction there was hardly more than a glimpse of other roofs, and far off, above trees, the beautiful, terraced mountain-side above "The Strip." This house, near the center of Hollywood, seemed secluded as a villa in Marakesch.

Dreiser's Seventy-Second Birthday

A few days after our arrival, Dreiser celebrated his seventy-second birthday, with a garden-party.

The long table under the avocado trees was covered with a white cloth, and laden with dainty sandwiches, cakes, glasses and a huge punch bowl.

This day had a special significance for Dreiser and Helen, and they always dressed in white for it. Dreiser was a striking figure in a heavy-cream linen suit, with his soft white hair, thick iron-gray brows and deep gaze, more magnetic than ever, now that his body seemed less strong. Helen wore a fitted, long white hostess gown—the type of dress particularly lovely on her and that she had often worn at the big parties in New York and Mt. Kisco.

About four o'clock, guests began arriving, all in their best summer finery. Helen greeted and introduced everyone with such warmth that immediately they all felt at home, and started talking to each other. Here were several Russians, the current Soviet Consul in Los Angeles and Ivan Butnikoff, composer and balletomane. There were a number of writers and scientists, a pale—Ibsenesque woman, Dr. Chiang, Chinese Doctor of Letters, with his exquisite Chinese wife and young daughter dressed in pale blue.

Among more intimate friends, was Marcia Masters, attractive writer-daughter of Edgar Lee Masters; Esther McCoy, the writer, with her husband, Berkeley Tobey. The presence of a Hungarian couple named Otvos, who had a bookstore in Beverly Hills, reminded me that Dreiser had always had a number of Hungarian friends, including Ralph Fabri and Maria Samson, a singer whose beautiful picture stood on the piano, and who had died tragically, some months before.

Now again, you could hear those colorful fragments of conversation, the stirring up of creative thought, which a Dreiser party always inspired. People did their best in talking to him because they saw in his deep penetrating eyes, the interest, the appreciation of any real thought, any sincere variation of temperament. This was particularly true of women; in Dreiser's presence they felt themselves heightened, built up to any superior quality they might possess, in looks or mind.

Even homely women felt at ease with Dreiser because he could and did admire qualities other than physical charm and went out of his way to find them in women not favored with an obvious appeal. Just as he was fatally attracted by female beauty he was also drawn by feminine intellect and sensitivity, often going out of his way to explore the mind of a bashful, lonely type, who could not easily project herself. One woman at this party seemed quite radiant as she exchanged ideas with him, whereas later, she went unnoticed in the crowd.

Suddenly, a young man, standing on the steps leading into the living-room, burst into song. Chords of a piano heard through the open French doors behind him, accompanied a glorious voice. Dreiser's face lit up with happy surprise. This was a broad, red-headed tenor who had been brought by Lillian Goodman, a close friend of Helen's, and herself a singer and coach. So another Dreiser party turned into a musicale. For both Dreiser and Helen loved music as much as ever, in their direct, emotional fashion.

As night began to fall, some twenty-odd guests who were left, moved into the house. Then Miss Chang, the sixteen-year-old girl in blue, modestly sat down at the long, black piano and, without notes, began to play excerpts from the Grieg Piano Concerto. People grouped themselves around the long room, some in the big armchairs, some perched along window sills, some leaning against tables or the rough stucco walls. With the background of the rich furniture and colors of curtains and clothing, the whole scene had the warmth of one of the old studio parties at 57th Street. The sleek, black instrument was like a living thing, as the young girl made it sing out.

Dreiser's eyes glowed as he listened to the music and drained the end of his delightful party. Much as he treasured solitude and, for the most part, felt alone in mood, he loved his friends; a group of friends at the end of the day, united by the common enjoyment of the piano's voice and the fellowship of the moment, wove something around him from which he was loathe to part, as from the warmth of a great cape on a night growing colder.

Dreiser's habits of life—Places

In those days, Dreiser rose about eight o'clock, breakfasted around eight-thirty and then liked to go out into the garden for awhile. By nine-thirty, he was usually ready for work.

Sometimes, he went into his study, but there he always wanted to be alone. Helen kept her large typewriter at the end of the long dining-table. Dreiser would sit here beside her, when answering his mail, dictating statements, or going over business matters. He still had no regular secretary, but Helen was tireless in her efforts to help him with routine work, although there was far too much to do for one person who was also housekeeper and lady of the house. But this was one of the many ways she showed her devotion.

With most of the mornings spent in work, Dreiser and Helen seldom took more than a sandwich or bowl of soup in the middle of the day. Around three or four, they usually made a break. While Dreiser sometimes went out alone, Helen often planned late afternoon errands, when she would drop him off somewhere, or they would go together to an art exhibition, or cocktail party. Often, they would simply take a drive, and stop to have their main meal of the day around five or six o'clock, according to the California custom.

Helen generously began including my son and me in these late afternoon drives, showing us the country-side and taking us to dinner. They chose restaurants without fuss or show, but they were always on the look-out for places that had some atmosphere, and where the food was good but inexpensive. Dreiser was no gourmet, but he was fond of certain dishes, German or Italian, or Mexican meals if not too strongly seasoned. If he was disappointed in a dish, he seldom complained, and often, he did not seem to be hungry. But if he sat without eating much, he would usually be interested in watching the faces of other people in the room, speculating about them and their relationships:

"Now just look at those two—what do you suppose they

have to say to each other?" Or—"watch that fellow over there. He eats like some sort of bird—What business do you suppose he's in?"

We were ourselves an odd foursome, the rugged Dreiser than seventy-two, Helen and I in the middle of our lives, and Hilary, a thoughtful boy of fourteen. Often only Helen and I chatted gaily if Dreiser was in a quiet mood. But then sometimes he would begin to talk in his roughly eloquent way, about some personality he had known, some strange occurence, or, as he did after we had visited Mt. Wilson, about the stars. Here, Hilary might put in some remark or ask a question. Once, Dreiser suggested that we go together to the Mt. Hollywood Planetarium and he and Hilary were particularly enthralled by the show there. Hilary remembers looking through a telescope for the first time. Indeed, Dreiser introduced Hilary to this cosmic world which ever after fascinated him as it did Dreiser.

During this period we visited many beautiful places. Helen was an excellent driver, as she had been in the east, and motoring seemed a natural outlet for her high-strung temperament. She was proud of her western country and took us to special spots where we could admire the dramatic sea-scapes of the California coast or views of deep canyons and far hills.

One Sunday, driving under the shoulders of the Sierra Madre, we visited the village of Montrose where Dreiser and Helen had once owned a building lot. There had even been rough plans made for a house, but nothing had come of it. This was one of the many dreams they had had for a home, and only *Iroki* had materialized. Yet now that, too, had been abandoned. It was not Dreiser's destiny to be rooted in any place, to leave behind a house which had meant much to him, and might have become a memorial, as Tolstoy's home at *Yasnaya Polyana*.

Even his birth-place in Terre Haute, Indiana, had no great meaning to him. We described it to him, as we saw it, motoring through. It was a small stiff little house, on a wide flat street, shaded with trees, and near a sprawling, red-brick brewery. We did not go in, because a sign on the door said

"Occupants Sleeping." They probably worked on a night-shift. The walls were covered with a modern, asbestos shingle, now a faded green. One had the impression that little of the original atmosphere was left.

Dreiser did not even remember this house, for his family had moved to another, cheaper one, in the same town a few months after his birth. But the *Banks of the Wabash*. Yes, this was a sentimental memory, perhaps more because of his brother Paul who called himself Dresser. The song which he composed, and to which Dreiser wrote the words, had become so nationally popular that the town created a Paul Dresser Memorial Drive which follows the river down for about a mile out of Terre Haute, making a sort of park, with huge, far-spreading trees reaching to the broad banks of the sluggish brown Wabash some fifty feet below.

Little House on Cadet Court—we work on The Bulwark

Dreiser was not particular about the place where he worked, but he wanted it to be cut off from distractions. He had loved the bareness and simplicity of his cabins at Mt. Kisco, and *The Shack* on Long Island Sound. Now he wanted me to find a place where he could come to work during the day, and keep papers relating only to *The Bulwark*.

Because of war-time crowding, it was impossible to find a furnished apartment. Then luckily, while walking up the hillside beyond our motel, my son saw a family moving out of a tiny house. We went back, and found a smiling, blue-eyed Irishman painting the inside walls, preparing it for sale. He did not want to rent. For several days we came around and chatted with him while he worked. We told him this was like a place we had had in Switzerland, with blue walls framing the mountains, and we thought this would be a good color for the smaller bedroom. The next day, when we came by, he was painting this room blue and said we could rent the house.

There were only three rooms; two bed rooms, and a larger, rectangular living room, entered from a long flight of cement steps coming up from a little Court, or dead-end street, cutting into the mountain, near Cahuenga Boulevard. The front and sides of the garden were terraced in European Villa style, with stone walks, privet hedges, masses of rose bushes, oleanders and other flowering shrubs. The right-hand path continued past two small peach trees, to a large square patio cut into the hillside.

The living-room also opened into this patio, through a pantry-kitchen. The white retaining wall of another, higher villa was barely visible through a tangle of rose-bushes and vines. To the west, the patio ran into a low diagonally mounting embankment where weeds and nasturtiums grew between rounded rocks, and the hill stretched up and out, burnt brown now in the summer heat, but rising in the distance to a clump of dark green live oaks. Still further back, another rise showed roofs and slim Eucalyptus trees swaying against the sky.

To the east, and facing the front of the Court, the beautiful pointed shoulder of Cahuenga Peak stood clear and farther away, along the other side of the San Fernando Valley, you could see the great march of the San Gabriel Mountains.

Dreiser teased a little about the place looking run down, and grumbled about the long flight of steps, but he loved the quiet, the view, the patio, and the fact that there was no 'phone and nobody near by.

We got only essentials in the way of furniture—a long table, the rumble seat of our convertible brought in to serve as a couch, and three stiff-backed chairs. Dreiser sat patiently on one of these, until we could afford to buy a pair of Mexican wicker arm-chairs, one of them with long, ample rockers.

From then on, this was Dreiser's chair. He sat in it, rocking almost imperceptibly as he worked, whether bent over sheets of paper at the big table, or sitting back, dictating or pondering over his lines. He did not smoke, and this slight, rhythmic movement seemed to soothe the restlessness that was ever in his body and in his mind, perhaps a part of his creative energy itself.

Now each day he became more absorbed in the idea of

finishing this novel which he had begun and abandoned, at least six times.

Each morning, about ten, I called for him and he would appear with some new bundle of manuscript under his arm. One day it was a heavy package, tied with blue string. Another time, a clothes-box, filled with papers; or there would be bunches of notes stuffed into bursting manila envelopes. We would sort them out on the long table.

"This is stuff on Isobel," he would remark. "She's the homely one." Or "This is about Stewart at school," and he would begin to talk about the Barnes family as though every one must know them. Just when he seemed to have everything sorted, he arrived with another very worn and over-stuffed manila envelope. "Fifty thousand words more," he chuckled. "Now this will send you back to Connecticut!"

Finally I moved an empty steamer trunk into the room, to store these endless manuscripts. The bottom of the trunk was half full and the tray filled with material already typed, before he was through adding to the collection. Often, this trunk stood open as we worked. When not in use, it was locked—although I never locked the door of my house! But this was our treasure-chest, full of literary slag and gold.

Solemnly, Dreiser showed me a special piece of manuscript made up of little, note-paper pages, pasted on larger sheets. It was written in that small, flowing hand which came out of his moods of deepest concentration; a touching scene in which a father creeps downstairs at night, to view the body of his dead son.

"I wrote this," Dreiser said, "when I first thought of the idea of *The Bulwark,* to see if it had the germ of a great tragedy in it. After I wrote this, I felt that it did."

The passage had never been copied before. I wanted to type it at once, feeling that it was something very precious that might easily have been lost. Where did it fit in?

"Nearer the end—No, I never got that far in any of the typescripts. I knew exactly what I wanted to do, but I could never get beyond a certain point."

Only then, he began to tell me what had happened to *The*

Bulwark and why he had never been able to finish it before. It had a curious history.

He had started it much earlier then 1917 when it was first scheduled for publication. We found a page of manuscript written on the back of a letter to H. L. Mencken, dated in 1910.

He said he had his own father in mind when he decided to portray a man dominated by religion and forced to face the modern world. This character must stick to his belief and yet be utterly crushed and defeated by the disasters which overtake him, because of his refusal to accept life "realistically." He has driven his children to opposite extremes, because of his own religious fanaticism. This, Dreiser felt, was the case of his own father, a strict German Catholic.

The hero of *The Bulwark*, however, was to be a Quaker—a sect which Dreiser felt to be more typically American, and his life was modelled after that of a certain family whom Dreiser had known near Philadelphia.

In order to build an authentic background for his story, Dreiser had felt obliged to read a number of books about Quakers, notably the *Journal of John Woolman*. This had made a deep impression on him. He found that he was facing something which he could not reconcile with his own views; Quakers simply did not give up when disaster struck them. They did not lose their faith. He had quoted a verse from the Prophet Job, in his first *Bulwark* attempts, which is often found in Quaker writings: "Though He slay me, yet will I trust Him . . ."

If Dreiser had not had such great integrity as a writer, he could easily have finished this novel years earlier, for the plot was clearly in his mind. But it was the psychological or spiritual aspect of it which, again and again, blocked him. He was too honest to write anything which he did not believe was true to character, nor to write about characters he did not fully understand.

Much of his writing and thinking was done at what was then a high point of cynicism and materialism in human history, and Dreiser was extremely sensitive to world currents.

The time had not come for him to produce a book on a religious as well as a social theme and the public that acclaimed *An American Tragedy* was not ready for *The Bulwark*. Indeed, the book is still ahead of its time, as was, when it was first composed, the disarmingly simple, religious music of Bach.

Then, in Dreiser's own life, had come the passionate search for truth through science, which in turn, had led him to a vague, cosmic faith, belief in a *Creator*.

He had not found the time nor the peace to finish his *Philosophy*, because of his involvement in political causes. Yet through one of these very involvements—his attempt to help the starving people of Barcelona, he had come into contact with the great Quaker, Rufus Jones, and they had become friends. Here was religion in practice, and here was the very man who, in a practical way, could help him finish *The Bulwark*. He spoke to Jones about the book, and when he returned to it again, relied heavily on the story of Jones' own youth, in *Finding the Trail of Life*.

Dr. Gerhard Friederich of Haverford College has made a careful study of Dreiser's debt to Rufus Jones in *American Literature* (Vol XXIX No. 2. May 1957).

When Dreiser first started to examine one of the old versions of *The Bulwark* he felt he must *paint in*—a phrase he loved—some of the earlier phases of his hero Solon's youth. The long introduction submitted to Earle Balch of Putnam in 1944, had incidents literally "lifted" from Jones' book, and Dreiser's own writing was bogged down by this following of another's story. It was only when he immersed himself more peacefully in the early versions of *The Bulwark* that his thought began to flow.

Yet even in the little house on the hillside, it took him some time to reconcile himself to his material. He was at times depressed and strangely silent. "I thought I was through with novel-writing" he said one day. "I wanted to do something bigger, more important." And he would take certain sections, and go out in the patio with them. He would sit and brood; get up and come in for another section. It was weeks before he felt that he was living with his characters again.

"You can't just make characters do what you want, anymore than you can people," he said once. "Sometimes, they just won't do certain things. The only way to tell what they *will* do is to live along with them 'til you *see* what they are going to do—sometimes they can really surprise you!"

Certainly, the whole drama was going through his mind, though it seemed as though he would never get on with it.

Bulwark *Material on Hand, September, 1944*

Besides the fifty-page introduction written by Dreiser in 1943 *The Bulwark* material on hand that September, 1944, consisted of hundreds of pages of handwritten manuscript and four different type-scripts, all written well before *An American Tragedy.*

The earliest type-script had been discarded and Dreiser put it aside again. Though it contained some very smooth and beautiful writing, he felt it was not dramatic nor swift enough.

The second type-script began, as does part II of the published book, with the wedding of Solon and Bencia and continued with the story of their married life, the arrival of the children, the gradual development of qualities disturbing to their parents, leading to the youngest son, Stewart's entrance into boarding-school. This we called The Family Version because it provided the framework for the present novel, giving most of the details and incidents that reveal the characters of the Barnes family and the atmosphere of their home.

The third type-script we called The Financial Version. It related, in brilliant successive steps, the banking career of Solon Barnes, from the time the young man enters his father-in-law's bank, to his final discovery of the questionable dealings of his associates, when he is already an aging director.

The fourth type-script seemed to be a much-cut family version, with certain changes in a hand unlike Dreiser's, chopping into what was already a too short coverage of the

colorful Barnes household. This version was valuable only
in that it led a little further into the story of Stewart, up to
the eve of his tragic adventure with Ada Maurer.

Seeing that the Family and Financial versions combined
would make a novel of no mean size, Dreiser felt encouraged
to plan what remained to be done.

The Financial Version was drastically cut, whereas the
Family Version was very little cut in Dreiser's final type-
script. It was supplemented in many incidents by bits from
handwritten descriptions which Dreiser had assembled, trying out various word pictures to illustrate the characters of
the children he loved most; Etta, Isobel, Stewart. Certain
traits or colors of their temperaments he had experimented
with, endlessly—Isobel's loneliness, neglect and sense of
frustration; Etta's dreaminess and longing for beauty and
romance; Stewart's consuming desire for excitement, loveli-
ness, sex.

There were lengthy, hand-written descriptions of a certain
Bendisher family which had bought the estate adjoining
Thornbrough and from whose porches on summer evenings
came the gay sounds of music and dancing, frivolities such
as were never allowed in the Barnes household. The children
would stroll up the road to hear them more plainly and
Stewart never missed a chance to catch a glimpse of young
Flora Bendisher walking around her grounds, plump and
beautiful, with ribbons in her thick, flying hair.

The little drama of the Naked Indians—when the Barnes
children in their play took off their clothes and painted themselves red, to the horror of their conservative parents, Dreiser had written in several variations. He had only to choose
the most effective one, to be fitted in to the Family Version.

Dreiser never used a typewriter nor carbons, and yet, in
his small neat hand, some pages seemed complete duplicates
of others. This was true especially at the beginning of chapters. The same, opening sentence and perhaps two or three
identical lines would be followed by others with different
emphasis or meaning. This was because Dreiser could get so
lost in a creative mood, so deep in the music of his own

special rhythms that he would begin all over again, rather than cross out a sentence, or chop his writing line. The flow of his language was all-important to him. When he was *in the swing*, page after page of his manuscripts were beautifully rhythmic to the eye, as well as to the ear, his lines flowing without a single correction or change of spacing.

Another characteristic of these pages was the round or golden sentence. Sometimes, at the beginning, or again at the end of a not unusual, realistic description, would appear one rarely beautful or evocative statement which would ring in the literary mind, like a bell:

"There is a wisdom related to beauty only, that concerns itself with cloud forms and the wild vines' tendrils . . ." When we came to passages like this in the old chapters which were not to be used, or paragraphs which had to be cut, in Dreiser's new plan for the novel, I could not bear to let them go. I would copy them out and we would try to fit them in elsewhere. But then Dreiser would sometimes laugh:

"Will you quit bothering about those old sentences? I'll make up another." But some of them were like pure gold nuggets that might not be found again.

One of the most delightful pictures of the Barnes children was lifted from an early, discarded chapter. It shows Old Joseph driving them back and forth to school in the family carryall; First Isobel, "in neat but trim little clothes, with her few small books" and later, the other children as they came along and were driven to Letitia Brigg's school at Red Kiln, in the same carriage. "House-wives and farm-hands along the road to Red Kiln, actually timed their clocks by it. 'There goes Old Joseph with the Barnes children—it must be after half-past eight.' "

I have always felt this would make a wonderful sequence for a film of *The Bulwark;* this carryall with the children in it, at different periods, growing in age and numbers, and finally only the restless little Stewart left, teasing Old Joseph to let him drive!

Descriptions of Stewart's growing restlessness, his use of slang, his longing for the gay life of restaurants and hotels such as he had seen at Atlantic City and in New York, and below and through all, his smouldering, almost terrifying desire for feminine conquest, filled many pages of curiously exciting and often autobiographical manuscript. Much of Dreiser's early hunger and yearning for a fuller life is in Stewart's bright and fatally impetuous temperament.

In order to get the new plan for the novel under way, we worked on a double-shift, Dreiser organizing the material with me in the daytime, and I typing over at night certain chapters in their new arrangement. We figured that about eighty-six chapters were already done, and only eighteen or twenty more were necessary to complete the story.

A diagram made hastily one day when Dreiser was discouraged about finishing his task, showed clearly how little entirely new material need be written. There was also the key scene, which had been composed, like a piece of grave music, long ago, and the last line of the novel, which Dreiser had had in his mind since its first conception. Actually, when it came to the writing of the last chapter, the line was placed a paragraph before the end, as Dreiser had a great sense of style about his endings, which few critics have understood.

Already written about Barnes Family, to Ch. 44   Left, 6 Chapters:
                                                   Etta Leaves Home

Already written about Stewart—2 yrs. more—to Ch. 55 | Left—12
                                                       Chapters
                                    Crime   Etta   Decline
Also Financial Version complete to Crime Suicide returns Death
                                                          of Solon

Dreiser also made a careful synopsis of the chapters already written, and an outline of those to come. This first résumé ran to fourteen pages and read like the summaries found on the first pages of classic Russian novels.

These outlines were ready about the end of November, 1944. A few minor corrections, and Dreiser sent them to his new publisher, Doubleday & Co., who had taken over *The Bulwark* from Putnam, and was also in need of encouragement.

Then Dreiser announced that he was ready to go on.

IX. THE NEED OF LOVE TOWARD ALL CREATED THINGS

—master of tragedy—master of style

Etta—Quaker Books

Dreiser loved his characters, and Etta, in *The Bulwark* was modelled on a girl to whom he had once been deeply attached. It was with her that he picked up the threads to weave his novel to the end.

He described her first at boarding school, where she has begun to see something of the world beyond the quiet Barnes household; then coming home, she begins to revolt against the restraint she feels there.

It was no easy task to make this sensitive, dreamy girl run away from her parents—yet this she must do—and that is the way Dreiser wrote, taking the part of his characters, one by one, and living through their experiences. He wanted to have Etta's conservative father find that she had been reading French novels, and so cause a scene which would lead to her departure. But what books—what passages?

As a young newspaperman Dreiser had come upon just such books, in the libraries of the Midwest, and by them had been inspired to write the realistic *Sister Carrie.* Now he wanted to refresh his memory of them, so he sent me down to the library. I found Balzac's *La Cousine Bette,* Flaubert's *Madame Bovary* but Daudet's *Sapho,* which he particularly wanted, was not there. Finally, I located a copy with an old-style florid cover in a second-hand book-store. Since it was near Christmas time, I wrapped it up and presented it to Dreiser as a gift. He was delighted, and read it through, as he had done forty years before. "It's still a remarkably honest book," he remarked, and then he picked out the scene from Sappho which Solon must find, when he opens the book, in Etta's room.

It took him another week to complete his chapter on Etta's leaving home. He really suffered over it, knowing how she herself had felt torn apart.

Because of the very accurate way in which Dreiser wanted to paint his hero Solon, he had read and studied a number of Quaker books. He brought them to me, and wanted me to copy certain passages. I was amazed at the many, slightly wavering lines and marginal comments he had made. Even the Quaker's solemn *Book of Discipline* seemed to fascinate him, in its stern nobility of thought. There were odd, touching stories in *Annals of the Early Friends* which he had marked. All the simple, Christian virtues which he had not himself followed, now won his unqualified admiration. From the old books he picked a motto such as Quakers used to hang in their homes, and he had Solon buy a framed sample and bring it home to Benecia his wife, on their wedding anniversary. It was stitched in yellow wool, and at sunset, the light struck it, through the tall windows of their dining-room: "In Honor, prefering one another"

"Solon really *gets* this religion—it leads him all through his life," he remarked almost apologetically one day, and then he used his deepest diapason tone to emphasize the Spirit which the Quaker's believed dwelt within them, *The Inner Light.*

Rufus Jones had suggested Dreiser's looking for a book of his that was out of print, at the Whittier College Library.

Dreiser drove out to this Quaker college, some twenty-five miles south of Los Angeles, found the book in question, and amazed the professors there by his interest in Quaker thought. Consequently, he was asked to speak to the students, at a Chapel Talk.

Dreiser spoke to the students and faculty for some forty minutes, stirring them deeply. "Did they realize that George Fox's Journal and John Woolman's Journal were among the world's great books? Were they aware that these men, along with St. Francis and a few others, were among the spiritual leaders of all times?" He seemed genuinely excited about all this.

Dreiser said then, that if he could belong to any church— and he seemed to imply a conscientious inability to belong to any—that he felt more drawn to the Quaker faith than any other. He spoke with such honesty, warmth and discernment that students and faculty remembered him vividly, seven years later, when I visited there.

Charles Cooper, dramatist and head of the English Department said that he had begun to read Fox and Woolman more carefully from that day: "I'm afraid Dreiser was disappointed in us," he said candidly. "I think he considered this a Quaker seminary, whereas it is a non-sectarian college. Only one half of the faculty are required to be Friends. Dreiser really wanted to find out what people were like who had this spiritual heritage. I had the feeling that his own discovery of Fox was rather recent and he was seeking to know more people who felt inspired by Fox as he did."

Dr. Paul Samual Smith of Whittier also spoke of Dreiser's intense curiosity about the college and about spiritual things. "I know he was disappointed in us," he said not knowing that Dr. Cooper had said the same thing. "He was so wholesome, so whole-hearted in his interest. He made a terrific impression on us.

"He was also deeply concerned with the matters of the world. He talked about Quakers and connected them with social work and said how he admired Rufus Jones. He talked about Russia, too, and he said devastating things about Hearst and the American press. His interest in religion was constructive. He seemed right on the point of things, vital, hard up against the problems of all people. Later, he sent me a letter on some political subject.—What a force he was!"

Dreiser never said that he was disappointed in Whittier—
On the contrary, he told me of his visit there with justifiable
pride:

"I told them some things about their Quaker books they
didn't know themselves," he laughed.

Services

Because of Dreiser's new interest in religion, it was only
natural that he was curious about various church services.
Unfortunately, there was no Quaker Meeting nearby. Whittier was too far away and with wartime gas rationing we
were limited to neighborhood churches.

Helen had long been interested in Christian Science with
its attempted synthesis of Eastern and Western thought.
Years before she had also studied Yoga Philosophy, in its
various aspects, and used to go up on the roof of the Studio
on 57th Street, to practice breathing exercises. Now she
favored Christian Science because of its impersonal way of
presenting the Scriptures and the interpretations of Mary
Baker Eddy, through *readers*. There was usually good hymn
singing and solo music by a professional. She said that
Dreiser had enjoyed such services when he would not go to
any other church.

So once we went to the Beverly Hills Church of Christ,
Scientist. It was a handsome, white building with airy hall,
blue carpet, and a dignified, if somewhat lifeless, atmosphere.
Another time, we went to the smaller church on North Hay-
worth, which Dreiser had attended when living on that street.
It had the charm of an old structure and my son then hoping
to be an engineer was fascinated by the open-truss roof.

Then we discovered the Mt. Hollywood Congregational
Church, where Allan Hunter was minister.

We had been told that Allan Hunter was a liberal, a tireless worker for peace and social justice. Indeed, the Congregational Church has always specialized in social action for
the underprivileged, but we did not realize what an extraordinary person he was until we heard him speak. He stood

there in a dark-blue business suit, talking with perfect natu-
ralness, about contacting God through thought and meditation. He used plain but beautiful language—a man of medium
height, slim, with wearing, sandy hair and features sculptured by what emotional or spiritual experiences. He might
have been anywhere between forty and sixty. His face
changed easily from expressions of seriousness, intensity, to
amusement or great tenderness. As he explained a parable
from the Gospel, he gave one a feeling of the closeness, the
intimacy of the Christ.

The service itself was the conventional Protestant ritual
of sermon, hymns and prayers. But one thing was noticeable;
the slower pace of the prayers—and for a few moments,
complete silence, for meditation, like a Quaker Meeting. After
it was over, Allan Hunter stood out on the broad, white steps
of the Church, greeting his friends, and all who came out,
with kindly humor, his blue eyes crinkling in the bright sunshine.

"That man has something," mumbled Dreiser, on the way
home. "What a character, and yet, nothing at all—" he waved
his hand to indicate that kind of simplicity which disappears
when you talk about it. Then we spoke of something else.
You didn't feel like discussing Allan Hunter's sermons anymore than you felt like arguing about music after a satisfying concert. You just thought that you would like to hear him
again.

Christmas Day Incident
The mood around Dreiser's work deepened. He did not want
to see anyone or do anything unless it had some import for
his work. As Christmas approached Helen turned down
many invitations, and we all decided to take as little time out
for celebration as possible.

On Christmas day, Dreiser and Helen asked us to have
dinner with them in an attractive restaurant just outside of
Hollywood. Here a strange incident occurred which affected
us all.

At a family gathering of some six people around a horse-shoe table in a niche next to ours, a commotion suddenly arose. A man from another table struck one of this family, a middle-aged, almost bald individual, who sprang from his seat. Before he was able to defend himself, another younger man sitting next to him, pinioned the heavy frame with his arms. The first man struck again and again, the blows thudding into the face of the victim who could not move, pinned back as he was and trapped in the horse-shoe niche, behind the table.

Dreiser rose with a growl of indignation, almost the first in the room to protest. Waiters finally pulled the men apart, but the room was charged with horror. A more merciful member of the family led the victim out, his face covered with blood.

Our meal, fortunately near its end, was all but spoiled. Dreiser was speechless, grieving in an almost personal way. I thought of the woman in the cafeteria, in New York, and of all the long procession of accidents, corpses, victims that Dreiser had seen in his newspaper days, recorded and unrecorded. Surely the palimpset brain of this master of tragedy had been spared little vicarious suffering over the world's pain.

Depression

Shortly after the New Year, Dreiser contracted one of his typical bronchial colds. He stayed in bed a few days, but there was no way to keep him quiet. He was seized by one of those periodic depressions that had always tormented him. Although he had fever, he would suddenly get up and wander out in the garden, his dressing gown hung loosely over cotton pyjamas, no slippers on his feet. Or he would go out to the kitchen, looking for something to drink. He would take a handful of vitamins, or a few slugs of whiskey rather than the medicine the doctor had recommended.

Coupled with his physical depression was a gloomy mood in regard to *The Bulwark*. He had passed the difficult chapter where Etta leaves home, but now Solon must go after her. Can he force her to come back? Or must he give up trying?

What would he really do? Dreiser seemed stuck, at this emotional impasse. And this was just the beginning of the agonizing period of the children's revolt. He began to suffer so deeply with Solon that he doubted whether he could ever finish his story. So strong was his pessimism that it communicated itself to me, although I tried not to show it. He could be so difficult at times, so sunk in a negative mood that death, and all sorts of disasters seemed actually lurking around him, as if he were deliberately drawing them to himself.

Helen and I did everything we could to get him through this period. I came every day to the house on King's Road, and he dictated to me, or had me type scenes he had thought of during the night. But the work was not going well.

Then one morning, when I came in, he seemed much happier and laughed:

"Well, I had a sort of dream last night. At least, I woke up knowing just what I would do. For I *was* Solon, and I seemed to be in a nice hotel room, opposite the campus at Wisconsin. Things were not as bad as I thought."

He went on to describe the family with whom his daughter, Etta, had taken refuge, at the college town, and how he gained confidence to leave her there. I started writing down everything he said, and now he felt the deadlock in his new chapter was broken.

After that, he seemed to grow better. A few days later he announced that he wanted to go out. He had not been fully dressed for two weeks, but nothing would stop him. He marched out to my car, a camel's hair bathrobe over slacks and shirt. The afternoon was indeed mild and beautiful, one of those Southern California winter days, clear and blue-skied, and spattered with a hundred bright flowerings. We drove into the hills, Dreiser humming and happy again, in his peculiar, quiet, brimming way.

Etta and Kane

Now came the love-story of Etta and Kane. Again, Dreiser wished to immerse himself in the atmosphere of the place in which they were to meet and live. This was Greenwich Village, that section of New York, bounded roughly by 14th Street and Bleecker Street, on the West side of Fifth Avenue. A hundred years ago, it had been the aristocratic center of the city, its four or five-storey houses of brick well built and trees and vines along its walls. The center of New York had long since shifted uptown, to marble palaces and great apartment houses. These old homes, with large, cozy rooms, made ideal studios and lodgings. Painters, writers, artistic people of all sorts moved in to this section which developed an interesting character; small restaurants, shops, art galleries, cafes, gave it a certain European quality. There were the French Hotels Brevoort, and Lafayette, in those days, and many Italian places especially toward Bleecker Street. Of course, pseudo-Bohemians and odd characters of all sorts also moved in, and by the nineteen-forties and fifties, many modern buildings threatened the whole aspect of The Village. But at the time of which Dreiser wrote, the Village was at the height of its colorful career.

For a day or two, he talked about places and people he had known there. He himself had had several rooms in various houses and an attractive apartment on 10th Street, where Helen first came to see him.

He spoke of Paula Holladay, a delightful woman who ran a small restaurant with the aid of a Hungarian friend and supercook. This man was dark, undersized and fired with energy. He had left his own country for political reasons, and happened to have extraordinary culinary talents. On numerous occasions, he would come storming out of the kitchen to deliver some speech on economic ills. There was also the restaurant of Romany Marie, where you could have your fortune told, and always get into interesting conversations with musicians, painters and other artistic personalities.

Dreiser talked for a long time about a man named Krog, and I jotted down some of his remarks:

"He was a writer, a brilliant, subtle mind. He had sold a number of articles to leading magazines and was on his way to success, if it had not been for an erratic streak in his nature that ended, finally, in insanity. But he was so entertaining, so charming, so stimulating that his friends literally fought over him . . .

"A fellow we called *Affinity Earl,* who was very popular with the ladies, invited Krog to stay with him in the country and immediately a well-known illustrator tried to get him back to the city, to stay with him. Like any genius, people fell in love with him, both men and women." (How often Dreiser had experienced this himself . . .)

"He shared my apartment for a while. I had a hall bedroom that I let him use, off my big studio. While he was there, he had a sudden attack of appendicitis and had to be taken to the hospital. The whole *Village* knew of it and talked about him, until he got out again. After that, he lived in various cheap hotels, but he would invariably get into some trouble, because of his bills, or his unusual behavior. One day, he showed up at my place, completely out of his head. He was raving about some deal or other, but still charming, delightful. I tried to make him stay with me that night, being really afraid of what might happen to him in his excitable mood.

"Shortly after that, he was taken to a mental institution. No one could handle him. There was some trouble I never quite understood, pressure on the brain, or something like it—But what a man! What a temperament!" And, as often when he talked about someone he loved, Dreiser's eyes filled with tears: "Yes, Krog, Krog . . . I'll write about him sometime."

So now into this atmosphere, Dreiser introduced his little Quaker Etta. She had come from college in Wisconsin, with her bland beauty and her longing for life. She must fall in love with a man who was worthy of her. This was to be no vulgar, Village seduction.

In the outline Dreiser had just made, he had given Etta's lover the odd name of Stanislaus Fiva. But he decided that this would be a false note in his story. Etta must not be swept off her feet by the sophistication of a European, but her lover must be someone like herself, with whom she could feel a natural, fatal affinity. Some one who would love her, too, yet be destined, by his artist temperament to make her unhappy.

As in the case of the artist Witla, in *The Genius,* Dreiser put much of his own psychology into the character of the painter, Kane. He faced the old problem of how much a creative person can give to love, without sacrificing his work, or thwarting that natural—or necessary—inclination toward *variety,* which seemed to him a part of the creative process itself.

Etta was the type of girl that could appreciate and deeply love a man like Kane (or Witla, or Dreiser) and yet be fatally weak and unpossessive, as far as holding him was concerned. Dreiser felt that there was a subtle beauty in this kind of weakness. He said he would like to write a novel just about such a couple as Etta and Kane, exploring their whole approach to life, and art, as well as to each other. This was to be a love just short of meaning everything that human love can mean.

"I don't see how Kane can leave a girl like Etta—yet he must," said Dreiser sadly, brooding over a page. In his mind was much of his own pain as an artist when—how often— he had felt he must tear himself away from a woman he had loved.

In order to make it convincing that Kane must leave, Dreiser wanted to put in his mind some irresistible urge toward creative work that would be stronger than the tie of love. With Dreiser, there were no easy solutions; he dug into his own imagination. If he were a painter, what would he feel urged to paint? What would obsess him passionately enough?

He thought of a valley in California through which he had motored at different times and which, each time, had strangely affected him. He would put this haunting attraction in the mind of Kane. He began to talk about this valley, and I scribbled along, but he waved his hand:

"Don't put all that down. Just let me tell you how it was . . ."

He described it as high and barren—perhaps a hundred miles from the coast: "Nothing but sands, moved by the winds—or perhaps there were great rocks, too, that had been sand long ago. They seemed to suggest figure after figure, stretched out in the sun. Far up on the slopes, down in the dry river,—male and female bodies, powerful ones and graceful ones—forms indescribable—and then, out of nothing—" (How Dreiser could hollow out all the eeriness of that word with his long hand)—nothing at all, except perhaps heat and universal energy, a sense of thousands and thousands of spirits, invisible, and yet almost visible, the whole evoking such a feeling of awe and mystery that I have never forgotten it.

"And when, years later I motored through here again, I had the same feeling, and I thought, Who are these? What? Why can I not see them, since I sense them, here and now? How am I to tell the world convincingly of these, inhabiting hot, dreary spaces which, without the sand-formed figures, could not suggest anything except endless time, motionless, undesigned space? What was this sense of life out of nothing but heat and sand?"

The desire to paint this valley could be strong enough, Dreiser decided, to motivate Kane in his growing restlessness under the spell of love:

"His work—His work—His work—From then on, there was an effort, half-conscious, half-unconscious, to express the need of a change. A word here. A phrase there. The necessity for his excusing himself for this period and that— quite swiftly conveyed to the sensitive Etta that her dream of union with someone—since evidently it was not Kane— was over."

With such odd subtleties of thought and word, Dreiser made of this parting a simplified, poignant symbol of the artist's essential egotism, or obedience to his creative urge, and the idealistic woman's longing for fulfillment.

Allan Hunter's Visit

Allan Hunter called on us one morning when Dreiser was working in the little house on the hill. It was one of those clear winter days, when the mountains seemed very near, and flowers and shrubs bright with color. We went out into the patio; there had been a few days of rain, and already on the brown hillsides, patches of fresh grass had made their appearance. "How beautiful, that new grass coming up there" said Allan, his eye roaming over the slope, to a tall poplar—"and that tree, unusual to see that out here, those bare branches"—his voice was as light as the tracery of the twigs. He was a person to whom all beauty was important.

The talk swung to India, where Allan had recently travelled and talked with many followers of Ghandi: "Easily, the greatest man of our time" he said casually as if the truth needed no emphasis. He explained to Dreiser the principle of *satyagraha,* the force of non-violence, with which Ghandi had finally won freedom from the British Empire.

Then Dreiser related how he had visited England after his visit to Russia in 1928. He had lunched with Churchill, who said to him that the Soviet power would not last another seven years! He also told how Churchill had shrugged off his questions about the "dole" and how he had visited the Welsh miners on that trip.

Lost in one of the poorest villages, Dreiser had gone into a tiny stone house, unbelievably bare, cold and gloomy. A middle-aged woman almost in rags, greeted him with stoic indifference. When he asked her how she could get along in this house, she shrugged her shoulders: "O, we have a little oil"—and with his lowest tone, and a gesture of his hand, Dreiser put all her pathos into that phrase.

I left the two men alone, and they seemed to enjoy each other immensely. When I came back with coffee, I was sorry they had not reached the subject of religion, or Quakers, for here was Dreiser in the midst of writing a deeply spiritual book, and yet he was still sometimes depressed, and bogged down in moods of defeat. I ventured to ask Allan what he thought was the secret of happiness. Should we be able to find joy, even though there is suffering all over the world?

Allan smiled, his keen lined face and blue eyes crinkling:

"I don't know that I can say off-hand. We make a mistake in being too glib, sometimes. But I know one person who was happy—who seemed to have the secret of happiness. His name was Philippe Vernier, a simple Protestant pastor in a small, Belgian town. During the Nazi invasion he used to swim across the river to bring back a bag of potatoes to his starving parishioners. Earlier, he was imprisoned for refusing military service. In jail, he experienced the nearness of God, in such a remarkable manner that he was filled with joy. One night he burst out singing, and so exasperated the warden, that he put him in solitary confinement. When asked what kept him through this trial, he said it was the continual sense of God's presence. 'It was,' Vernier said, groping for the right word in English, '*un chant dans le fond du coeur* (a song in the depth of my heart). My happiness was like that of a rescued child. As if I was in an ocean, drowned, and then God's arms were under me, lifting me up.' "

Dreiser was greatly impressed with this story and asked Hunter to write it up for him in note form. "I'd like to write about a character like that," he said, recalling his *Doer of the Word*, from *Twelve Men*.

"Delightful chap," exclaimed Dreiser as Allan left. "Be sure that he sends me that stuff about Vernier." As a matter of fact, Hunter did send him a six-page sketch, which he intended to use in a short story, when he got through his novel.

Conference at UCLA

One day, Allan Hunter phoned to ask if Dreiser would like to attend a Conference on Religion at the University of California, in Los Angeles (UCLA). He picked Dreiser and Helen up at King's Road, and I also came along.

The chairman of the morning session was Arthur H. Compton, cosmic-ray expert and head of the metallurgical laboratory in Chicago, where some of the most important discoveries related to the atomic project were made. Discussion centered around the existence of God. Besides Compton himself, a number of scientists, outstanding in their fields, defended the theory of a Divine Power, calling It various names from Super-intelligence to an Unknown God, but still a God. Only one held a negative view.

Dreiser was amazed—not that he needed to be further convinced in his own mind of what he called The Creative Force, or *My Creator*. But to hear these men make public confession of some kind of belief was very different from earlier days, when a belief in science seemed to exclude a belief in anything supernatural, and he had been pushed by scientists into his own peculiar brand of determinism.

The afternoon session was equally impressive. Here a new voice arose, protesting the inadequacy of the definitions given in the morning discussions. Hugh Miller, Professor of Philosophy said that for scientists merely to concede the possible existence of a God was not enough—Almost as bad as nothing. It was only in the conscious effort to learn more about the nature of God that man can begin to understand the Universe.

"Science can and must pursue religious truth in order to advance," he challenged. This grasped Dreiser's imagination as something very new; he left the Conference in a thoughtful mood.

As he rode along in the front seat beside Allan Hunter, Dreiser began to talk about plant life. They spoke of winter rye, about how one plant may have as many as fourteen billion hairs, or fine rootlets, totaling sixty-six hundred miles in length. Dreiser seemed to rejoice in this fact which seemed to him to defy a mechanistic view of life.

"You can't tell me there's no meaning in those little roots reaching out toward the nourishment that's in the soil. I've studied the thing under a microscope and I tell you it's not just a machine. There's something more than we had thought in this process by which these plants grow and add life to themselves."

We remembered the gesture of his long hands as he said this, his fingers emulating the roots pushing through the soil to find the moisture and minerals there.

Holy Week

By odd coincidence, it was toward the end of Lent that Dreiser was working on his concluding section of *The Bulwark*. He heard that Allan Hunter was holding services each night, reading the story of the *Passion,* according to the four Gospels.

On Good Friday, he asked if there would be another service. "Yes, but it will be more formal," I answered, really trying to discourage him, for I knew he had not taken part in a communion service since he attended Catholic Mass as a boy.

"I want to go," he said.

Allan Hunter's church was hushed and beautiful that evening, decorated as though for a country wedding. The women had put a long white cloth on the communion table and at the foot of a rustic Cross there were candles and white flowers in abundance. Only a few people had gathered when Dreiser came in with Helen, and took a place about four rows from the table. I remember how white his hair seemed and how it shone in the light of the candles.

Dreiser had a special look when he was in a church. It was easy for him to be reverent, to enter that meditative mood in which he often sat, at his desk or in his garden, sometimes for half an hour without moving. In the pew he was a little more conspicuous than most people, sitting taller, but very subdued. His round, domed head, rough-hewn, with slightly sagging jowls, his mobile mouth, usually hanging open, suggested primitive power not altogether tamed.

His eyes would seem almost hidden under the heavy iron-gray brows; grave, thoughtful, inward—then suddenly they would look out, quizzical, intense, able to laugh by themselves, without changing a muscle of the face. Not a word, not a subtlety of the Gospel would he miss, but glancing, seemed to catch each deep or mystically exciting meaning.

There was something more than interest in those eyes—a gleam of age-old participation—as if this intercourse with the Divine was an old matter with him; as if he frequently indulged in it and would relish it always were it not for the opposite pull of some force buried in his own flesh—something diabolic, perhaps, that held him back.

For he had always been aware of dark forces—as Powys was—had seen evil faces around his bed and run to mediums, seeking communication with any spirit who might be able to lift a corner of the curtain between life and death. So he had listened spellbound, when Powys described meetings with his own ancestors on the night-blackened moors of his native Wales. Both men believed in the reality of the unseen as much through a sense of psychic power as through any faith in a supreme God.

In many of Dreiser's plays and short stories, he has shown his fascination for the supernatural. And in his *Moods,* he had seemed to fly into a cosmic world of mystery, seeking to rise on spirals of wild dream or plunging into a pit of despair, his great spirit often troubled and crying out from depths, as had the psalmist David: *De profundis clamavi ad te Domine . . .*

But now, the very choice that Dreiser had made of looking for design, or placing things in relation to a Creator, had begun to bring order into the chaotic spiritual world he had long inhabited.

When Allan Hunter began the stark recital of the Crucifixion Dreiser followed each step. At last: "Darkness over the land—Jesus cries out. The centurion says, *This was indeed the Son of God . . .* O Father, help us to understand something of this mystery, to partake of this experience."

The Deacons passed the bread, the tiny cups of wine. Dreiser took his, with the others, melted entirely into this humble and holy mood.

The congregation filed slowly out into the California night which, as Allan had pointed out, was about like the nights in Palestine at that time of year; the same kinds of hills and palms and olive trees, the same moon and many of the stars that Jesus must have seen.

It was only when we were going down the street and near our cars that we were aware of each other again.

"Want to come and have coffee with us?" murmured Helen.

Dreiser was silent, still very deep in mood. "No, Teddy must be tired," I answered. And as Hilary and I said good-night, Dreiser gave one of his rumbling sighs:

"Well, that's the most unusual service I've ever been to—"

Dreiser—Master of Tragedy

Dreiser was nearing the climax and final chapters of *The Bulwark.* All that he had written that winter, and over the years before, must come together and be resolved, after the involuntary crime and tragic death of Stewart. How was Dreiser going to manage all this? Step by step, I was privileged to follow the technique, the creative moods of this master of tragedy.

The actual plot of Stewart's ill-fated adventure, Dreiser had found in a newspaper story many years before. For Dreiser always felt that an occurrence from real life carried more conviction with it, more human truth, than any purely imagined disaster. So also, in *An American Tragedy,* he had found his plot in a newspaper story, after studying many typical crimes of our days, as related in the press. Indeed, in his files, he kept many clippings, giving potential plots of great power, which he had come across in his scanning of newspapers.

The crime in question concerned the rape and unintentional murder of a young working-class girl by three rich youths, somewhere in New Jersey. Dreiser felt that this could be fitted into his story of a well-to-do boy, longing for life and sex, driven to extremes by the restraints of his religious and conservative family.

The original clipping was lost or buried somewhere deep in his files, but he remembered the plot with complete clarity: Three young boys, one of whom owned a car (a luxury only for the rich, in those days) had invited a girl out "to have some fun," and had put some kind of knock-out drops, or an aphrodisiac, in her drink. A little while later, she collapsed suddenly, while they were making advances to her. In terror, the boys abandoned her body, thinking that perhaps she had merely fainted. They had been assured that the drops were not harmful. Indeed, an autopsy revealed that she had not died directly because of the drug, but only because of the circumstance that she happened to have a weak heart—a fact which the boys did not know. They were soon traced, and accused of rape and of murder. Since their families were wealthy and prominent, the case was given a great deal of attention. The boys, all in their 'teens, were finally given long sentences of imprisonment.

This frightful coincidence of the drops and the weak heart was the sort of thing that Dreiser could brood over for hours. It was so merciless, so Greek, in its arousal of pity and fear.

But Dreiser did not know what this fatal medicine had been. For probabilities, he consulted with his doctor, and after discussing the effects of various drugs at some length with him, decided on the one best for the purpose.

With the same accuracy of mind, he went, a week later, to the sheriff's office on Fairfax Avenue in Hollywood, to ask the police there certain questions as to the possibilities of Stewart's killing himself in jail. For he had decided that his young hero must be overcome with remorse and so take his own life, before facing his stern, religious father.

He had already dictated a scene for Stewart's suicide, but it did not satisfy him, because it did not seem plausible that the boy would be able to conceal a knife on his person, yet this was the method of suicide he had envisioned.

Two and then three uniformed men gathered around this big, interesting old creature who declared himself to be a writer. They laughed as he apologized for disturbing them, and began to describe as many murders and suicides as he could bear to hear, illustrating their advice about Stewart's case with recent incidents in the County jails.

"Better have'm do it the first day or so in jail. Then he still might have a knife hidden on him. Sometimes, when fellows are locked up temporary, before there is a formal charge against them, they can keep their own clothes—'specially such young boys, and ones that had rich parents with pull that might bail 'em out. Then he might get away with it—sure— why, only last week, right in there, a kid hung himself with his belt—" He pointed to a cage-like cell, open on all sides.

"But if they got into the regular prison, they would be classed as felons, have their own clothes taken away—Yes, better have'm do it the first day—"

Dreiser made a few remarks about his newspaper days, when he had to cover jail stories, and they all laughed and were sorry to see him go out.

However, Dreiser did not find it as easy to write this scene as it had been to talk about it at the Sheriff's Office.

Thinking of what Stewarts' thoughts would be in jail, Dreiser sat in his rocker beside the table, moving almost imperceptibly, silent, grave.

Stewart must do this thing quickly. His despair would, of course, be greatest, at the very first. This was all he said for an hour, talking more or less to himself. Then he began to dictate, slowly but almost without a stop:

"In this situation, hour after hour, facing iron bars on four sides, observing guards parading to and fro, receiving an occasional drink of water . . . while they brooded over their own errors and the miseries of their families, Stewart more depressed and degraded in his own mind than any of the others . . .

"His father! His beloved mother! How to do? How to reduce this shame?"

As Dreiser said these words, he was weighed down by a great load. He was not thinking, what adjective shall I now use? He was simply speaking, with a breaking heart of this boy whom, at that moment, he loved as a son, and with whom he was also fully identifying himself.

When he stopped there was a silence so momentous that no one could dare to break it. If there was a word I had not understood, I could ask him about it later, and of course, he might change much when he went over his typescript. But now he had reached a new level of concentration, almost a communication with his characters:

"How would he ever be able to face his father—considering his father's reproachful language in connection with incidents so trivial that they could not be compared with any phase of this present situation. How could he answer him now, when even then he had not been able to say anything.

"He could not. Under no circumstances, would he be able to confess to the reality of his act. . . .

"And how would he face his mother, who, as he knew, loved him so much that she would forgive his every sin. How face her forgiveness?"

A few more sentences and Dreiser had reached the fatal act:

"And thinking of his beloved mother, the misery of whose love for him he sensed, he proceeded to pry open the larger blade of his pen-knife—and once it was so opened, to turn his back to his neighbor's cell, and saying *Mother, forgive me*—plunged it into his heart."

"And then once more, the blare of the press. The attractive son of the distinguished Barnes family had committed suicide."

"Fortunately, for the—. . . ."*No!*" Dreiser abruptly got up.

"That's enough." Now he had reached the bottom of his story. This was *the works*—he used this slang expression, to laugh at his own sorrow, to gather himself together. There was also relief. He gave one of those great, heaving sighs: "Well—ten dollars!" He held out his hand, in a weary, comic gesture.

Sometimes, when an unusually fine sentence rolled out of him, he would look at me, and smile: "Two dollars" he would add, with sardonic tone. If it was exceptionally good, I would say; "Three." Sometimes, we would raise it to five, and now this special corner was turned. It was worth ten. It was a silly little device to get out of an over-sensitized, almost agonized mood. A few lighter sentences, a little affectionate jesting, and he was covered up again, not raw, bleeding for the grief of the world.

The next chapter was still harder to write. Each character must now be made to feel the shock of Stewart's tragic death.

Sitting in front of a white piece of paper, Dreiser waited for the right idea to begin this recital; then he suddenly thought of the Quaker community, that visible sign of the spiritual forces which alone could make tolerable such dire events.

His main theme, that of the Quaker faith, the *Inner Light*, took hold of his mind, and he dictated, slowly, but without hesitation, the paragraphs about the loving, commiserating attitude of Solon's Quaker friends.

Then he stopped and said: "This is where I could use some of those wonderful passages from the old Quaker books. Get them out, and let's look over them," and the rest of that day was spent in considering these.

The next day, Dreiser wrote about Benecia, and the eldest daughter, Isobel, who returns to her home. His style began to take on that simple, and almost Biblical or Bach-like quality which has great beauty for the discerning, literary ear.

And then at last, Dreiser came to that scene which he had written long ago—perhaps some thirty years before—to see if *The Bulwark* story had in it, the seeds of tragedy.

If there is a passage in modern literature comparable to this, I have not seen it. It can more readily be compared to music, a Beethoven slow movement, or some parts of Bach's *Passion according to St. Matthew.*

I had copied it very slowly, anxious to keep every comma, every spacing of the original. And Dreiser did not change a word of it. The editors of *The Bulwark,* however, saw fit to cut certain phrases and sentences, including Solon's use of the *Lord's Prayer.* I would like to give the original ending here: Solon has come downstairs at mid-night, a candle in his hand, to view the body of his son which has been brought to the living room of their home.

"My boy, My boy" he whispered at last. . . . His mood was added to by a sudden and deep spiritual uncertainty, so much so, that he sank to his knees putting the candle he had carried to light his way on the floor beside him, for he could not hold it, and then beginning to pray only whispering to himself as he did so, Our Father who art in heaven—help me, help me!" And then the tears began to flow from his eyes.

"I have tried" he ventured to say—"but I have not known how to do. Forgive me—and him, my boy—for I have sought to do Thy will and I have erred. Yes, yes, I must

have, Father—Forgive us our trespasses as we forgive
those who trespass against us—Perhaps I have not under-
stood. Perhaps I have been too hard"—and he sobbed.

But at that moment, Benecia who had heard him leave
his room and followed him, came forward, her own eyes
wet, her heart aching for him as for Stewart and putting
her arms around him said: "Come, Solon, Please. Come
Darling. . . . You have done all that a father should
always. . . . Come, rest. You must not weep. Come, Dar-
ling, come—" and she drew him so affectionately that
at last he rose, she taking up the palely flaring candle—
and went with her to their room, sobbing as he did so,
yet less and less as he went because of Benecia's plead-
ings.

Yet down below in the great living room was his boy,
his favorite son—and dead, by his own hand. And the
sorrow! the shame! Almost, like Jesus on the Cross, he
was ready to cry, "My God! My God! Why hast Thou
forsaken me—"

There remained only the last two chapters of *The Bulwark*
to be done. During the next days, Dreiser dictated some of
the most disarmingly simple, curious passages of literary
sad-music which he had yet composed. Something different
in style from any of his other novels—pages of emotion which
can hardly be read without a deliberate slowing down of the
modern reader's tempo. Since many were cut or dropped out
entirely by the editors, I would like to quote some. Yet, out
of their context, they seem incongruous, and one must know
Solon, as Dreiser has shown him to us throughout the novel,
to understand this depth of mood, the background of Quaker
faith, and the new element of acceptance and harmony with
nature which Dreiser was creating for the first time. Again,
I cannot help comparing Dreiser's quality of expression in
these last chapters, to that of some of the minor works of
Bach which lay for so many years, unappreciated, considered
dull or stumbling. (I think particularly of that now popular

fragment from *The Organ Buchlein,* long ignored: *Come, now, Savior of the Heathen.*)

But all was not dirge for the dead. There was the living tragedy of Etta's desertion by her artist-lover, and her return to the side of her father who now, in the humility of his own grief, had no reproach left in him, but only love. Etta herself, however, does not seek to escape her own conscience. Here Dreiser brings her tragedy into focus, as a part of the theme of the whole novel. For it is the lovely, sensitive Etta who in the end, emerges as the true, spiritual daughter of her *Bulwark* father. But first she, too, must go through the depths of suffering. Slowly, Dreiser had dictated:

How bitterly she now reproached herself for her part in Stewart's downfall, she who had first stolen her mother's jewelry and run away from home—and later abandoned herself to every desire of the body. If only she could weep in Kane's arms tonight, be joined with him in the love that had meant everything to her . . . But he had left.

Everywhere she had failed and was alone, standing in her own mind, rejected and forsaken.

By what deceptive road—to what miserable well of disappointment had she been led,—and this by moods and desires which she herself had not created and even now, did not know how to master—As yet, she had not learned that beauty of spirit must hang upon a cross."

Financial theme—Resignation from the Bank
It seemed as if Dreiser had forgotten his financial theme, but one morning he dictated a passage which suddenly came back to it. He had plunged already into the nature moods, which were to lift the heavy burden of tragedy, but as yet he could not manage to make them do so.

Only rarely did Solon walk out into the garden . . . For the sight of the flowers and trees and birds, and even the fishes in the stream all the more emphasized the life

that Stewart, but for his tragic folly, might still be en-
joying. For it was spring and here was the great Creative
Force, showering beauty on every hand—His boy! His
boy!

Only now and then, in between his darkest thoughts,
would intrude some aspects of the practical world which,
up to this time, misery had excluded. One of the things
that returned sharply to his consciousness was that he
was after all, connected with a bank ..."

Here Dreiser stopped abruptly, and got up.

At last, Dreiser had roused himself, as he had determined
to arouse Solon from his long pain. "Now," he said, with a
lift of voice, "let's have a look at the financial section, and
see where we can bring in the last scene at the bank."

This was another turning point for Dreiser in the writing
of the novel. The darkness of his mood gave way to the business of winding up his financial theme. He got a certain glee
out of imagining what Solon would say to surprise and con-
found, his cold-blooded bank associates.

He wrote two scenes before he was satisfied that Solon had
put in simple language all that he, and Dreiser himself, felt
about the injustice of modern banking manipulations, and
especially the misuse of funds by Solon's bank, from which
he then dramatically resigns.

Benecia—Theme of Love and Unity with Creative Force
Now when Dreiser came to the little house in the morning,
he would usually go out and sit in the patio. Then slowly, he
would begin to talk about his work, telling me something
that had occurred to him in the night, or to speak so fluently
about the coming scenes, that I would get a pencil, even though
he was not dictating. Lines came to him that were completely
beautiful. Once, when I did not have a piece of paper, I wrote
one out on a white box, not wanting to jump up and disturb
his meditative mood.

Sometimes, he did not do more than a page or two of his
book, but the sense of rush was over. He was living fully but

calmly in each moment, each day. Thinking deeply of life itself, he seemed to be on the border of a great understanding and simplification of all the questions and principles that had long been warring in his mind.

It was spring, which even in Southern California comes over the hills with a new light step. Masses of ice-grass and flowers were blooming; the little peach trees along the walk, were covered with blossoms. This all seemed miraculous to Dreiser, as if he had never seen it before. His love of nature had become something more—a sense of unity with the *Creative Force* he now believed was behind it and which he now could identify with these Quakers and their faith.

Dreiser's skill as a tragedian had decreed that Benecia must die first, and then Solon. But would this mean that Solon's heart would be torn again? No, a different factor had come in. Dreiser looked up from meditation in the patio; a queer, intense gleam in his eye:

"Don't you think that a religious person—someone like Solon, would think of Benecia as *not really dead?* It was harder to feel that way about Stewart, but Benecia?" He was questioning himself, rather than me. I waited for him to go on.

Then he dictated two of the most beautiful passages which are intact in the present edition of *The Bulwark* (see Chapter Sixty-four). Benecia was in the presence of *Him in whom there is no shadow of turning.*

A few days before, Dreiser had asked me to find the first Chapter of the Epistle of James, which he said contained his favorite definition of religion, which he also quotes in *The Bulwark* (Chapter Sixty-five, James I:27).

Then he had gone back to the 17th verse of the same chapter: "Every good gift and every perfect gift is from above and cometh down from the Father of Lights with whom is no variableness, neither *shadow of turning.*" The phrase had stuck in his strange spirit, so troubled often on the surface, yet now far down, so very clear and still, and the image had welled up, as did many verses of the Bible, in these final chapters, coming unexpectedly from his hidden store.

Now he had reached a new level in his story. The tragedies have occurred, and Solon has accepted them—*Not my will but Thine*. Moreover, he is possessed by an overwhelming sense of peace. The result of such a mood is not negative, as Dreiser saw it, but generative of a spiritual power which can best be described by the word *Love*.

Dreiser himself had always felt this love—for nature, for science, for the sea, for small flowers. For animals and people he had felt it, too, and this was perhaps a reason for his seemingly over-strong love for women. Because sex was also strong in him, his love for people often took this form. But even if mixed with sex, his love was of a broad and universal sort—a warm emanation or vibration that was felt by all who came near him. And it had risen to great heights in his love for the needy and unfortunate, and had inspired all his political attitudes and struggles.

But now it was the quieter, fuller aspect of this *Love* which he wished to give Solon, to raise his spirit. The pages about his going out into the garden and observing a green fly, marvelling over its color and movement, implying the wisdom and art of the Creative Impulse, were dictated very slowly, as if Dreiser was expressing his own belief.

Then there was the story of the snake which had run across the toe of Dreiser's shoe, at Mt. Kisco; he wished to use it here, as an experience of Solon's in his garden. When he began dictating, I was surprised that instead of telling the incident as if it were happening directly to Solon, he told it first through the eyes of Etta and Isobel, who are watching their father through the window. Dreiser wanted them to be included in the experience as they would not have been had he merely related it to them afterwards. This was because Solon's mood of love to all created things was now especially concentrated in his daughters, and the snake furnished him with a point at which to draw them all together. When they questioned him about the strange fact that the snake seemed to have responded to his voice, Dreiser was able to make Solon state what might have been the key to his own *Philosophy*, had he been able to finish it: "Daughter, I know

now that we know so little of *that infinite something of which
we are a part*—and that there are more languages spoken
than we have knowledge of."
    And he spoke further to them of *the need of love to all
created things.* . . .

Another device that Dreiser used to draw Etta into closer
understanding with her father, was to have her read portions
of *John Woolman's Journal* to him. We got out the volume,
marked by Dreiser in many places. John Greenleaf Whittier
had said in an introduction to the works of Woolman: "His
religion was love. His whole existence and all his passions
were love."
    "That's what I want to start with," said Dreiser. At first,
he was only thinking of using the last part of Woolman's
vision. But after poring over it for perhaps an hour, he said,
"No, I've got to use it all. It has everything in it, whether
people understand it or not."
    In his extraordinary vision, as he lay near death, Woolman
had seen "a mass of human beings in as great misery as they
could be and live, and that I was mixed with them and that
henceforth I might not consider myself as a distinct or separate being . . ." This represented the mass of the southern
slaves, for Woolman, long before the days of Lincoln, worked
to abolish slavery.
    "I was then carried in spirit to the mines where poor, op-
pressed people were digging rich treasures for those called
Christians, and heard them blaspheme the name of Christ
at which I grieved, for His Name was precious to me. I was
then informed that these heathen had been told that those
who oppressed them were followers of Christ and they said
among themselves, 'if Christ directed them to use us in this
way, then Christ is a cruel tyrant . . .' "
    Then comes the passage explaining the words he had heard
"John Woolman is dead which meant nothing more than the
death of my own will."
    This question of the *will* had always haunted Dreiser, and
he expresses it here, in the simple Christian terms of Wool-

man, who has deliberately sought to give his will over to God's will. Dreiser had always believed in the direction of the human will by a superior force. He used to call it Destiny, or blind determinism, feeling that man himself had nothing to say in the matter, that man does not have the free-will to resist. Perhaps this was the very evidence of the God-pull on him, of that closeness to the Creative Force, which he had always felt and which he now recognized.

In any case, he was saying something here, through Woolman, that he had never said before. He had seen through these Quakers, the meaning of God's *Love,* which was also Christ's Love and identification with a suffering world. He was saying that the way of Christ was the way of the submitted, or subjected will. But he let Woolman say it for him, as Woolman himself, had quoted the words of the Apostle Paul: "I am crucified with Christ, nevertheless I live; yet not I, but Christ liveth in me."

So Dreiser wove another mystery into the rich texture of *The Bulwark.*

Etta

It remained for Etta, brooding alone, to conclude Dreiser's philosophy of love and mystical closeness to a *Creator.* She felt that her own frustrated passion could now be transformed into this universal love shared by Woolman and her father, and it could reach out to the mystery of some final union, or even a partial union, which could bring her joy:

It was this greater love which . . . was moving through her father and which had literally raised him out of the black shadow of grief. . . . Now she felt it moving through her, too, and she was ready to receive it.

In this love and unity with nature, as she now sensed, there was nothing fitful or changing or disappointing— Nothing that glowed one minute and was gone the next. This love was rather as constant as nature itself, everywhere the same, in sunshine or in darkness, the filtered

*splendor of the dawn, the seeded beauty of the night. It
was an intimate relation to the very heart of being.*

Finale

Now the final pages could be written. Dreiser had long thought
about the scenes which would bring Solon to a realistic end.
Dreiser had wanted Solon to look at himself in the mirror
while shaving. He was to use the kind of old-fashioned razor
which Dreiser always used himself—and say: "Where is that
poor old man whose son killed himself?"—as if he had reached
a kind of detachment from his own body, or identity.

Etta, standing beside him, is sadly puzzled. "She waits on
him, as might a servant," he had dictated in an early outline,
wanting to bring out the closeness of their final relationship.

Solon's death was another one of those scenes that seemed
actually to be going on in Dreiser's inner vision, and to which
he had only to attend, in order to describe.

The whole passage in its stark originality, was spoken out
gravely, with frequent, easy pauses. Yet nothing was lacking,
to bring all Dreiser's themes together. Once, Solon mur-
murs, almost as if dreaming: "The poor and the banks . . .
the poor and the banks . . ."

When Solon asks suddenly, as if to a stranger: "If thee
does not turn to the Inner Light, where will thee go?" Etta
turns around to see if anyone has entered the room. That is
all that is said, but there is the implication that Death has
come in. Solon's eyes then close. But Etta speaks another
line before she looks up and sees that he is dead. This is
the simple, subtle literary style of which Dreiser was master.

Finis

"And so at last, the final obsequies for Solon Barnes at
Thornbrough, that originally so beloved home of his father
and mother and after his father's death, of him and
Benecia . . ."

Again, Dreiser created some indefinable literary music
by going back to his first theme, the announcement of his
first *motif*, and sweeping through the years, as a master of

symphony picks up all the musical skeins of his composition for the last thematic climax.

Dreiser had written two versions of his *Finis* in pencil and brought them to me to type, in the middle of the winter. He looked over them now, and combined the best sentences of both. Each had started with the same, long, backward-going passage.

Then Etta, too, must look back and make her sweep of emotion go from her earliest dreams to her lover's desertion —and now the loss of her father whom she had grown to love.

At last came the line that Dreiser had been waiting for Etta to say at the end of his novel, for more than thirty years:

"I am not crying for myself, nor for father—I am crying for *life.*"

Another, curious long sentence brings this cry to a natural close. The family walks out toward the carriages that will take them to the burial ground.

It was done; the lives of the Barnes' were rounded into literature.

X. WORK COMPLETED
—a cosmic tool

Another month and *The Bulwark* must be ready for the publisher. Dreiser was checking over the second rough draft, adding in pencilled corrections.

One night in his home, he suddenly had a severe pain which turned out to be a serious kidney condition. His doctor warned him that he must take better care of himself, eliminate all alcoholic drinks and not mix drinks and medicines, as he had been doing.

It was several days before he came back to work in the little house. He had a chastened and subdued look, but his mind had not been as brilliant all winter. He glanced through whole sections of his novel; everything was as clear to him as objects on a fall day: *This* must go out; *This* must stay; That—"put a piece of paper in the typewriter, I'll dictate that over right now . . ."

And so everything that had been doubtful or unsatisfying to him was put in order during those intense days. Never had he worked harder, felt happier, surer of his art. When he looked over the first introduction he had done for Putnam, he was amazed: "Did I let this go to Balch?" he questioned, "I must have been crazy when I wrote some of this."

The long introduction which he had written, drawing heavily on Rufus Jones' recital of his own childhood, was

very repetitious, and Dreiser had decided in the beginning
of our work on *The Bulwark* manuscripts to leave it aside
until we had finished the book as a whole, and then he would
better see how much of the introduction was needed. Now he
cut it drastically. He also asked me to check and cut repe-
titions, but he did not want me to copy it. He said he had
promised Helen that she might type this section, since she
had originally typed it for him, and wanted to have some part
in the work.

When I was busy making a third typescript and had
almost finished the long job, Helen came up one day to get
the introduction she wished to copy. Dreiser was not with her,
and she was quite upset because so much had been cut of the
original chapters which Dreiser had dictated to her. I tried
to say that they had been very repetitious, but this did not
please her. I was too rushed at the time to think much of
this. Helen had seldom done literary work for Dreiser,
having so many other duties to perform and having had her
own life, often away from his. But later, I realized that she
now felt as capable of helping him as anyone else, and that
she resented particularly that this introduction had been cut
and changed. It must have had a bearing on the way she
subsequently acted, when the proofs of *The Bulwark* were
sent for correction.

Now there was only the task of checking the third type-
script, which Dreiser resolutely set about. He never liked
such routine work. Once a book was out of its creative stage,
he was almost bored with it.

"I want to do a series of sketches on why women leave
their husbands," he said one morning. "For goodness' sake,
don't do anything until we've finished these corrections," I
pleaded. But his mind was already leaping ahead, the cocoon
around *The Bulwark,* broken.

Dreiser would take one chapter at a time out into the
patio, to brood over or revise, while I was typing in the house.
Sometimes, I would hear him humming to himself, or see that
he was looking off, over the hill.

He got amusement out of watching my son's guinea pigs

that ran loose around the patio, peering from under the hedge, or venturing forth to eat carrots he would offer them. "Come out and watch these little things," he would call, and make me sit awhile beside him.

The manuscript was handed in on May 3, 1945. The next day, Helen suggested, with her typical generosity, that we take a week-end trip to Mexico, to celebrate. We motored to Ensenada, the white beach across the border.

Now Dreiser let Helen accept any invitation she wished. He was glad to meet his friends again, and he went to see Elizabeth.

Elizabeth

About this time, a friend and collaborator of Dreiser's, Elizabeth Kearney had come back into town. There was a romantic quality about her that was particularly appealing to Dreiser. Her features were small, with eyes set far apart in a pale, sensitive brow. She had Irish dark hair and eyes— different from the quality of Latin darkness, a Celtic airiness of voice and manner, and she played the harp. Dreiser loved to go to her small Spanish-style house, where a tall, gold concert harp stood in the corner. She would play folk-songs or melodies appropriate to this strange instrument, accompanying them with a small, harmonious voice, creating an effect of music both primitive and modern, poignant, having a bare poetry of its own. So it seemed to me once, as I heard her play it, watching her small, white hands pluck the heavy, singing strings and seeing her delicate face through them, as through a Spanish *reja*.

Dreiser had first met Elizabeth for a brief moment in New York at the funeral of her twin brother Pat Kearney, young writer of great promise, who had just then dramatized *An American Tragedy* for its successful Broadway production. Elizabeth was then happily married, with three small children.

Shortly after her twin brother's death, her young husband was stricken with pneumonia. She was left a widow with almost no funds, and an undeveloped talent for writing.

She had come to Hollywood, hoping to write for the movies, and got in touch with Dreiser shortly after he came to California, in 1938.

Then came their successful cooperation on an ice-show for Sonia Henie and finally a script for *The Banks of the Wabash* which came out under the title: *My Gal Sal;* the name of another Paul Dresser song which was used in the production.

Charlie Chaplin

Dreiser had known Charlie Chaplin since his first visit to Hollywood with Helen in the early 'twenties. That spring, Helen gave a little dinner party for him and his vivacious, young wife, Oona, daughter of the playwright Eugene O'Neill.

Clifford Odets and his wife, Florence, Sylvia Sydney, The Russian Consul in Los Angeles, Esther McCoy Tobey and Berkeley Tobey were the other guests.

My son Hilary and I were also invited, and came early to help with the preparations. Helen had an excellent old Hungarian cook whom she employed on such occasions, but could not find anyone to wait on the table. This Hilary volunteered to do and attired in a white coat, he looked tall and acted with almost professional dignity, much to the amusement of the guests who knew him.

Wharton Esherick's long, graceful table was used for the eight *couverts*. After Vodka and canapés, a delectable Hungarian Chicken Paprika was served, with excellent Chilean wine.

Conversation was animated. At Dreiser's end of the table, Charlie Chaplin was sounding off against religion—at least against certain actions of some churches he had knowledge of, in England.

Dreiser did not contradict his opinions, nor did he agree with them wholly. But he did not argue that night, did not thunder, as he used to of old, when some subject stirred him. He was very quiet, intensely interested, really animated by a love for this fiery Chaplin who talked so colorfully, dynamically—leaping from humor to hatred, from irony to conviction, with his irrepressible actor-skill.

After dinner, Chaplin was amused to see Hilary slip in, his white jacket exchanged for a dark one. He went up to him, laughing and shook his hand: "Thank you, my son, for your service!"

A minute later, he jumped up to illustrate a Japanese *Noh* play. Charlie Chaplin had visited Tokyo for some months before the war, to make a study of the classic form of the Japanese drama which dealt mostly with the traditional feuds and conflicts of the *Samurai*. The play he now described to us with words and gestures, became as real as if we had been seated in a Japanese Theatre.

A Japanese couple in their small home receive a desperate friend for whom political enemies are searching. As they hear his pursuers outside the house, they hide their friend in a flimsy wardrobe in the center of the wall. The political warriors, flourishing huge swords, enter and search the house. The couple converse with them, hoping to distract their minds.

They are about to leave, when they notice the wardrobe. Without bothering to open it, one of the warriors arrogantly runs his sword through its paper-like door, and pulling it out again, looks to see if there is blood on it—(Magnificent, chill-evoking gesture on the part of Chaplin!)

There is no blood, and the warriors leave, apologizing to the couple for having disturbed them. The couple hasten to open the door of the wardrobe, and out falls their poor friend, pierced through, but dying happily, because he has not been discovered. "But how was it that they found no blood on the sword?" they inquire.

"As they pulled it out—I grasped it—wiping it with my kimono, *like this*—" Chaplin made a gesture of diabolic cunning in the midst of agony.

Dreiser gave a tremendous growl—one of those great sounds with which he responded to strong emotion, an explosion of delight at Chaplin's performance.

Charlie was wound up, too, by his act and our enthusiasm. He went on, to describe experiences in India, in London. He

told of his own boyhood in the slums of that city, and showed
how he had taken flowers from an old pedlar who could not
dispose of them, and sold them all in a short time. He represented himself as a miserable orphan, whereas in reality his
parents were very much alive but cared little for him. After
a few such successes, he decided he could become an actor,
and procured a job in vaudeville.

It was with a third-rate troupe that he came to the United
States. When Hollywood of the early days offered him eight
hundred dollars a week, he said he did not want eight hundred,
thinking he would not know what to do with it. But they
thought he wanted more and offered him a thousand!

Yet with all the money that rolled into his hands since, he
he had not become spoiled, not indifferent to poverty. On the
contrary, it was obvious as he talked that his heart was
still with the poor of London, and the victims of the struggle
for money, all over the world.

Inevitably, the discussion became political. The Soviets
were not radical enough for Chaplin; they had compromised
too much, according to him. Others defended the views of
modern Russia. Again, strangely enough, Dreiser did not
thunder, did not take over the argument with one of his
famous diatribes in favor of the Soviet Union. He seemed
more interested in listening to the younger men. Now more
and more, though not always, he was beginning to retreat to
a higher place, feeling that the final reality of things was
spiritual rather than intellectual, that truth was hardly
debatable, if not *sensed,* perceived by an inner sense.

It was after midnight when the party broke up. Dreiser
hated to see Charlie go—this delightful soul, always in flux
between comedy and tragedy, overflowing with creative
energy like Dreiser's own, but having a more facile charm,
a contagious volatility. He had given us a gala evening.

Paul Robeson

Paul Robeson came to Los Angeles at this time, in his famous
performance of Shakespeare's *Othello,* which Dreiser had
seen in New York the spring before.

These two had been friends for twenty or more years, since the young Robeson had sought Dreiser out in his Tenth Street studio, to ask what he thought of his interpretation of *The Emperor Jones.* This was Paul's first role on the stage, and the first production of Eugene O'Neill's sensational play at the old Provincetown Theatre in Greenwich Village.

Helen had arranged a tea for about fifteen people, to meet Robeson and when he came into the room, the simple impact of his presence was enough to seem to make everyone else shrink into anonymity. Dreiser himself was the only temperament to match him, and soon the two were talking together as if no one else were in the room.

What they were saying was enough to give everybody pause, for Robeson told Dreiser of his travels to every part of the world, to study the conditions and problems of the Negro race. He talked to Dreiser as I think he would have spoken to very few people, his natural eloquence expressing the burden on his heart for all his African brothers as well as for the American, and for all the human race.

Dreiser was drinking in his every word, laughing and scowling, with that intense participation he could turn on and radiate, like an electric current. He had always been deeply concerned about the Negroes in America, but he had not realized to what extent Robeson had investigated the hardships, and also the power of other Negro communities, and the new spirit arising amongst them. Indeed, many of the things Robeson said at that time were prophetic.

When Robeson realized it was time for him to go back to his theatre, Dreiser embraced him and held him back with his hands: "Sing one thing for me, Paul, on the way out."

Robeson leaned back on the long living-room table, his arms bracing him in an easy pose, and slowly opened up his voice, like the stops of an organ, first low and soft, then louder, seemingly unlimited in potential power. *Old Man River*—as if singing before a great audience, he brought out all the lilt, the pathos, the revolt, the deep philosophy of that song. Did he sing so beautifully for Dreiser because he sensed that he might never see him again?

Dreiser stood watching him in that old, fierce pose, his legs apart like a sailor's, his arms akimbo, his eyes under the heavy brows, ablaze with love and admiration.

The Stoic

There was about a month left before my son finished his school year and we would return to Connecticut. Dreiser wanted to continue our working arrangement and there were a number of things he wanted me to do.

For one thing, he wanted to go over the manuscript of *The Stoic*, third book in his *Trilogy of Desire*, of which *The Financier* and *The Titan* were already well-known studies of the famous and infamous Cowperwood, business magnate of Philadelphia and Chicago. The third book was to follow his life to its very end, and tell of his financial ventures in London. But Dreiser had never finished it, simply because he had not found the time to do so.

The material for this book was far from as bulky or abundant as that for *The Bulwark*. It was contained in a medium-sized grocery box!

Again, Dreiser's hero was to be Charles T. Yerkes, whom he had called Cowperwood, and whose business ventures and amatory escapades he had paraphrased in the first novels of the Trilogy.

Dreiser had actually made a trip to London to gather data on the financial history which went into this true, or based-on-truth story of Yerkes' last great business adventure, the building of the London subway system. In this grocery box were bundles of financial statements from subsidiary companies which Yerkes owned or controlled; press clippings from London papers of that period, and a detailed map of London, with its few old, unrelated subway lines, and the new proposal which revolutionized the transportation of that day.

Here were also elaborate outlines of the lives of the principal characters in *The Stoic*, giving the dates when they made moves, back and forth over the Atlantic.

Yerkes, or Cowperwood; Aileen, his wife; Berenice, one

of his mistresses; another protégé who was an actress; and still another, who was studying music; Tollifer, society *gigolo,* paid by Cowperwood to dance attendance on his wife, so that she would not so greatly mind what he was doing— all these had biographical outlines drawn up for them, as if they were historically important personages.

This seemed a rigid and completely un-Dreiserian way of marshalling up a novel. But more distressing still, the type-script of the story, extending up to the time of the maturing of the London Subway deal, and the settling of Berenice on a country estate near the city, seemed not at all like Dreiser's way of writing. He admitted that it had been *fixed up* by someone.

(This reminded me of the famous story told by Horace Liveright, the publisher, about a Dreiser manuscript which he had handed in. It was given to a young college girl editor to prepare for the printer. But soon she brought it into Liveright's office, saying that it was so bad that she thought it was better just to rewrite it completely rather than try any small revisions!)

This typescript covered some interesting ground, but it did not ring true. Dreiser was never at home in describing great luxury or the lives and psychology of the rich. They were too far away from his own experience, even though now he belonged to the aristocracy of genius. Nor did the character of Berenice seem real or alluring, but inexcusably affected and dull.

Another thing was obvious: that Dreiser could never again wrestle with all the facts and figures which could make the financial story of the subway convincing and dramatic. Nor did he feel interested in doing so. He was chiefly concerned with winding up this man's life, and he had fascinating de-tails about his return to New York, when he felt he was dying, and about the way his wife refused to take him into his own home. That his friends actually sneaked Yerkes' corpse into the house at night, after he died in a hotel, was confidential information Dreiser had gathered through old newspaper friends. This was a climax too good to miss! So Dreiser felt he could make a human interest ending to his *Trilogy*, without bothering about too many business details.

He also felt that it would be best to leave out the characters of the two other mistresses of Cowperwood, in order not to make the whole situation too confusing, the deadly conflict between Aileen and Berenice being quite sufficient to provide the drama which took place at the end of his life.

To see how he could simplify and finish this book, we made an outline of some fifteen chapters, which woud cover essential points, between the end of the typescript and Cowperwood's death in New York. This Dreiser felt, was sufficient.

The spirit that emanated from this book was disturbing. It was so cold-blooded and false, so different from *The Bulwark*.

"If I come back," I said, "I would rather see what you can do with the *Philosophy* file."

He had also hoped to do a few more short stories, based on some of his Quaker material, and to write the story of Vernier, the Belgian pastor, about whom Allan Hunter had sent him notes. But now he was afraid that he had put too much religious feeling in *The Bulwark* and that people would not understand it. He had just received a discouraging letter from Louise Campbell, who had helped him edit *An American Tragedy*, and to whom he had sent a carbon copy of *The Bulwark*. She had utterly failed to understand his new attitudes. And he had heard nothing as yet from his new publisher.

One day he sat looking at *The Stoic* papers in a very gloomy mood. He said he did not feel well, and this was always the case with Dreiser when he was sinking into a depression. I offered to stay on a few more weeks, to help him finish *The Stoic*, but this did not cheer him.

The next day, however, the pressure of his mood had lessened. He went out and sat in the patio, and everything straightened itself in his mind.

As for *The Stoic*, he said, it was best to put it aside now, since we did not feel happy about it, after working on *The Bulwark:*

"I don't know if it's a good book," he said, humbly of
The Bulwark, "But I don't think I could have done it any
other way." And after that, he was serene again, watching
the birds and the hill, with its swaying grass and graceful
trees.

Short Stories

For a day or so, we busied ourselves looking over and
bundling up the original *Bulwark* material. Then standing
by the car, as he was about to go home, Dreiser had an idea:
"I've thought of the title for a story we could do—*The Total
Stranger.*" I asked him what he had in mind. He stood with
one hand on the door of the car, and with the other, made
gestures which accompanied his sketch:

"It's about a man who happens to get a room in a boarding-
house. He's right next to a couple that keep quarreling all
the time. He can hear them through the walls; it's just a
cheap place.

"Finally, he can't stand it any more. He's a stranger, and
all that, but it's the same situation that he had with his own
wife. And she went off and left him. Now he sees the same
thing happening to them—and this woman, too, will go off and
the man will realize too late what he's lost. . . ."

"Can he save them in time?" I asked.

"Well, it's not at simple as that. I'll start writing it out,
and see what happens."

The next morning, he had several pages of pencilled manuscript for me to type. Then he talked on about this man, and
I jotted down what he said. Just as he had seen Solon in that
hotel room in Wisconsin and knew what he would do, so now
he saw *The Total Stranger* plainly before him:

"He's a mechanic or skilled worker of some sort, maybe an
electrician. He's clean, middle aged, nice-looking without
being handsome. He's big, broad-shouldered. Bigger than the
man next door who's abusing his wife. The husband is small,
wiry, dark and nervous—the kind who talks a lot, but it
wouldn't take much to lick him.

"The woman is plain, but nice looking. She has a good

body; she's in her thirties, wears her hair very simply, just a house dress, no fuss—"

So the story was born out of his thought around a title. Often, Dreiser would get an idea in this way, and test it out, to see if it would "hold water." He never felt that a good title was enough to go on, but it was a starting point, if you could think of appropriate action to go with it.

Once we talked about a story idea, *Sign in the Fog,* but he abandoned it because it did not have enough plot. "Things have got to happen," he said. "You can put all the thought and emotion you want into characters, but they're not convincing to the reader unless something really happens to them. I mean real drama, an accident, murder, death, change of some sort to hold a reader's attention."

The work on *The Total Stranger* made Dreiser think in terms of short stories. As he was riding along in the car one morning, he said slowly and low:

"I have a swell title—*That which I Feared*—"

"*Has come upon me?*" I questioned, trying to complete the quotation from the Bible.

"Not necessarily. It might be treated either way. Something you had feared might come upon you, or it might never happen at all. The *fear* is the thing—"

And after a while, he said it over, like a grave musical phrase, in his darkest tone, accompanied by a wave of the long hand: "*That which I Feared*—"

There was about Dreiser at this time, such a brimming quality that it is hard to find words for his mood. I had never seen him so near happiness, so at one with nature and the creative force. His book was done. Though he was not sure of its critical acceptance—he was always truly humble about that—he had heard that Doubleday would publish it the following winter. Whatever comments or editings might follow, he did not worry about them now. He had delivered himself of this story of a man's life and death, and put enough of himself in it to feel purged and freer than he had felt for a long time.

The fact that he would not rest now, but worked along on the short stories, was only an indication of that joy-in-creation which had carried him through life, literally dragging him through his worst depressions as well as bearing him up to his hard-won successes. There was nothing that satisfied him so much as to feel he was fulfilling that strange destiny which had called him to be a writer.

For throughhout his life, he had felt he was being impelled, or actually driven, by a force beyond himself. That he was a "cosmic tool," as he put it, a part of some cosmic purpose.

This was both his greatness and his weakness. In his work, he was sustained and guided by this belief, but this did not keep him from making a plan, from doing his best to cooperate with this force. He wrote with pain and care, waiting with endless patience, at times, for the right idea, the right words to come to him out of the depth of some unknown but superior wisdom. When John Cowper Powys called him a *mediumistic genius,* this is what he meant.

But in his personal life, he had not taken the same care, the same amount of time, to order his days. After his first unsuccessful marriage, he began to live voraciously by his emotions, avoiding plans and decisions whenever possible. He wanted always to keep free to respond to the strongest impulse of the moment.

His awareness, his physical and spiritual sensitivities were so great that he was spoiled by them, as a person possessing great riches is tempted to spend and squander. If he had chosen to conserve his spiritual resources and discipline himself, with the great love and compassion which was natural to him, he might have become a St. Augustine, or a Saint Francis.

Instead, he blundered exuberantly along, believing that destiny was pushing him, anyway. The Satyr in him was as strong as the Saint. Once Helen said, with her refreshing directness: "Something has him by the foot."

Perhaps it was the women in Dreiser's life who suffered

most from this duality in his nature. They were drawn to him because he loved women, understood them, appreciated each feminine quality and gave them, for the moment, all the poetry and fulfillment that a creative person can bring to love.

Even in his books, women sensed this, and his fan mail would have surprised anyone but a movie star. Even as late as the year he died, a woman reader had written him a letter full of yearning, and in a curious, sardonic mood, he had answered her with one line from Genesis: *Male and female created He them.*

A short time afterwards she arrived in Los Angeles having come some thousand miles to see him. She was a tall, dark handsome woman, lonely in soul, one of the many drawn to him by the deep magnetic love in him for all people.

But many were injured by this love, wanting it more durably, for themselves. Dreiser never wantonly hurt any creature, much less a woman whom he had held in the light of romance. But in him was always that varietistic impulse which he has ascribed to so many of his characters. And because he felt driven by an exterior power, to fulfill a pattern not his own, he did not feel that it was obligatory, or even possible, for him to plan his emotional life, or to limit himself to one love.

To Helen, on the contrary, must go the credit for having made a plan for her life; devotion and unrelenting adherence to Dreiser. And so, out of all the tangled emotions, and in spite of separations and almost unsurmountable defeats, her love emerges clear and triumphant, a thing of great, human beauty.

We leave Hollywood

Dreiser came to work each day of the last week in the little house. Perhaps we spent more time in the patio, trying to make light of my departure. Knowing how Dreiser felt about making plans, I did not want to promise to come back to Hollywood in the fall. Nor did he insist on a promise. He did not want me to go at all. He went over the reasons, my aging mother, my son's interests at home.

"If you go you may not come back," he said glumly, as if it were something beyond our control. At any rate, I made an arrangement to reserve the little house for another year, the owners to live in it during the summer.

Nevertheless, a sense of destiny hung over those last days. We had reached a plateau of work and companionship, where time seemed suspended.

One day, we talked about Solon and Benecia, and their innocence and love made us feel infinitely sad. Could one have lived one's life differently? Certainly, he could not have been a Solon. He had had no Benecia—yet, how beautiful the pure in heart!

I tried to make him say something about religion, but readily as he would discuss politics or philosophy he seldom said anything about his feelings for people, intimate relationships, or things that touched his heart. Now it was the same with his changing belief. It went far too deep.

Still, a word here and there, a grumbled phrase could sometimes show what was below the surface of his mind. There were certain old-fashioned expressions he liked to use, because they had passed from the cliché stage to an almost Aesop-like exactness of connotation.

For instance, as he raised his glass to drink some horrible mixture of wines or whiskey, he would say with sardonic tone, yet frightening realism: *"The Drunkard's Grave. . . ."*

In the same way he had stood in the patio door, looking down at me, with that intense scowl, the day after he had taken Communion on Good Friday, in Allan Hunter's church, and murmured: "Well—*The Mourner's Bench. . . .*"

This was the humble, reverent Dreiser, the man who belonged to no religion, but took all truth and beauty and love into his heart. The love that was not for one person only, but for all mankind and for the Creator of all. This love was nothing new in him, for it had run all through his life, and he had expressed it in a poem, one of his *Moods,* many years before. This timeless love that all could share:

ST. FRANCIS TO HIS GOD:

Hold me close to your heart
Always
And let me whisper
Sing
Breathe
Dance
Act out
My love to you
Over and over.

*   *   *

You are the wonder flower
Of all the passions
All the ills
All the joys
Of life
You—
Who create
And destroy
Extend
And recall
Demand
And repay

*   *   *

In your expressions
And extensions
Your suns,
Moons
Stars
Your universes
In your flowers,
And jewels
Your behemoths
And midges
Your doers
And undoers
Your wars
And long restful periods
Of dream-like peace
Have I not seen,
As in eyes,
Heard,
As from lips speaking

Felt,
As in the very arms of love,
The strength
And the bliss
Of your miraculous love
And by it
Been exalted
Above this world?

XI. LETTERS LITERARY AND POLITICAL
—Dreiser and Russia

At Dreiser's request, I went to see his publisher when I got back to New York. I discovered that Louise Campbell had sent from Philadelphia a much edited copy of *The Bulwark*, with most of the religious parts eliminated! Donald Elder, the young editor in charge of Dreiser's work, agreed that this would take the very heart out of the novel. He had written to Dreiser, asking his permission to reinstate the cuts.

Then a long letter came to me from Dreiser from Portland, where he had motored with Helen to visit her sick mother:

"I received your letter concerning Doubleday and the editor, Donald Elder, and the fact that the book might not come out before February first next—a period of time which to me seems excessive, but which, all things considered, I am not inclined to quarrel with, . . . seeing that we slaved together over so many phases of it and that later, I sent the Ms. to James Farrell, the critic, who seemed to feel that it had some minor errors or inconsistencies which he wanted to correct and even suggested how it should be done."

"Here, Helen's mother being so ill, I could do nothing much. I did send a copy to Mrs. Louise Campbell of Philadelphia, a former editor of mine who seems satisfied that the book is a strong piece of work likely to do better than I think. Incidentally, she is suggesting a few corrections. (If only you were here to discuss these matters with me!)"

He had obviously forgotten that I was with him at the time
he had received the first negative reaction of Mrs. Campbell
to *The Bulwark.* Fortunately, Elder understood the value of
the book as Dreiser had written it, and I could only hope
for the best, as far as other changes were concerned. Strange,
that after all these years *The Bulwark* was still not on a
clear track!

(This correspondence about *The Bulwark* was published
in *Collected Letters of Theodore Dreiser,* University of Penn.
Press, 1959.)

There was also the question of Dreiser's style. In *The Bulwark* there was a new tempo and rhythm. Long, involved sentences coming directly from his inner ear, the odd little
phrases, so easily cut, which he loved to use . . .

Also the *connectives.* As he once explained in a tone of
secrecy, "I always like to have something that connects one
paragraph with another—a handle, as it were. It makes
things smoother."

And so there were *for's* and *but's* or *And's* and *So's* before
almost every block of words. How many of these had been
dropped by editors through the years. (Many were missing in
the published *Bulwark!*)

How many would understand his new literary tone; grave,
slow, clumsy at times, but coming out in the end, with heavy
grace like that of an elephant moving logs, or walking in
long, swinging lines, according to its own pattern of action.
This final development of Dreiser's curious, original and
often rarely beautiful style was here, in his last great novel
—perhaps it had been eliminated, along with the religious
parts!

From that time on, I was uncannily disturbed about what
might happen to *The Bulwark* manuscript, as well as what
was going on around Dreiser.

Tomb of Charles T. Yerkes

Dreiser had asked me to visit the tomb of Charles T. Yerkes,
the *Cowperwood* of his *Trilogy,* in case he wished to describe
it in *The Stoic.*

On a hot sultry afternoon, with thunder in the air, I reached the cemetery in Brooklyn. A long, up-grade walk through monuments and greenery led at last to a large mausoleum, a Greek temple, in form though not in feeling, its mechanically cut gray facade suggesting a small bank building, impressive rather than beautiful.

Heavy bronze doors with lion-head handles, and a small rear window glazed in some formal pattern, showed no personal taste or thought. Nor was there a religious symbol of any sort, but the heavy square letters, in abbreviation, cut across the pediment:

CHAS. T. YERKES

The only other words were on a small oblong plaque, among the dark green leaves around the stone base: "In Perpetual Care of Greenwood Cemetery." This seemed, in lieu of religious sentiment, a slight exaggeration.

Taking a note about the construction of the tomb, and sitting on its step, I thought long of Dreiser: Yerkes had built this monument to himself with his millions; but Dreiser had built his novels with his accumulated inner riches, and perhaps the only thing that would be remembered about Yerkes in the future would be his portrayal in *The Financier, The Titan,* and *The Stoic*—in spite of the "perpetual care" of Greenwood Cemetery!

The summer wore on. My son had only two weeks before school would start again. I was still waiting for definite word from Dreiser as to whether I should come back or not. His last letter had said:

"I need an action program, something constructive that will stir me to labor. If I did not feel so sickish, so lethargic, I could think something out. As it is, no important thought has arrived to drive me. But it will, I hope. What I need most I guess, is you. Write me and suggest something."

It was his bewildering way of letting someone else make the decisions. I finally wrote, offering to come, but asking for a straight answer.

Then came a long, disturbing letter. I will quote only a sentence here:

". . . . If you came of your own accord and were settled, had that little house and a position in a movie that required only a portion of your time—rest to be devoted to us—to work— how quickly this dream of serious, constructive labor might be realized."

It was enough to make me decide to go back, if only for a period, at least until the proofs of *The Bulwark* were done.

Dreiser and Russia

The most surprising communication that had come to me from Dreiser that summer, was a mimeographed statement which he had taken the trouble to sign in ink, at the bottom of the page. It was entitled *Why I joined the Communist Party,* and was a copy of a letter asking for membership, explaining his step in language which was not his usual way of writing, but rather like something gotten up for him to endorse. I remembered what he had said to me in a letter just after his visit to New York in 1941, when he had been asked to sign certain statements and resented that he was "being pushed to the fore as a leading Communist," whereas, as he said:

"I have avoided (always) joining the Party on the ground that it is better to be an independent American campaigner for the social equities that would, if emphasized here, bring the equivalent of Communism and actually gain a swifter support for all of them rather than a prolonged and delaying quarrel over a name."

Unfortunately, the words *communism* and *socialism* arouse a fierce antagonism in the average American, who is generally ignorant of their social ideals. Dreiser always hoped that a vigorous alignment of progressive forces could some day bring about those *equities* which he desired for all mankind. His very choice of this word was an attempt to find a ground-expression on which all men of good will might agree. He had had great faith in the reforms of Franklin D. Roosevelt, but was disheartened that many opposed them, and still clung to the American dream of making big money, each man a potential millionaire.

Robert Elias discussed this step with Dreiser, and says in his biography, *Dreiser, Apostle of Nature:* "Conscious of his numbered days, Dreiser thought of the fact that after he died, he would no longer be able to speak out in behalf of any cause. . . . what would remain of his social view, his long and independent struggle to promote the cause of equity? He discussed the matter with John Howard Lawson and other persons enrolled or interested in the Communist Party who hoped Dreiser would formally commit himself to its program. They could point out that distinguished European artists and scientists were members. . . . Finally, some of his friends drew up a letter, and Dreiser, after some comments and slight revisions, signed it."

It touched me that the letter was addressed to William Foster, whom Dreiser so loved and admired, and I remembered how the two big-bodied men had sat together on that small couch in the hotel room in New York, holding hands, as they talked about the problems of the day, and the old fights they had been through together, in California, and with the miners in Harlan County.

Dreiser was no Marxist, and had not made any serious study of theoretical politics. Robert Elias goes on to say "Dreiser was asked whether he intended to submit to Party discipline or whether he was still going to disagree and criticize publicly, if he wished. He replied that he would say what pleased, and if the Party did not like that, they could throw him out. He did not care. He was interested only in their objective which seemed to him selfless in a way that proved of greatest advantage to the greatest number of selves. The principles of Communism were, as the Red Dean of Canterbury had explained, like the principles of Christ. 'What the world needs is more spiritual character,' Dreiser said, then he added: 'The true religion is in Matthew.'" (Conversation of Elias with Dreiser, September 10, 1945)

Dreiser meant here, The Sermon on the Mount and The Beatitudes, to which he often referred in books, and in speeches, such as that to the factory workers of Newark. He did not see any contradiction between the social teachings of Christ and Socialism which upholds the ideal of brotherhood, unselfishness and equity for all. Add to this the concept of *Love*, in its broadest sense, and you have the social and spiritual ideal which Dreiser finally expressed in his unique novel, *The Bulwark*.

In it, as we have seen, Dreiser quotes long passages from the journal of John Woolman who, one hundred years before Abraham Lincoln, spoke out against the slavery in the South. Dreiser wrote: "Here was no narrow morality, no religion limited by society or creed, but rather, in the words of Woolman, 'a *principle* placed in the human mind which, in different places and ages hath had different names; it is, however, pure and proceeds from God. It is deep and inward, confined to no forms of religion, nor excluded from any, when the heart stands in perfect sincerity. In whomsoever *this* takes root and grows, they become brethren.' "

To Dreiser, this was politics, this was religion.

At the end of his life, he spoke of these truths, as if he had reached a great simplification, and an inner peace, knowing that he could no longer fight in a political way, but that his message, on the social and spiritual level, was clear and unified.

There was another reason, going deeper than political considerations, that made Dreiser wish to draw nearer to the Soviet Union. He had always felt akin to the Russian temperament, to the special character of Russian genius. Now he felt that the creation of a new order was taking place in this "Russian Land," and that, in spite of difficulties and blunders, a trail was being blazed for all mankind. I believe he wished to identify himself with this destiny of the Russian people.

Long before the revolution of 1917, Dreiser had been impressed and influenced by Russia's great writers. He had read Tolstoy as early as 1897, and around 1906 discovered Turgenev and Dostoievsky. Through these men, and later through Gogol, Pushkin, Gorky, and others, he had seen the picture of life under the Czars in all its emotional richness, color and pathos. He was aroused by the artistry of these masters and filled with compassion for the characters they described. Many Russian books were found on Dreiser's shelves wherever he lived. He particularly loved Dostoievsky; *The Brothers Karamazoff*, with its legend of *The Grand Inquisitor*, and *The Idiot*. This last, he said, was his favorite novel of all literature. He could not "get over" the character of Prince Mishkin, but actually chuckled when he spoke of the simplicity and truth this hero represented. When a critic of the Stalin era once asked Dreiser to state that Dostoievsky was not a true revolutionist, he refused, saying:

"He is a Russian. He is a great artist; his temperament, twisted by torture or not, does enormous credit to the race from which it springs." (Letter to Smirnov, Aug. 5, 1932, in *Collected Letters of Theodore Dreiser*)

The stories of Chekov were a constant delight to Dreiser. He said to me once that his favorite was *The Darling,* and when I told him I had not read it, he began relating the plot in moving language, dwelling on the fact that the simple heroine could not live without having someone to love and care for. First, her husband; and after he died, a second one. Then when he, too, was gone, she took in a poor, backward boy. This seemed wonderful to Dreiser; he read into it all the pathos and nobility of a woman's destiny. When I finally read the story, it seemed small compared to the large place that Dreiser had given it.

Dreiser often referred to Russian writers in discussions about literature. Once he wrote in a letter to H. L. Mencken: "Why do we not have more real, literary achievements, such as a play by Chekov, or a satire by Andreyev?" In another letter to Mencken, as late as 1943, trying to explain to his old friend how he had felt about the Russian people since his visit to them in 1927, he writes:

Better educated and higher thinking and more kindly and courageous men and women, I have never met in my life. In my humble estimation, their equals in this coun-

*try are few indeed. In sum, I conceived a passionate
respect for that great people and still retain it,—a people
who, in so far as I could see, wished humanity to survive
on a better plane than ever it had known before. . . . And
the love I conceived for them then and that passionate
admiration I also developed there, I still retain, as also,
I have for their writers, artists, and musicians since
ever I became aware of their enormous gifts. If you question my judgement here, show me a Chekov, a Dostoievsky, a Tolstoy, a Gogol, a Moussorgsky, in all the
history of American art and American reaction to American life, and I will sit up in silent reverence, for their
equals I do not know.*

His book, *Dreiser Looks at Russia,* published after his
trip in the winter of 1927-28, is a rich document of experiences, with Dreiser's reactions, political and artistic. In spite
of the poor living conditions of those early days, Dreiser
was convinced that difficulties were shared by all alike. He
writes:

*Still another fact that I harvested in Russia and which
I will never forget is this—that via communism, or this
collective and paternalistic care of everybody, it is possible to remove the dreadful sense of social misery in
one direction and another, which has so afflicted me in
my own life in America and ever since I have been old
enough to know what social misery was. The rich dis-
tricts as opposed to the poor ones in all our great cities
and our poorer and smaller towns and villages . . .*

Dreiser had many encounters with leading figures in the
art world. He and Eisenstein, the film producers, Tretyakov,
the playwright, Meierhold, of the Meierhold Theatre, Tairov,
an able director, using new, simplified scenery. He saw many
theatre performances, opera, the ballet.

The great director of the Moscow Theatre, Stanislavsky,
impressed Dreiser tremendously. He describes him as a tall,
striking personality, looking sixty when he was actually over

eighty. Stanislavsky said that he thought the communist theatre had produced some good plays, none great so far. He deplored certain "revisions" of the classics, and said: "The white line of art is eternal and passing conditions cannot even fundamentally affect it."

Dreiser's visit to the home of Leo Tolstoy, about sixty miles south of Moscow, was another memorable experience. I often heard Dreiser repeat the story, adding details not in his book. *Yasnaya Polyana,* or *Clear Fields,* stands at the edge of a birch forest, about a quarter of a mile back from the main highway. Dreiser walked up a mounting drive, along pine trees, to the simple country house in the snow. At that time Tolstoy's daughter Olga was living there, as well as his niece. Dreiser went through the wide, old-fashioned rooms with low ceilings. Tolstoy's white iron bedstead and washstand stood just as he had used them. Here were photographs, family portraits, manuscripts. In a lower study, where he used to work, were Tolstoy's desk, and another table. Dreiser examined everything carefully and questioned Olga about her father. She told how he loved to put on his old blue peasant blouse and go out to work or plough in the field near the house, even in his last years when he was frail and there was little need for his effort. But he wanted to keep contact with the soil, and live his philosophy of the simple life. Often, she said, when her father knew guests were coming, he would go out, so that they would find him in the field; then he would return and entertain them graciously in his home.

As they spoke, school children began to gather around the house. This was the anniversary of Tolstoy's death, and there was a procession to his grave, a long walk through towering birches, to a small mound, where he had wished to be buried, without a stone. Here, an old man who had been a friend of Tolstoy's read a poem he had composed in his honor. Then the children and a large group of villagers sang an old chant— *There is no death.* It was very cold as they trudged back in the snow. Dreiser returned to Tula, the nearest station, some twenty miles away, in a horse-drawn sleigh.

In Moscow, Dreiser dined with the dynamic writer Vladimir Mayakovsky. I first read the story of this evening in a Providence, Rhode Island newspaper, where it was written up by Ruth Kennell, Dreiser's American-born Russian-speaking guide. This attractive young woman had come to the Soviet Union with a group of American engineers, planning to build a manufacturing center in Siberia. Her unusual story is told by Dreiser in his sketch *Ernita* from *A Gallery of Women*.

Visiting Moscow in 1964, I was able to find the house where Mayakovsky had lived with the talented couple, Osip and Lily Brik. Osip Brik was a literary critic and his wife, a beautiful and accomplished hostess. Their home was a salon for writers and intellectuals. Others present that evening of Dreiser's visit were Professor Tretyakov and his wife. I was fortunate in finding Madame Tretyakov in Moscow and was also most graciously received by Lily Brik, now living in a modern, souvenir-filled apartment with her third husband, an art expert. They belong to that Soviet elite which are free to travel and she frequently visits her sister, Elsa Triolet, wife of Louis Aragon, in Paris.

Lily Brik is still a fascinating woman, as Dreiser described her in his book, *Dreiser Looks at Russia:* "She had the broad, white brow which is the charm of so many Russian women, clear, sensitive, comprehending eyes and a dazzling smile." On the same page, he described Mayakovsky:

". . . A very much talked of poet, large, blond, dynamic who looked like a prize-fighter and dressed like an actor. He was all for the machine age and as soon as possible on the ground that it would liberate Russian energies—mental energies—to better things. . . . Unlike some, however, he was not the least bit afraid that his individuality would be submerged by the lockstepping Communistic program. On the contrary. . . . he seemed to think that individuality was to endure, Communism or no Communism."

Unfortunately, Dreiser did not describe their dinner together. But it has was not hard to imagine it, seeing the little house where he had come on a cold November evening.

The wooden structure is one of those old Moscow houses

which seems left over from some village, absorbed into the great rambling city. It is now preserved as a literary museum with manuscripts, portraits, statues and photographs of the handsome poet, as well as drawings, satirical sketches and posters made by him. To Lily Brik he had written some of his most impassioned love poetry. And here was a head of him, strongly sculptured by his versatile friend.

To the right of the small entrance porch, ornamented with wood-carving, were the four rooms which the Briks had occupied. Mayakovsky's room was in the far front corner, and the nearer front room had served for living and dining. On one wall stretched a long, preposterously high book-shelf which Mayakovsky had built for himself, since he was over six feet tall. In this room, the little dinner-party for Dreiser had taken place. A fire had been burning brightly in the central, white-tiled stove.

All said that Dreiser had seemed shy and diffident when he first came in. But soon after, with the aid of Ruth Kennell and Madame Tretyakov who spoke English, communication was established and every one began to have a good time. Vodka and various Russian dishes pleased Dreiser. Madame Tretyakov remembered that there was caviar and fish, served on elegant old china. "Lily always knew how to do things well" she said. It was difficult to procure fruit or any kind of luxury in those days, but prunes and whipped cream were brought out for dessert. Mayakovsky was taken-aback when Dreiser poured Vodka on his prunes and roared with laughter. Dreiser responded, and teased him in return. Unfortunately, no one could recall much of what was said that evening, but all agreed that a feast-like atmosphere prevailed.

Lily Brik remembered particularly Dreiser's warmth and humor. She said: "When it was time for him to go, he stood in the low doorway for a long time, still talking and reluctant to leave. Mayakovsky urged him to spend the night and said he would put up a bed for him in the dining-room. We were all very gay."

Mayakovsky gave Dreiser a copy of his long, revolutionary

poem *Harasho—(Excellent!)* which had just been published. He inscribed it in Russian, in his big, sprawling hand:

"To Mister Dreiser from Comrade Mayakovsky, 18th of November, 1927."

Mayakovsky declared he would never forget this evening, and indeed, the two men made a strong impact on each other, each big, dramatic figures, Dreiser some twenty years the elder, but both equally young in spirit, unruly geniuses of a rare pitch. Mayakovsky had just written his satiric play against bureaucracy, *The Bed Bug.* His poems ranged from intensely personal and even spiritual experiences, to the flaming polemic verses which had caused him to be acclaimed as the Revolution's First Poet. Swinging between poles of emotion and mood, as Dreiser did, about two years later Mayakovsky took his own life in a fit of despondency. Dreiser was truly shocked and grieved when he heard this, calling him one of the greatest writers to come out of the new era.

Gorky was, of course, a bridge between the old and the new. Dreiser admired him greatly, and was sorry that he was in Italy at the time Dreiser came to Russia. A few years later, in 1934, Gorky invited Dreiser to attend a writers Congress in Moscow, and Dreiser felt obliged to refuse, because of troubles with his publisher at the time. However, in his answer to Gorky, he said:

"You know my best wishes go to you and the Congress; with your presence and your efforts, it can only be vastly successful and inspiring." In 1936, Dreiser wrote a statement as a memorial to Gorky after his death. It ended with the words: "In spirit, I lay a wreath on the grave of this great human being."

When Dreiser returned from his trip to Russia, he was seized upon by newspapermen, made various critical and commendatory statements, and at first, seemed depressed because all was not as perfect, in retrospect, as he had hoped. But ever afterwards, his heart was on the side of the heroic people he had been struggling with the stupendous task of building socialism out of chaos and need.

When I first encountered Dreiser in the fall of 1928, he

was still brimming over with his Russian experience. It was then he conceived the idea of bringing over the Russian Ballet, which unfortunately did not materialize. However, his very efforts made for better understanding of Russia. Through the following years, Dreiser was in frequent touch with Russian affairs. He exchanged letters with Dinamov, the young critic whom he had met in Moscow, and with Eisenstein, Cherniavsky, Anisimov and others. The Russian Consuls in New York, and later, in Los Angeles, were received in his home, and he consulted with them about matters of publishing his books and articles in the Soviet Union. He had a number of Russian friends, both White and Red, because he relished the Russian temperament. Men such as the composer Butnikoff, and Boris Chaliapin, the painter and son of the famous singer, for whom Dreiser sat for a portrait, were always welcomed guests.

When the threat of the Fascists and Nazis began to spread over Europe, we have seen how Dreiser joined the popular movements against them, fighting with his pen and in a bodily way, by going to France and Spain, and later, by lecturing in this country.

When the Second World War was raging, he agonized over the desperate struggle of the Soviet Union, as it bore the full brunt of the Nazi war machine, and rejoiced when the tide of the war turned at Stalingrad. His feelings were eloquently expressed in his article, *The Russian Advance,* published in *Soviet Russia Today,* in 1944. A few months later, the dream of United Nations—the United States and the U.S.S.R., great allies of the war united with others against all future wars—seemed near realization. Dreiser, with many others, was glad because of our better relations with the Soviet Union, and foresaw many useful exchanges. He hoped for better understanding on the part of Americans and more intellectual freedom for his Russian colleagues. Was not his gesture of joining the Communist party in that year of 1945, a tribute to them and to the millions of Soviet soldiers who had laid down their lives for their country, and for us? (The Cold War had not yet begun!)

But it was not any one act nor any one article in his long career that proved Dreiser's love for Russia and the Russian people; rather it was a partaking in their own temperament, their courageous pioneering for a better future that united him to them in the common love of humanity.

It is no wonder, then, that the Russian people have reciprocated this love of Dreiser's for them. This interrelation of Dreiser and Russia must be understood not as a political matter, but as a human phenomena; a great writer of one country, adopted by another. This is true of all universal genius—the classic authors of the past, and near past. But it does not often happen in the lifetime of a writer, that both temperament and circumstance play together to make him a hero in a strange land.

At the time of Dreiser's death, the Russian newspapers were full of articles about him. In the words of the Moscow journalist, Isbach, writing in *The Literary Gazette:* "The Soviet people know Dreiser very well, value and love him." And Professor Anisimov, said in his *Necrology,* in *Pravda:* "All Dreiser's creation serves humanity . . . because of this, he is loved in every corner of the world—and in our country where his popularity is already great."

Far from being exaggerated, these opinions are understatements of the widespread fame of Dreiser in Russia. Taxi drivers, maids in hotels, school children, not to mention intellectuals in every field, always seem to know about him and respond warmly when asked if they have read his books. I have tested this on some hundred ordinary citizens, particularly on taxi drivers, during a recent visit to the Soviet Union. If you take a taxi alone in a Soviet city, the polite and friendly thing to do is to jump in and sit by the driver. After a few sentences in halting Russian, I would ask "Ever heard of our American writer, Theodore Dreiser?" Invariably, the answer would be an enthusiastic "yes," and the book most generally read, *An American Tragedy.* But one taxi-philosopher thought this "too soft" and preferred *The Financier* and other books of the *Trilogy* which he considered more typical of American life. Another gentle English specialist preferred

Dreiser's books about women: "We weep over them," she said. *"Sister Carrie, Jennie Gerhardt*—How well Dreiser understood life!"

Russian school children are taught about Dreiser when they have reached world literature courses, at about fifteen or sixteen, and students of English read a shortened version of *Sister Carrie,* or some of Dreiser's short stories, which have appeared in pamphlet form, or "mass printings." Later, of course, almost all his books are available to them in English editions, both published here, and the more popular ones, also published in the Soviet Union.

Practically all Dreiser's books have been translated and published in the Russian language. There have been three different editions of his collected works, the first, of seven volumes, published in 1929. A twelve-volume set in 1950, and a new printing in 1955, with another volume added. A fourth comprehensive collection of 20 volumes is planned for the near future.

In addition, Dreiser's most popular books have been published in at least twenty other languages of the Soviet Union; Armenian, Georgian, Latvian, Mongolian, Tadjik, Churvash, Uzbek, etc. Three books have been given out in the Russian equivalent of Braille, for the blind.

Dreiser's books are found in libraries all over the Soviet Union. Very complete files of his books and books written about him are to be found in the Library for Foreign Literature and the Lenin Library, in Moscow. Leningrad, also, has an impressive collection. Smaller cities, and even rural communities, number Dreiser's works among their own classics. One day I strolled into an old estate in a park on the Moscow River, which had been converted into a library. It was a drowsy, Sunday afternoon, people were reading on benches in the grass or in the wide-open country rooms. Yes, at the librarian's desk they had *An American Tragedy,* and even a copy of *The Bulwark,* which I took in my hand, reading Solon's Quaker musings, perfectly translated in Russian!

An American Tragedy has been staged many times in Russia, not only in Moscow and Leningrad, but in Rostov,

Tiflis, and Vladivostok, to mention only a few other cities where it has been played. It was also published in a theatre edition, which has made production easy. *Sister Carrie* has also been dramatized and widely produced, as has Jennie Gerhardt. I saw a beautiful staging of this play, with an excellent cast, in Leningrad, at the Bolshoi Dramatic Theatre, in 1958. It played to packed houses all summer.

Another tribute which Russians have paid to Dreiser, is the issuing of memorial pamphlets, on the tenth anniversary of his death, and another, on the 85th anniversary of his birth. These were sent out by the Library of Foreign Literature, to aid in the celebration of such occasions, by lectures, readings from Dreiser's works, in clubs and libraries; the writing of newspaper editorials, etc. This is typical of what the Russians do to honor their own great writers, and here Dreiser is ranked with them. Such pamphlets have excellent bibliographies, quotations, and pertinent information about Dreiser and his work.

I have made a study of newspaper articles and critical studies about Dreiser, which is in itself another chapter, too long for inclusion here. Dreiser's own articles, written for the Soviet Union, or reprinted from newspapers and magazines in this country, are also familiar to Soviet readers. His work as a "publicist" is widely acclaimed in the more politically minded Soviet milieu.

Talking to Ilya Ehrenburg, the Soviet writer who holds a unique place in the literary world, and has just published the third volume of his *Memoirs,* he told me that he regretted not meeting Dreiser. "If I had met him, it would be engraved in my memory, in gold," he said. "Dreiser is one of the great. He writes with texture, thickness. He *describes* a man. Hemingway *shows* a man, through his dialogue. Your writers of the thirties have had much influence on us; we love Hemingway; Steinback's *Of Mice and Men,* Erskine Caldwell's *Tobacco Road.* Dreiser is already a classic. He prepared the way for them. Dreiser was the first American writer who began to *break through,* to start an American culture. Whitman, Poe, were too original, too isolated. Mark Twain, Jack London, are not in the same class. . . . Dreiser is comparable to our great writers, *in place,* but he is different. He is American."

So Dreiser, during his lifetime, functioned almost single-handedly as a cultural link between America and the Soviet Union. And he continues to do so, through his books, and that personality of genius, that lives on in the works of big men.

XII. NO SHADOW OF TURNING

—Death of Dreiser, December, 1945

The temperature stood in the nineties, when we found Dreiser again, at the house on North King's Road. He greeted us with the same affectionate scowl, and rich, inscrutable presence. But he seemed a little more subdued and said he had not been feeling well.

Helen was dressed in beach slacks and looked very glamorous in spite of the heat. She seemed nervous, however, and took me up to her tower boudoir saying she was worried about Dreiser. He was seeing some new kind of health specialist who gave him massages to "get his circulation going." (He had not been to his kidney specialist for a long time.)

Helen said that Dreiser was working with her on *The Stoic*, and under no circumstances, could he work on anything else, because he was not strong enough. She also said that they had grown very close again, as in the days of their first love.

Later, Dreiser took me out into the garden, and said that Helen was upset because she thought I would disturb their work on *The Stoic*. He said it was not going well and he wished he could discuss it with me, but for the present, there was nothing to do, until Helen calmed down. He would try to finish the book shortly with her, and then turn to other things. I would have felt immediately that it was a mistake for me to come back, had it not been for Dreiser's grip on my hand, his eyes searching mine, with that sad, questioning look.

There was nothing to do but accept the situation, and Dreiser sent me to his agent, to see if I could get a temporary job. Days passed quickly enough. The heat spell changed into a fruit-filled autumn. The little trees along the path to the patio were covered with rose-and-yellow peaches, as they had been when Dreiser first came there, the year before.

If I did not drop into see Dreiser almost every day, Helen would call and ask me to come. She was her usual generous self about inviting Hilary and me to drive off occasionally, for dinner, although Dreiser did not go out as often as formerly. He preferred to have me come and sit in the garden with him, and Helen took advantage of these visits to do errands or go off in the car, since she did not like to leave him alone.

There was about Dreiser now a vagueness and sometimes, distress when he talked about practical matters. His memory had grown worse and he seldom went out alone, except to walk down to the corner drug-store. This he liked to do, and would buy small items, make telephone calls, or pick up an extra newspaper. It kept up his sense of independence, for it seemed as though Helen was really running his life for him now, as she had never been able to do before. It was only natural that she should wish to do this, in view of his health, but for the first time, he seemed to fear her. He wanted to come up to the little house on the hill, but was afraid she would not like it:

"Come by at this time tomorrow and meet me at the drug-store, so we can go up there," he said one day.

"Why, no, Teddy, I won't do that," I laughed. "I've always been perfectly open with Helen—"

"Elizabeth picked me up there the other day, and Helen knew nothing about it," he said, casually.

"No—Helen and I have always been friends—She'll get over this," I said lightly. Another time, we discussed this more seriously. We spoke of Helen's loyalty and how we must do what she thought best:

"I guess she deserves it," he said, "She stuck to me a long time" . . . He made a gesture towards the small pool: "Look, she put those blue flowers in there, yesterday." There was a new bunch of dwarf ageratum in the rocky border over the water, where Dreiser loved to watch the gold fish glimmer and disappear.

These hours in the garden with Dreiser were a beautiful extension of the deep sense of companionship we had had always, in moments of quiet. It seemed that we said little of importance, compared to the joy of being together in this contemplation of nature. Near the pool were the rustic table and garden chairs which Dreiser would arrange for me, with his old gallantry. Although he was not quite steady on his feet, he would not let me carry as much as a pillow, when we emerged from the house. Then he would pull the heavy furniture around with that show of sturdiness which he loved to ascribe to his male heroes such as the young Solon.

One day, a large, bluish-gray bird came and perched in the thick avocado tree right over Dreiser's head:

"There he is," he chuckled. "That's my bird. He comes here every day, whether I feed him or not and never seems afraid of me. Watch him—now he'll come nearer."

Sure enough, the big bird hopped down the branch, toward him. He was within easy reach of Dreiser's hand, had he stretched it over his shoulder. "You know," he continued with one of his eloquent hand-sweeps, "We put something out for the birds in the morning, that is, most of the time, not always; and off and on, certain ones become almost tame, and we see them around every day for awhile—and then they go off— Now this fellow's been around for several weeks. I talk to him and he really knows me. Lately, I'm hardly ever out here that he doesn't come around after a few minutes."

Dreiser spoke in that very same detailed, accurate way, as he had when he had described the incident of his talking to the snake at Mt. Kisco. Perhaps it was something about his vibrant voice that had also attracted this gray-blue bird who had become his friend in the garden.

Visit with Bob Elias

That fall, Robert Elias came out to Hollywood to see Dreiser. He was collecting material for the biography which Dreiser had sanctioned.

Elias had the same serious yet easy quality about him which Dreiser liked and again, he talked freely with him, and enjoyed his visit. He had no men of his own generation to chin and jibe with, as he had done with Masters and Mencken and Powys. But Elias understood this background, and could gain Dreiser's confidence, as before.

During this visit, Helen told him that Dreiser was going to introduce ideas of Eastern Philosophy into the conclusion of *The Stoic* through Cowperwood's young mistress, Berenice. Since she was already such an artificial character, this did not seem to make much sense to me. What could the classic beauty of the *Vedanta* teachings have to do with the end of Dreiser's *Trilogy,* based on the cynical study of international banking and a rather cold-blooded polygamy. But I did understand that these ideas had meant much to Helen, in the difficult times of her relationship with Dreiser, when it seemed as if she could not accept his varietistic attitudes and her own love for him had become an obsession which was driving her to despair.

The letter which she had written me when I asked her if she would like me to come to Hollywood, also revealed her own effort at detachment through realizing the fleeting quality of purely human love.

And only a few months before, she had lent me her book on *Hatha Yoga,* the physical aspects of *Yoga,* which included breathing exercises she used to practice.

Quite by accident, I heard through a mutual friend of Allan Hunter that Dreiser and Helen had been to consult the Swami Prabhavananda, head of the *Vedanta Center* in Los Angeles. Since the Swami was a friend of Allan Hunter's, I asked him later about this visit. "It was she who did the talking," said the Swami. "She wanted to know if they were right in their expression of the *Vedanta* teachings. I told them I could not tell this, unless I saw the manuscript itself.

This they did not have with them. Mr. Dreiser said nothing at all."

I tried to ask Dreiser about his use of these Eastern ideas the next time we sat together in the garden. But he seemed unwilling to talk about them just as he also avoided talking with me about his joining the Communist Party. It seemed in those days words fell away, in the brief enjoyment of being together.

Sunset

Dreiser came only once with Helen, to the little house on the hill. I had invited a delightful painter-friend of mine to meet him. Hilary was also with us; we had arranged appetizers and drinks in the patio, and we were all going out to dinner in the San Fernando Valley, afterwards.

We sat a long time over our drinks, as the light faded slowly from the hill and the flowers along the border began to lose their color. Dreiser sat in his old chair, rocking ever so slightly, hardly saying a word. When it was time to go, he said:

"You go along and let me sit here. I'm not hungry and I'd just like to sit here till you come back." But of course, we said he must eat something, and so persuaded him to come with us.

This was October. Dreiser was not really sick nor unhappy in those days, but he was growing more detached from practical details. Moreover, he felt a deep gratitude and loyalty to Helen. They had had so many stormy years together, and he truly wanted her to have a sense of happiness that she had not always had; he felt a revived tenderness toward her, wanting her to have the reward of her long devotion.

Later in the month, Helen came driving up to the little house one morning obviously very upset. "Come down quickly," she said. "Something's the matter with Teddy. He doesn't know me, and he keeps asking for Helen."

When we got down to King's Road, Dreiser was lying on the couch in the living room. "I don't know what's the matter with me," he said dully. "I feel terrible."

His eyes were gleaming, and his hands felt feverish: "I don't know where Helen is—" he said. "There was a strange person here this morning. Maybe you can find out for me."

Helen's coming back soon," I said casually. "I'll stay 'til she comes." He seemed relieved and got up for a drink.

It was obvious that he would never take care of himself properly, but still relied on whiskey and vitamins of all sorts, to buck him up. It was some time since he had seen a doctor.

After a while, Helen came into the room, and he recognized her as usual. She had phoned for their regular doctor, and I went off, to consult a psychiatrist.

This man was Dr. Fritz Kunkel a noted writer as well as a doctor, whom we had met through Allan Hunter. His advice was curiously discouraging:

"There is nothing you can do about such a condition, with a person of his age. It might be more disturbing to question him about past experiences, than to leave him alone. He should have plenty of rest, no conflicts, and peace of mind." Certainly, that is what we were trying to give him. But what could Helen or I or anyone do for this great strange spirit who seemed at times to be drifting into a shadow.

For a while, Dreiser seemed better. I did not see him very often the following month, for I had taken a job, but Helen and I kept in touch by phone, chatting frequently about him or things in general. They were living a quiet but normal life, working on *The Stoic* and going out occasionally, to the homes of friends. The weather was mild, and Dreiser spent much time in his garden.

One evening, Helen invited Hilary and me to attend an Ice-Show at the Pan American auditorium. Dreiser was delighted with the beauties of color and motion displayed by the groups of swift skaters, turning, swooping, seeming to fly or move without weight.

One blue-and silver ballet created a dream-world lovely as anything of its kind could be on any stage. Dreiser sat absorbed as a school-boy from the country, his mouth hanging open, his eyes gleaming and dancing with the forms he watched. Comic numbers made him roar, tears coming to his eyes, from laughter. It was a gay, happy evening.

The Dybbuk

Early in December, Helen procured tickets for us to see that remarkable Jewish classic drama, *The Dybbuk*.

The play brings to life an old legend in which a young rabbi, not permitted to marry the girl he loves, begins to practice black magic. . . . He dies, and his soul enters into the soul of the girl, literally *possessing* her, so that she thinks only of him, spends most of her time in a trance, and refuses to marry another bridegroom her rabbi father has chosen for her.

In solemn conclave, the most powerful rabbis of the community meet to exorcise this evil, possessing spirit, and drive it from the girl. But *The Dybbuk* or damned spirit, refuses to leave her. Finally, under the most potent of all curses—the *Anathema* of Sacred Jewish Rite—he is torn from her, but literally rends her body, as he leaves it, so that she falls dead, beside her parents.

Dreiser, who had always believed in the supernatural world even in his worst days of scoffing at religion, was deeply shaken by this drama, as we all were. It was a strange thing that he should see this play at this time, a terrible and beautiful thing, for psychic phenomena had always seemed real to him as when he had gone to séances, and played with Ouija boards or glimpsed the strange, horrible faces he said he saw sometimes around his bed at night. He had a growing belief that the spirit lives on after death, in some mysterious way, a part of the Force of Creation. He had said of Benecia, through the mouth of Solon, that she was now in that *Presence in whom there is no variableness neither shadow of turning*. And again Solon thought of his young Benecia not as dead, but *now blended with those mysterious forces*.

All this time, I had been waiting for the proofs of *The Bulwark* to arrive, hoping that Dreiser would feel well enough to do them, and planned to take time off from my job to help him get through them as easily as possible. He had promised to let me know about this, and if I did not come to see him, he would complain; so I sometimes managed a late afternoon visit to the gray-bird's garden.

One week-end, I went on a retreat to the mountains above Redlands, with a group led by Allan Hunter. It was a new experience, and I stopped in to tell Dreiser about it on Sunday when I got back.

I found that he had already retired, though it was only about six o'clock. Helen asked me to go in and talk to him, while she prepared him a little supper.

He was in excellent humor, sitting up in bed with a fresh white pyjama jacket, looking very rested, his eyes full of fun and affection. We hit one of our old conversational strides— saying things dangerously near profanity, yet putting all the beauty and daring we could into words trying to express the infinite.

Dreiser's mind seemed dazzlingly clear and deep-blue in its brilliance. Always, in his worst days, he could surprise you like this, his spirit like a great mountain peak with clouds surrounding it, obscured, and then the sun of absolute clarity breaking through like shafts of light from the Creative Force itself, dispelling all mists, revealing his thought and his towering personality.

He talked about prayer, about Allan Hunter and Thoreau, and said he often did not know whether he was praying or not. Then I made him a little speech about how he was a natural mystic, with much more *love* than Thoreau. . . . When I stopped for breath, he laughed in that deep, sardonic way:

"Well, that's certainly encouraging. Maybe the Almighty will give me a chance!"

A few days later, when I came home from work, Helen telephoned and said that the proofs of *The Bulwark* had come, but I did not need to worry about them. She had read them over with Dreiser, and they were all right. I jumped into my car and drove down to King's Road.

As soon as I walked in I felt a strained atmosphere. Dreiser was sitting in one of his big chairs glowering at me unhappily. I had planned to go away over the following Christmas week-end with my son, but now I said I would stay to finish the proofs with Dreiser. Helen said it would not be necessary.

I appealed to Dreiser, but he seemed utterly lost in gloomy silence. This was too much for my patience. I had given up everything to keep peace with Helen, but this was my responsibility, this *Bulwark*. I had labored with Dreiser over each word. I had seen some of the brutal cuts, the insensitive "corrections" already made. I felt as if the devil himself was trying to sabotage this book.

The following scene is painful to me and I would not describe it, had not Helen and others told of it inaccurately. It is also a part of the strange timing of Dreiser's life and the story of *The Bulwark*. It is particularly distressing because I was always fond of Helen and felt I understood and admired her.

I was later to learn that *The Bulwark* proofs were returned to Donald Elder of Doubleday with hardly a mark on them showing that Dreiser had not gone over them with any care. Certain omissions and changes in style would certainly have been troubling to him, if he had read them with the same eyes as the previous spring. His last great novel, short enough as it was, had been seriously injured by cutting. I have elsewhere illustrated the difference between the final third typescript and *The Bulwark* as published. An untouched first carbon of this original typescript is in the University of Pennsylvania Collection of Dreiser's manuscripts, and it is my hope that some day this manuscript will be published as written. Let literary historians of the future judge whether this is not a finer, fuller piece of writing.

But now Helen refused to allow me to see the proofs, even to glance over them alone, which would have reassured me as to their general fidelity to the original. I said that I was going to fight for this, that Dreiser did need me, and that she was making it impossible for him to say so.

At this Helen started to fight back—a tirade such as only she could make with her husky, emotional voice. Dreiser rose up and stood there, swaying—but it was not for long. I could not bear to see him like this; miserable, weak, like an old, tormented lion. I suddenly turned and went out.

The heavy door seemed to slam behind me. I waited. No— I must not leave like this, as though in anger. I rang the bell.

Dreiser opened the door and stood there, as if he had not moved, scowling in that terrible, silent way. Helen had disappeared but I knew she was nearby.

"I didn't mean to slam the door, Teddy," I said. "But I am desperate. I don't know what to do. Call me if you change your mind."

It seemed to me that he mumbled something in a very low voice, but I did not hear what it was. I stumbled out, this time closing the door very slowly behind me.

It was the last time I saw Dreiser alive.

Death of Dreiser

No word had come from Dreiser, and my son and I had been away on a Christmas ski trip. Two days after Christmas, when I came back from my work, my son was standing against the door, looking strangely tense.

"Mom, Helen phoned that Teddy died. She wants you to call her right away."

On the phone Helen said, between sobs, that Dreiser had had a kidney attack early that morning. He had fallen on the floor in agony, and in twenty minutes the doctor had come to ease his pain and get him into bed. After that, he seemed to rally for a while, but by ten o'clock, a male nurse was giving him oxygen. He had died about six o'clock. She asked me to come right down.

When I drove up to the house on King's Road, a large, ambulance-type hearse was at the door. Berkeley Tobey let me in. Esther McCoy Tobey and Lillian Goodman and her husband were with Helen in the living room. Helen and I embraced each other.

Just then the men from the undertaker's came out of Dreiser's room, wheeling a low stretcher-carriage. I had handled many such carriages in Red Cross work during the war, and it seemed perfectly natural now to reach down and help the men with their heavy burden.

"Do you want to see him?" Helen asked.

"I'd like to ride with him, if you don't mind," I said. She didn't object, so I followed the men out.

There was a low seat, such as that arranged to attend patients on the carriage. I sat beside him, and we rode along together, once more. It seemed perfectly natural to talk to him, to stroke his brow, which was only a little cool, and to hold his hand.

It was a long ride to Forest Lawn, a beautiful and timeless ride, because he seemed fully there, and his hand did not slip from mine.

Then there were the inevitable details of the funeral to be arranged. Helen seemed to want my assistance, and asked me to get Allan Hunter to conduct a service in The Rudyard Kipling Memorial Chapel at Forest Lawn.

In the meantime, various incidents were related by one and another. Dreiser had seemed quite well that Christmas week. He had attended a wedding with Helen, where an excellent picture was taken of both of them.

Mona Lasky, writer and member of the movie colony, had seen Dreiser at the studio of a painter who had just done a portrait of his friend, Butnikoff. "He seemed aloof," she said, "detached, although he looked at the portrait with intense interest. There was something magnetic about him. He sat in a fullness, in a silence that nothing could break through, although he did make some casual remarks. . . . He seemed like a man who had found something—a *whole* man."

Dreiser had also been to see Elizabeth the day before Christmas, and brought a present for her small son. She had played the harp for him, which he always enjoyed: "Don't talk to me about my work," he had said, and wished that Christmas were over.

When Dreiser was stricken, Helen had first called Lillian Goodman and her husband, who arrived even before the doctor, and later, the Tobeys came to be with her. Helen said that Dreiser made no significant remark that day, except to say: "A pain like that could kill a person."

When Allan Hunter came in to speak about the funeral service, and he told me in detail about a curious fact that Helen had already mentioned to me: how he happened to drop in on that afternoon when Dreiser was dying.

"It was a few minutes after two, and I was going to be late for a two-thirty appointment—every reason for driving past King's Road. Suddenly, I found myself making a turn and in a moment, ringing his doorbell. Obviously something strange and important was happening within. A stranger met me at the door.

" 'Mr. Dreiser is very ill.' Without explaining, I walked into the bedroom.

"Mrs. Dreiser was there, in some distress. 'Do you mind if I have a prayer with you and Mr. Dreiser?' She seemed very glad to have a prayer. It all seemed entirely fitting and natural. Without further words, I took his hand in my right hand, and as I recall, put my left hand on his forehead, and simply spoke intimately to God as father, committing the whole situation to His care, in confidence that He was nearer to us than we were to ourselves or to each other, and that the words of Christ could come home to us at that very moment. 'Peace I leave with you. My peace I give unto you—not as the world giveth, give I unto you. . . . In this world you will have tribulation, but be of good cheer, I have overcome the world.'

"It was only a couple of minutes. Dreiser was struggling with the oxygen apparatus that was placed over his mouth, breathing heavily and with some effort. But his eyes spoke clearly enough, it seemed to me, of his realization and appreciation.

"I left the room without saying anything, except near the door, 'Blessings on you, Brother!' Dreiser lifted his hand in a gesture of farewell. He died four hours later. . . . It was all very strange, the sudden impulse to go to his home, although I had not seen him since April. The stripping down to essentials with hardly any words, except the prayer and good-bye; the look in his eyes, not struggle alone, but the sense—or am I only reading this back into the experience?—of mystery, of getting ready for an important journey that was nothing to be afraid of really since there was meaning and presence to be encountered later but in a way already experienced, as if eternity were a reality *now*."

So Allan Hunter, this extraordinary, thin, vibrant, self-effacing man had been the last of his own stature to wish Dreiser God-speed from this earth.

But at the very moment that Allan and I were talking and walking around and around in Dreiser's garden, as an icy chill settled over the landscape, the pall-bearers inside were holding a conference as to how to dispense with Allan's services. A conflict had arisen. The Communist Party was to be represented at the funeral, and religion was being driven to the wall. Helen fluctuated in her opinions, and finally Allan was called in. Only a man of his bigness and liberal understanding could have mastered this situation. Finally, a compromise was reached; each one was to have his part in Dreiser's final tribute.

In the meantime, Dreiser lay in a slumber room at Forest Lawn, dressed in his black lecturer suit, with soft white shirt and black bow tie. He looked strangely large and real in his casket. Back into his face had come that solid, dynamic look, of an object coming at you through space.

Edgardo Simone, who had made a sculptured head of Dreiser some months before, was willing to come and make a death mask of his face and hand. I have these masks which preserve much of Dreiser's strength and nobility.

Dreiser's Funeral

The day of Dreiser's funeral was bright and clear.

People began arriving around one o'clock at the stone Church of The Recessional at the top of the high hill at Forest Lawn. This is a copy of an English Chapel associated with Rudyard Kipling, and it has a bland, wide look with a court of flagstones stretching along a gray parapet. Beyond it, the mountains flanking the San Fernando Valley could be seen, looking higher than they really were, in their stark dignity.

The Chapel was Gothic in style with fine stained glass and woodwork, the left side opening into a sort of conservatory, filled with plants and flowers. To the left of the long center aisle was the pulpit, and behind it, where in most churches would be the altar space, stood the casket, open and surrounded by flowers. There were floral pieces of all sorts, one a white cross. Over the foot of the casket was Helen's gorgeous blanket of red roses.

The pall-bearers sat in the first two rows behind the pulpit. Behind them, two friends, my son and I, and a secretary who was to take down the service in shorthand, filed in and took our places. The two front rows on the other side were strangely empty, for Helen and the official funeral party. The Goodmans, the Tobeys, and Vera Dreiser, Edward Dreiser's daughter and the only member of the Dreiser family present, were sitting in a special alcove reserved for mourners, behind a screen through which they could see but not be seen. This seemed strange to an Easterner, the family not seeming to participate in the service.

The organ began to play numbers of Bach and Händel; then Allan Hunter stepped out, wearing a black minister's gown, which he never used except for such occasions. It made him look still thinner, ascetic. He began: "Lord, Thou hast been our dwelling place in all generations, before the mountains were brought forth or ever Thou hadst formed the earth and the world, even from everlasting to everlasting thou art God."

"Mr. Lawson, a friend of Mr. Dreiser's, will interpret a little of this life which some of you loved deeply, others looked upon with great respect—this life that we trust, will remain a force of compassion and understanding in the wills of many men."

Then John Howard Lawson came into the pulpit and gave a warm, political tribute, referring to Dreiser by that Marxist term, *a man of culture*—somehow not quite fitting this untamed genius.

Then Charlie Chaplin stepped to the platform, small, tense,

his curly iron-gray hair smoothed back, handsome in his serious mood. Obviously shaken by his unusual task, he held in his hand a paper on which was written one of Dreiser's prose-poems from *Moods*. He read it slowly, in a hollow, English-sounding, palely emotioned voice:

> *O, inorganic*
> *Yet breathing*
> *The organic*
> *Inarticulate*
> *Yet voicing itself*
> *Articulate*
> *In heights*
> *Depths*
> *To which we rise*
> *Or sink*
> *Yet infinite*
> *And from which we take our rise.*
> *O, Space!*
> *Change!*
> *Toward which we run*
> *So gladly*
> *Or from which we retreat*
> *In terror—*
> *Yet that promises to bear us*
> *In itself*
> *Forever.*
> *O, what is this*
> *That knows the road I came?"*

As Chaplin stepped back, there was a profound hush, composed of his own communication of sincere grief and Dreiser's old questioning.

The organ broke through with Bach's believing *Come, Sweet Death*.

Allan Hunter then came forward again, and spoke very quietly. Most of what he said came from his own very sensitive, mystical approach to life, which Dreiser had also shared, although he expressed it differently:

"The highest cannot be spoken, and we cannot with words more than approach that which is most real, mysterious and strange to us. Many people have tried through telegrams and letters to suggest their sorrow and sense of loss; to communicate through an impossible medium of speech, their sense of desire to live in accord with the peace and justice—yes, and the truth, that moved Mr. Dreiser.

"One writer in California speaks of him as the man of the people, who wrote of the people and for the people. Upton Sinclair said: 'He was possessed by a warm and broad human sympathy which is essential to all true literary greatness. His books will be read as long as there are Americans to read them.'

"But nothing that any human being can say with words is able to plumb the depths of the meaning of his life, especially as we sense it, as it is taken from us.

"Mr. Dreiser had his limitations, which of us does not—but he had going in him, like a fire in his bones, not just a wistful desire, but a *demand* that power be cut up and passed around among men and that dignity of these men be recognized and that they be given a chance to fulfill themselves in this world, beginning *now*. . . . Insistence that ordinary men be looked upon as not ordinary but in their wholeness and their integrity and their dignity.

"I would like to read one or two sentences from Mr. Dreiser's book, not yet published, but which most of you will probably read. . . .

"At the end of *The Bulwark*, a woman going out of a room where her father lies dead, is crying. Someone asks her why she is crying—Is it for her father? What Dreiser is trying to communicate here is the yearning and longing in man. Listen to her answer: 'I am not crying for myself, nor for father, I am crying for *life*.'

"It is such a sense of compassion, of the poignancy of the world, that haunted Mr. Dreiser. . . . possibly, this is the most characteristic cry out of this man. . . ."

There was a verse that meant very much to him as he sought to see through his own integrity: *Lord, I believe. Help Thou my unbelief . . .*

Finally, he ended with a prayer:

"Oh, Thou who art so near that nearer Thou canst not be, Whose Spirit mingles with our own as sunshine with the air . . . May we know Who Thou art? May we dare to face Thee, the invisible, the eternal, the utterly good, who hast put something of Thy own nature in Thy children, *who hast made us restless until we find our rest in Thee; for Thou hast made us for Thyself.*"

"We are committing into Thy hands the spirit of this man who dared much, thanking Thee that he cared for his fellow man, thanking Thee that much of the creative was able to pour through him, that he was seeking truth, seeking through the unseen into that purpose that, Oh God, we are trying, each in his own way, to understand and obey. We thank Thee that he had friends, that there were those all over the world, that cared for him. . . .

"We pray that this world may be less of a jungle and more of a home for the human spirit, because of him."

The service was over. The ushers went noiselessly from pew to pew, forming those who wished to pass by the casket, into a single file.

The Church had been crowded, but only about a third of the people were Dreiser's personal friends. Few of the movie colony were there. Most of the crowd were simple people, perhaps political admirers or the sort of persons who were Dreiser readers, nondescript, humble people who loved him and loved his books.

Now they solemnly walked down the aisle. Dreiser was amazingly handsome in his black suit and bow tie. Only his mouth looked unnatural, that heavy, sensuous mobile mouth, now closed. But there were the long, beautiful hands, the soft, white hair, the great brow unchanged.

As each one went by, searching the face of death or turning from it, there was the quiet and finality of a stage passed, a curtain dropped.

Outside, as one stepped through the low stone doorway that lead away from the casket, was the full crash and brightness of the sunshine, and the great symphonic march of the San Gabriel Mountains.

Epilogue

Perhaps thirty people followed the hearse down to the knoll in Forest Lawn where Dreiser was to be buried. They walked in from the road over graves completely flat and one with the ground, marked only by brass plates set into the thick, green lawn, no stones rising above them, but only pines and swaying eucalyptus.

Allan Hunter stood beside the open grave and made a short prayer, saying in part: "O Father, with the sound of the wind in the branches, with the grass springing up at our feet, with the sunlight around us. . . . We commit this man to Thee. . . ." The casket was lowered into the ground. Now Dreiser himself was *blended with those mysterious forces.*

A bronze plaque, like all the others, was eventually laid in the greensward. It carried only his name, the dates of his birth and death, Aug. 27, 1871—Dec. 28, 1945 and the words from the *Mood* which Chaplin had read at the funeral:

> *"Oh, space!*
> *Change!*
> *Toward which we run so gladly*
> *Or from which we retreat in terror*
> *Yet that promises to bear us in itself*
> *Forever*
> *Oh what is this that knows*
> *The road I came?*

Six months later, *The Bulwark* made its appearance, carrying the message of his last years, his love of Nature, his sublimated political creed, his new philosophy, revelation of a Creative Force—all had gone into it.

There followed *The Stoic,* last of the *Trilogy,* and many books written about Dreiser, articles and comments from all over the world.

So the spirit of Dreiser lives on and he has taken his place in the company of universal genius, to influence not only his own generation, but many to come, and only the future will bring him into the fullness of his power—this Dreiser, great artist, great lover of mankind and tool of his Creator.